LONDON
SOUTH EAST
COLLEGES
BROMLEY

Learning **ux**
Centre Second Edition

Richard Petersen

Osborne **McGraw-Hill**

Berkeley ▪ New York ▪ St. Louis ▪ San Francisco
Auckland ▪ Bogotá ▪ Hamburg ▪ London
Madrid ▪ Mexico City ▪ Milan ▪ Montreal
New Delhi ▪ Panama City ▪ Paris ▪ São Paulo
Singapore ▪ Sydney ▪ Tokyo ▪ Toronto

Osborne **McGraw-Hill**
2600 Tenth Street
Berkeley, California 94710
U.S.A.

For information on translations or book distributors outside the U.S.A., or
to arrange bulk purchase discounts for sales promotions, premiums, or
fund-raisers, please contact Osborne/**McGraw-Hill** at the above address.

Linux Programmer's Reference, Second Edition

Publisher   Brandon A. Nordin
Editor-in-Chief   Scott Rogers
Acquisitions Editor   Jane Brownlow
Project Editor   Carolyn Welch
Acquisitions Coordinator   Tara Davis
Technical Editor   Eric Richardson
Copy Editor   Dennis Weaver
Proofreader   Susie Elkind
Computer Designers   Jani Beckwith, Michelle Galicia
Indexer   Valerie Robbins
Series Design   Peter F. Hancik

1234567890 DOC DOC 019876543210

ISBN 0-07-212355-9

About the Author

Richard Petersen, M.L.I.S., teaches Unix and C/C++ courses at the University of California at Berkeley. He is the author of Osborne's *Linux: The Complete Reference,* now in its second edition.

To my Uncle and Aunt
Gabriel and Bonnie

CONTENTS @ A GLANCE

CONTENTS

x Contents

---

3   Z-Shell Programming 111

---

4   Compilers and Libraries: gcc, g++, and gdb 159

xvi   Contents

INTRODUCTION

This book is designed to be a programmer's reference on Linux. It covers the commands, syntax, and operators for three major shells used in Linux: the Bourne Again shell (BASH), the TCSH shell, and the Z shell. All are enhanced versions of their corresponding Unix shells. The BASH shell is an advanced version of the Bourne shell, which includes most of the advanced features developed for the Unix Korn shell and C shells. TCSH is an enhanced version of the C shell that was originally developed for BSD versions of Unix. The Z shell is an enhanced version of the Unix Korn shell.

In addition, the book covers programming tools including compilers, libraries, debuggers, and project managers. The GNU C compiler used extensively on Linux is discussed, along with the different types of libraries available: static, dynamic, and shared. The **gdb** debugger and **make** utilities are presented in detail, as well as the Revision Control System (RCS) for managing complex programming projects.

The book also examines software distribution tools. **autoconf** and **configure** can automatically compile software source code on any Linux system. The Redhat Package Manager (**rpm**) automatically installs software packages, placing all appropriate libraries and configuration files in their proper directories. Even the **man** macros for developing online manuals are examined.

The second edition adds chapters on Gnome and KDE programming. KDE is very much a C++ programming operation whereas Gnome uses C function calls. The chapter on Gnome covers the basics of Gnome programming as well as GTK+. Numerous tables listing the different components of the various libraries used in Gnome programming are provided. The chapter on KDE covers the basics of KDE and QT programming. Tables listing the different classes making up the KDE and QT libraries are provided.

Three appendixes at the end of the book contain listings of Perl, Tcl/Tk, and TeX/LaTeX commands. Though these are cross-platform programming languages and tools, they are used extensively on Linux systems to create customized Linux applications.

Chapter 1
BASH Shell Programming

The BASH shell has programming-language-like capabilities that allow you to combine shell variables, control structures, expressions, and Linux commands to create complex shell programs. A shell program combines Linux commands in such a way as to perform a specific task. The Linux shell provides you with many programming tools with which to create shell programs. You can define variables and assign values to them. You can also define variables in a script file and have a user interactively enter values for them when the script is executed. There are loop and conditional control structures that repeat Linux commands or make decisions on which commands you want to execute. You can also construct expressions that perform arithmetic or comparison operations. All these programming tools operate like those found in other programming languages.

Usually, the instructions making up a shell program are entered into a script file that can then be executed. You can create this script file using any standard editor. To run the shell program, you execute its script file.

Shell Scripts: Commands and Comments

A shell script is a text file that contains Linux commands, which you enter using any standard editor. You can then execute the commands in the file by using the filename as an argument to any **sh** or dot command (.). The shell then reads and executes the commands in the script. You can also make the script file itself executable and use its name directly on the command line, as you would use the name of any command.

You make a script file executable by setting its execute permission with the **chmod** command. The executable permission for the **chmod** command can be set using either symbolic or absolute references. The symbolic reference **u+x** sets the execute

1

permission of a file. The command **chmod u+x hello** will set the execute permission of the **hello** script file. You can now use the script filename **hello** as if it were a Linux command. You only need to set the executable permission once. Once set, it remains set until you explicitly change it.

hello

```
echo "Hello, how are you"

$ chmod u+x hello
$ hello
Hello, how are you
$
```

An absolute reference will set read and write permission at the same time that it sets the execute permission. In brief, 700 will set execute as well as read and write permission for the user; 600 will set read and write permission, 500 will set execute and read permission; 400 will set read permission, 300 will set execute and write permission, and 200 will set write permission. Users most often set 700 or 500. In the next example, the user sets the read, write, and execute permissions using an absolute reference.

```
$ chmod 700 hello
$ hello
Hello, how are you
$
```

It is often helpful to include in a script file short explanations describing what the file's task is, as well as describing the purpose of certain commands and variables. You can enter such explanations using comments. A comment is any line or part of a line preceded by a sharp sign (#) with the exception of the first line. The end of the comment is the next newline character, the end of the line. Any characters entered on a line after a sharp sign will be ignored by the shell. The first line is reserved for identification of the shell, as noted in the following discussion. In the next example, a comment describing the name and function of the script is placed at the head of the file.

hello

```
# The hello script says hello
echo "Hello, how are you"
```

You may want to be able to execute a script that is written for one of the Linux shells while you are working in another. Suppose you are currently in the TCSH shell and want to execute a script you wrote in the BASH shell that contains BASH shell commands. First, you would have to change to the BASH shell with the **sh** command, execute the script, and then change back to the TCSH shell. You can, however, automate this process by placing as the first characters in your script, #!, followed by the path name for the shell program on your system.

Your shell always examines the first character of a script to find out what type of script it is—a BASH, ZSH, or TCSH shell script. If the first character is a space, the script is assumed to be either a BASH or ZSH shell script. If there is a # alone, the script is a TCSH shell script. If, however, the # is followed by a ! character, then your shell reads the path name of a shell program that follows. A #! should always be followed by the path name of a shell program identifying the type of shell the script works in. If you are currently in a different shell, that shell will read the path name of the shell program, change to that shell, and execute your script. If you are in a different shell, the space or # alone is not enough to identify a BASH or TCSH shell script. Such identifications work only in their own shells. To identify a script from a different shell, you need to include the #! characters followed by a path name.

For example, if you put **#!/bin/sh** at the beginning of the first line of the **hello** script, you could execute it directly from the TCSH shell. The script will first change to the BASH shell, execute its commands, and then return to the TCSH shell (or whatever type of shell it was executed from). In the next example, the **hello** script includes the **#!/bin/sh** command. The user then executes the script while in the TCSH shell.

hello

```
#!/bin/sh
# The hello script says hello
echo "Hello, how are you"
```

```
$ hello
Hello, how are you
```

Control Structures

You can control the execution of Linux commands in a shell program with control structures. Control structures allow you to repeat commands and to select certain commands over others. A control structure consists of two major components: a test and commands. If the test is successful, then the commands are executed. In this way, you can use control structures to make decisions as to whether commands should be executed.

There are two different kinds of control structures: loops and conditions. A loop repeats commands, whereas a condition executes a command when certain conditions are met. The BASH shell has three loop control structures: **while**, **for**, and **for-in**. There are two condition structures: **if** and **case**.

The **while** and **if** control structures are useful for general purposes, such as performing iterations and making decisions using a variety of different tests. The **case** and **for** control structures are more specialized. The **case** structure is a restricted form of the **if** condition and is often used to implement menus. The **for** structure is a limited type of loop. It runs through a list of values, assigning a new value to a variable with each iteration.

The **if** and **while** control structures have as their test the execution of a Linux command. All Linux commands return an exit status after they have finished executing. If a command is successful, its exit status will be 0. If the command fails for any reason, its exit status will be a positive value referencing the type of failure that occurred. The **if** and **while** control structures check to see if the exit status of a Linux command is 0 or some other value. In the case of the **if** and **while** structures, if the exit status is a zero value, then the command was successful and the structure continues.

Control Structures: AND, OR, and NOT	Function
command **&&** *command*	The logical AND condition returns a true 0 value if both commands return a true 0 value; if one returns a nonzero value, then the AND condition is false and also returns a nonzero value.

Control Structures: AND, OR, and NOT	Function
command I I *command*	The logical OR condition returns a true 0 value if one or the other command returns a true 0 value; if both commands return a nonzero value, then the OR condition is false and also returns a nonzero value.
! *command*	The logical NOT condition inverts the return value of the command.

Loop Control Structures: while, until, for, for-in, select	Function
while *command* **do** *command* **done**	**while** executes an action as long as its test command is true.
until *command* **do** *command* **done**	**until** executes an action as long as its test command is false.
for *variable* **in** *list-values* **do** *command* **done**	**for-in** is designed for use with lists of values; the *variable* is consecutively assigned the values in the list.
for *variable* **do** *command* **done**	**for** is designed to reference script arguments; the *variable* operand is consecutively assigned each argument value.
select *string* **in** *item-list* **do** *command* **done**	**select** creates a menu based on the items in the *item-list*; then it executes the *command*; the command is usually a **case** statement.

Condition Control Structures: if, else, elif, case	Function
if *command* **then** *command* **fi**	**if** executes an action if its test *command* is true.

**Condition Control
Structures:**

if, else, elif, case	Function

if *command* **then**
    command
else
    command
fi
	if-else executes an action if the exit status of its test *command* is true; if false, then the **else** action is executed.

if *command* **then**
    command
elif *command* **then**
    command
else
    command
fi
	elif allows you to nest **if** structures, enabling selection among several alternatives; at the first true **if** structure, its *commands* are executed and control leaves the entire **elif** structure.

case *string* **in** *pattern*) *command*;; **esac**	**case** matches the string value to any of several patterns; if a *pattern* is matched, its associated commands are executed.

Jobs: Background, Kills, and Interruptions

In Linux, you not only have control over a command's input and output but also over its execution. You can run a job in the background while you execute other commands. You can also cancel commands before they have finished executing. You can even interrupt a command, starting it up again later from where you left off. Background operations are particularly useful for long jobs. Instead of waiting at the terminal until a command has finished execution, you can place it in the background. You can then continue executing other Linux commands. You can, for example, edit a file while other files are printing.

Canceling a background command can often save you a lot of unnecessary expense. If, say, you execute a command to print out all your files and then realize you have some very large files you do not want to print out, you can reference that execution of the **print** command and cancel it. Interrupting commands is rarely used, and

sometimes, it is unintentionally executed. You might, however, interrupt an editing session to send mail, and then return to your editing session, continuing from where you left off.

In Linux, a command is considered a *process*—a task to be performed. A Linux system can execute several processes at the same time, just as Linux can handle several users at the same time. There are commands to examine and control processes, though they are often reserved for system administration operations. Processes actually include not only the commands a user executes but also all the tasks the system must perform to keep Linux running.

The commands that users execute are often called *jobs*, in order to distinguish them from system processes. When the user executes a command, it becomes a job to be performed by the system. The shell provides a set of job control operations that allow the user to control the execution of these jobs. You can place a job in the background, cancel a job, or interrupt one.

Operators

The BASH shell has a standard set of arithmetic, relational, and assignment operators, as found in most programming environments, and operators for shell functions such as redirection and background operations.

Definition and Evaluation of Variables: =, $

A variable is defined in a shell when you first use the variable's name. A variable name may be any combination of alphabetic, numeric, and underscore characters. The name may also include a number, but the number cannot be the first character in the name. A name may not have any other type of character, such as an exclamation point, ampersand, or even a space. Such symbols are reserved by a shell for its own use. A name may not include more than one word because a shell uses spaces to parse commands, delimiting command names and arguments.

You assign a value to a variable with the assignment operator. Type the variable name, the assignment operator (=), and then the value assigned. Note that you cannot place any spaces around the assignment operator. Any set of characters can be assigned to a variable. In the next example, the greeting variable is assigned the string "Hello".

```
$ greeting="Hello"
```

Once you have assigned a value to a variable, you can then use that variable to reference the value. Often you use the values of variables as arguments for a command. You can reference the value of a variable using the variable name preceded by the **$** operator. The dollar sign is a special operator that uses a variable name to reference a variable's value, in effect, evaluating the variable. Evaluation retrieves a variable's value—a set of characters. This set of characters then replaces the variable name on the command line. Thus, wherever a **$** is placed before the variable name, the variable name is replaced with the value of the variable.

In the next example, the shell variable greeting is evaluated, and its contents, "Hello", are then used as the argument for an **echo** command. The **echo** command simply echoes or prints a set of characters to the screen.

```
$ echo $greeting
Hello
```

Here: <<

Normally, a shell script contains a series of commands. However, there may be times when you want to include lines of data in the shell script to use as input for one of the commands. The Here operation allows you to do this and it is represented by two less-than signs (<<). It is a redirection operation, redirecting data within a shell script as input to a command. It is called Here because the redirected data is here in the shell script, not somewhere else in another file.

The << operator is placed after the command to which input is being redirected. Lines following the << operator are then taken as input to the command. The end of the input can be specified by an end-of-file character, CTRL-D, or you can specify your own delimiter. A word following the << operator on the same line is taken to be the ending delimiter for the input lines. The delimiter can be any set of symbols. All lines up to the delimiter are read as input to the command.

In the next example, a message is sent to the user mark. The input for the message is obtained from a Here operation. The delimiter for the Here operation is the word **myend**.

mailmark

```
mail mark << myend
Did you remember
the meeting
    robert
myend
```

Double Quotes, Single Quotes, and Backslashes: "", ", \

The values that you assign to variables may consist of any set of characters, but problems occur when you want to include characters that are also used by the shell as operators. In most cases, you will need to quote your values using either single quotes, double quotes, backslashes, or back quotes, which allow you to quote strings in different ways. Quoting a special character on a command line makes it just another character. It is not evaluated by the shell. Back quotes have the special function of executing a Linux command and using the results as arguments on the command line.

Double and single quotes allow you to quote several special characters at a time. Any special characters within double or single quotes are quoted. A backslash quotes a single character—the one that it precedes. If you want to assign more than one word to a variable, you need to quote the spaces separating the words. You can do so by enclosing the words within double quotes. You can think of this as creating a character string to be assigned to the variable. Of course, any other special characters enclosed within the double quotes will also be quoted.

The following examples show three ways of quoting strings. In the first example, the double quotes enclose words separated by spaces. Because the spaces are enclosed within double quotes, they are treated as characters, not as delimiters used to parse command-line arguments. In the second example, single quotes also enclose a period, treating it as just a character. In the third example, an asterisk is also enclosed within the double quotes. The asterisk is considered just another character in the string and is not evaluated.

```
$ notice="The meeting will be tomorrow"
$ echo $notice
The meeting will be tomorrow

$ message='The project is on time.'
$ echo $message
The project is on time.

$ notice="You can get a list of files with ls *.c"
$ echo $notice
You can get a list of files with ls *.c
```

Double quotes, however, do not quote the dollar sign—the operator that evaluates variables. A **$** next to a variable name enclosed within double quotes will still be evaluated, replacing the variable name with its value. The value of the variable will then become part of the string, not the variable name. There may be times when you want a variable within quotes to be evaluated. In the next example, the double quotes are used so that the winner's name will be included in the notice.

```
$ winner=dylan
$ notice="The person who won is $winner"
$ echo $notice
The person who won is dylan
```

On the other hand, there may be times when you do not want a variable within quotes to be evaluated. In that case, you would have to use the single quotes. Single quotes suppress any variable evaluation and treat the dollar sign as just another character. In the next example, single quotes prevent the evaluation of the winner variable.

```
$ winner=dylan
$ result='The name is in the $winner variable'
$ echo $result
The name is in the $winner variable
```

If, in this case, the double quotes were used instead, an unintended variable evaluation would take place. In the next example, the characters **$winner** are interpreted as a variable evaluation.

```
$ winner=dylan
$ result="The name is in the $winner variable"
$ echo $result
The name is in the dylan variable
```

You can always quote any special character, including the **$** operator, by preceding it with a backslash. The backslash is useful when you want to evaluate variables within a string and also include **$** characters. In the next example, the backslash is placed before the dollar sign in order to treat it as a dollar sign character, **\$**. At the same time, the variable **$winner** is evaluated since double quotes do not themselves quote the **$** operator.

```
$ winner=dylan
$ result="$winner won \$100.00"
$ echo $result
dylan won $100.00
```

Back Quotes: ``

Though you can create variable values by typing in characters or character strings, you can also obtain values from other Linux commands. However, to assign the result of a Linux command to a variable, you first need to execute the command. If you place a Linux command within back quotes on the command line, that command is first executed and its result becomes an argument on the command line. In the case of assignments, the result of a command can be assigned to a variable by placing the command within back quotes to first execute it. Think of back quotes as a kind of expression that contains both a command to be executed and its result, which is then assigned to the variable. The characters making up the command itself are not assigned.

In the next example, the command **ls *.c** is executed and its result is then assigned to the variable **listc**. The command **ls *.c** generates a list of all files with a .c extension, and this list of files will then be assigned to the **listc** variable.

```
$ listc=`ls *.c`
$ echo $listc
main.c prog.c lib.c
```

Keep in mind the difference between single quotes and back quotes. Single quotes treat a Linux command as a set of characters. Back quotes force execution of the Linux command. There may be

times when you accidentally enter single quotes when you
mean to use back quotes. The following examples illustrate
the difference. In the first example, the assignment for the **lscc**
variable has single quotes, not back quotes, placed around the **ls**
*.c command. In this case, **ls *.c** are just characters to be assigned
to the variable **lscc**. In the second example, back quotes are
placed around the **ls *.c** command, forcing evaluation of the
command. A list of filenames ending in **.c** is generated and
assigned as the value of **lscc**.

```
$ lscc='ls *.c'
$ echo $lscc
ls *.c

$ lscc=`ls *.c`
$ echo $lscc
main.c  prog.c
```

Positional Parameters: $

Like Linux commands, a shell script can take arguments. When
you invoke a script, you can enter arguments on the command line
after the script name. These arguments can then be referenced
within the script using positional parameters. To reference a
positional parameter, you use the **$** operator and the number of its
position on the command line. Arguments on the command line are
sequentially numbered from 1. The first argument is referenced
with the positional parameter **$1**, the second argument with **$2**,
and so on. The positional parameter **$0** references will contain the
name of the shell script, the first word on the command line.

These argument references can be thought of as referencing
read-only variables. For those familiar with programming
terminology, you can think of words on the command line as
arguments that are passed into positional parameter variables, **$1**
through **$9**. These variables are read-only variables. Once given the
initial values, they cannot be altered. In this sense, argument
variables function more as constants—constants determined by the
command-line arguments. Each word on the command line is
parsed into an argument. Quoted sets of words are considered one
argument. If you enter more than one argument, you can reference

them with each corresponding argument number. In the next example, four arguments are entered on the command line.

greetargs

```
echo "The first argument is: $1"
echo "The second argument is: $2"
echo "The third argument is: $3"
echo "The fourth argument is: $4"
```

```
$ greetargs Hello Hi Salutations "How are you"
The first argument is: Hello
The second argument is: Hi
The third argument is: Salutations
The fourth argument is: How are you
$
```

A set of special variables, **$***, **$@**, and **$#**, allows you to reference different aspects of command-line arguments. The **$#** argument contains the number of arguments entered on the command line. This is useful when a script requires a fixed number of arguments. The variable **$*** references all the arguments in the command line. A command line may have more than nine arguments. The **$@** also references all the arguments on the command line, but allows you to separately quote each one. The difference between **$*** and **$@** is not clear until you use them to reference arguments using the **for-in** control structure. For this reason, they are discussed only briefly here and more extensively in the section on control structures later in the chapter.

In the next example, the command-line arguments are displayed first using the **$*** special variable and then **$@**. The number of arguments is displayed using the **$#** special variable.

sargs

```
echo $*
echo $@
echo "There are $# arguments"
```

```
$ sargs Hello Hi Welcome
Hello Hi Welcome
```

```
Hello Hi Welcome
There are 3 arguments
```

The following table lists both positional parameters and process variables.

Positional Parameters	Description
$0	Name of Linux command.
$n	The nth command-line argument beginning from **1**, **$1-$n**; you can use **set** to change the arguments.
$*	All the command-line arguments beginning from **1**; you can use **set** to change them.
$@	The command-line arguments individually quoted.
$#	The count of the command-line arguments.

Process Variables	Description
$$	The PID number, or *process ID*, of the current process.
$!	The PID number of the most recent background job.
$?	The exit status of the last Linux command executed.

Arithmetic Operators

Arithmetic evaluation is performed in long integers with no check for overflow. Division by 0 is trapped and flagged as an error. The table of operators shown here is grouped by equal-precedence operators, with the groups listed in order of decreasing precedence. Precedence can be overridden by using nested parentheses.

Operator	Description
-, +	Unary minus and plus
!, ~	Logical and bitwise negation
*, /, %	Multiplication, division, remainder
+, -	Addition, subtraction

Operator	Description
<<, >>	Left and right bitwise shifts
<=, >=, <, >	Comparison
==, !=	Equality and inequality
&	Bitwise AND
^	Bitwise exclusive OR
I	Bitwise OR
&&	Logical AND
I I	Logical OR
=, *=, /=, %=, +=, -=, <<=, >>=, &=, ^=, I =	Assignment

You can use shell variables as operands. Constants beginning with a 0 are interpreted as octal numbers; a preceding x denotes a hexadecimal number.

Redirecting the Standard Output: >

Suppose that instead of displaying a list of files on the screen, you would like to save this list in a file. In other words, you would like to direct the standard output to a file rather than the screen. To do this, you place the output redirection operator (greater-than sign, >) and the name of a file on the command line after the Linux command. In the next example, the output of the **cat** command is redirected from the screen device to a file.

```
$ cat myletter > newletter
```

The redirection operation creates the new destination file. If the file already exists, it will be overwritten with the data in the standard output. You can set the **noclobber** feature to prevent overwriting an existing file with the redirection operation. In this case, the redirection operation on an existing file will fail. You can overcome the **noclobber** feature by placing an exclamation point after the redirection operator. The next example sets the **noclobber** feature for the BASH shell and then forces the overwriting of the **oldletter** file if it already exists.

```
$ set -o noclobber
cat myletter > oldletter
cat: file exists
$ cat myletter >! oldletter
```

Though the redirection operator and filename are placed after the command, the redirection operation is not executed after the command. In fact, it is executed before the command. The redirection operation creates the file and sets up the redirection before it receives any data from the standard output. If the file already exists, it will be destroyed and replaced by a file of the same name. In effect, the command generating the output is executed only after the redirected file has been created.

In the next example, the output of the **ls** command is redirected from the screen device to a file. First, the **ls** command lists files, and in the next command, **ls** redirects its file list to the **listf** file. Then the **cat** command displays the list of files saved in **listf**. Notice that the list of files in **listf** includes the **listf** filename. The **listf** file is first created by the redirection operation, and then the **ls** command lists it along with other files.

```
$ ls
mydata intro preface
$ ls > listf
$ cat listf
mydata intro listf preface
```

Errors occur when you try to use the same filename for both an input file for the command and the redirected destination file. In this case, since the redirection operation is executed first, the input file, since it exists, is destroyed and replaced by a file of the same name. When the command is executed, it finds an input file that is empty.

In the **cat** command shown next, the file **myletter** is the name for both the destination file for redirected output and the input file for the **cat** operation. The redirection operation is executed first, destroying the **myletter** file and replacing it with a new and empty **myletter** file. Then the **cat** operation is executed and attempts to read all the data in the **myletter** file. However, there is now nothing in the **myletter** file.

```
$ cat myletter > myletter
```

Appending the Standard Output: >>

You can also *append* the standard output to an existing file using the >> redirection operator. Instead of overwriting the file, the data in the standard output is added at the end of the file. In the next example, the **myletter** and **oldletter** files are appended to the **alletters** file. The **alletters** file will then contain the contents of both **myletter** and **oldletter**.

```
$ cat myletter >> alletters
$ cat oldletter >> alletters
```

The Standard Input: <

Many Linux commands can receive data from the standard input. The standard input itself receives data from a device or a file. The default device for the standard input is the keyboard. Characters typed into the keyboard are placed in the standard input, which is then directed to the Linux command.

If you combine the **cat** command with redirection, you have an easy way of saving what you have typed to a file. As shown in the next example, the output of the **cat** operation is redirected to the **mydat** file. The **mydat** file will now contain all the data typed in at the keyboard. The **cat** command, in this case, still has no file arguments. It will receive its data from the standard input, the keyboard device. The redirection operator redirects the output of the **cat** command to the file **mydat**. The **cat** command has no direct contact with any files. It is simply receiving input from the standard input and sending output to the standard output.

```
$ cat > mydat
This is a new line
for the cat
command
^D
$ cat mydat
This is a new line
for the cat
command
$
```

Just as with the standard output, you can also redirect the standard input. The standard input may be received from a file rather than the keyboard. The operator for redirecting the standard input is the less-than sign (<). In the next example, the standard input is redirected to receive input from the **myletter** file rather than the keyboard device. The contents of **myletter** are read into the standard input by the redirection operation. Then the **cat** command reads the standard input and displays the contents of **myletter**.

```
$ cat < myletter
```

You can combine the redirection operations for both standard input and standard output. In the next example, the **cat** command has no filename arguments. Without filename arguments, the **cat** command receives input from the standard input and sends output to the standard output. However, the standard input has been redirected to receive its data from a file, and the standard output has been redirected to place its data in a file.

```
$ cat < myletter > newletter
```

Pipe: |

You will find yourself in situations in which you need to send data from one command to another. In other words, you will want to send the standard output of a command to another command, not to a destination file. Suppose you want to send a list of your filenames to the printer to be printed. You need two commands to do this: the **ls** command to generate a list of filenames and the **lpr** command to send the list to the printer. In effect, you need to take the output of the **ls** command and use it as input for the **lpr** command. You can think of the data as flowing from one command to another, and to form such a connection in Linux, you use what is called a *pipe*. The pipe operator (vertical bar character: I), placed between two commands forms a connection between them. The standard output of one command becomes the standard input for the other. The pipe operation receives output from the command placed before the pipe and sends this data as input to the command placed after the pipe. As shown in the next example, you can connect the **ls** command and the **lpr** command with a pipe. The list of filenames output by the **ls** command is piped into the **lpr** command.

```
$ ls | lpr
```

You can combine the pipe operation with other shell features, such as special characters, to perform specialized operations. The next example prints only files with a **.c** extension. The **ls** command is used with the asterisk and **.c** to generate a list of filenames with the **.c** extension. Then this list is piped to the **lpr** command.

```
$ ls *.c | lpr
```

Whereas redirection simply places output in a file, pipes send
output to another Linux command. You may wonder why this
cannot be accomplished with redirection. You need to keep in
mind the difference between a file and a command: A file is a
storage medium that holds data. You can save data on it or read
data from it. A command is a program that executes instructions.
A command may read or save data in a file, but a command is not
in itself a file. For this reason, a redirection operation operates on
files, not on commands. Redirection can send data from a program
to a file, or from a file to a program, but it cannot send data
directly from a program to another program. Only files can be the
destination of a redirection operation, not other programs.

You can, however, simulate the piping process through a series of
redirection operations. You could send the output of one command
to a file. Then, on the next line, you could execute a command
using that file as redirected input. The next example uses two
redirection operations in two separate commands to print a list
of filenames. This same task was performed in the previous
examples using a single pipe operation. The pipe operation
literally takes the standard output of one command and uses it
as standard input for another command.

```
$ ls > tempfile
$ lpr < tempfile
```

Up to this point we have been using a list of filenames as input, but
it is important to note that pipes operate on the standard output of
a command, whatever that might be. The contents of whole files or
even several files can be piped from one command to another. In
the next example, the **cat** command reads and outputs the contents
of the **mydata** file, which are then piped to the **lpr** command.

```
$ cat mydata | lpr
```

Suppose you want to print out data you are typing in from the
keyboard, instead of printing data from a file. Remember that
the **cat** command without any arguments reads data from the
standard input. In the next example, **cat** takes input from the
keyboard instead of a file and pipes the output to the **lpr**
command. The **cat** command is executed before the **lpr** command,
so you first enter your data for the **cat** command on the keyboard,
ending with the end-of-file, CTRL-D. The input for a piped byte
stream may come from any source.

```
$ cat | lpr
This text will
be printed
^D
$
```

Linux provides **cat** with a -n option that outputs the contents of a file, adding line numbers. If you want to print your file with line numbers, you must first use the **cat** command with the -**n** option to output the contents of the file with line numbers added. You then pipe this output to the **lpr** command for printing, for example:

```
$ cat -n  mydata | lpr
```

You do much the same thing for displaying a file with line numbers. In this case, the numbered output is usually piped to the **more** command for screen-by-screen examination. You can even specify several files at once and pipe their output to the **more** command, examining all the files. In the next example, both **mydata** and **preface** are numbered and piped to the **more** command for screen-by-screen examination.

```
$ cat -n mydata preface | more
```

Be careful when you use redirection with pipes. A standard output redirection specifies a destination for the standard output. The standard output is saved and stored in that destination file. Once saved, there is no output to be piped into another command. Though redirection can take place at the end of a series of pipe operations, it cannot take place *within* pipe operations. The next example is a valid use of pipes and redirection. The output of the **sort** command is piped to the **cat** command with the -**n** option to number lines, and then the result is saved in the **nfile** file.

```
$ sort mylist | cat -n > nfile
```

What if you need to save the result in **nfile** and print it out? You cannot do something like this:

```
$ sort mylist | cat -n > nfile | lpr
ERROR
```

The only way to save the output in a file and print it is to use the **tee** command:

```
$ sort mylist | cat -n | tee nfile | lpr
```

You can use **tee** anywhere in the piping sequence. The next example saves a sorted version of the list while printing the numbered version.

```
$ sort mylist | tee sfile | cat -n | lpr
```

Redirecting and Piping the Standard Error: >&, 2>, |&

When you execute commands, it is possible that an error could occur. You may give the wrong number of arguments, or some kind of system error could take place. When an error occurs, the system will issue an error message. Usually such error messages are displayed on the screen, along with the standard output. However, Linux distinguishes between standard output and error messages. Error messages are placed in yet another standard byte stream called the *standard error*. In the next example, the **cat** command is given as its argument the name of a file that does not exist, **myintro**. In this case, the **cat** command will simply issue an error:

```
$ cat myintro
cat : myintro not found
$
```

Because error messages are in a separate data stream than the standard output, error messages will still appear on the screen for you to see, even if you have redirected the standard output to a file. In the next example, the standard output of the **cat** command is redirected to the file **mydata**. However, the standard error, containing the error messages, is still directed to the screen.

```
$ cat myintro > mydata
cat : myintro not found
$
```

Like the standard output, you can also redirect the standard error. This means that you can save your error messages in a file for future reference. This is helpful if you need a record of the error messages. Like the standard output, the standard error's default destination is the screen device, but you can redirect the standard error to any file or device that you choose using special redirection operators. In this case, the error messages will not be displayed on the screen.

Redirection of the standard error relies on a special feature of shell redirection. You can reference all the standard byte streams in redirection operations with numbers. The numbers 0, 1, and 2 reference the standard input, standard output, and standard error, respectively. By default, an output redirection (>) operates on the standard output, 1. However, you can modify the output redirection to operate on the standard error by preceding the output redirection operator with the number 2. In the next example, the **cat** command again will generate an error. The error message is redirected to the **myerrors** file.

```
$ cat nodata 2> myerrors
$ cat myerrors
cat : nodata not found
$
```

You can also append the standard error to a file by using the number 2 and the redirection append operator, >>. In the next example, the user appends the standard error to the **myerrors** file, which then functions as a log of errors.

```
$ cat nodata 2>> myerrors
$ cat compls 2>> myerrors
$ cat myerrors
cat : nodata not found
cat : compls not found
$
```

To redirect both the standard output and the standard error, you need a separate redirection operation and file for each. In the next example, the standard output is redirected to the file **mydata**, whereas the standard error is redirected to **myerrors**. If **nodata** actually exists, **mydata** will hold a copy of its contents.

```
$ cat nodata 1> mydata 2> myerrors
$ cat myerrors
cat : nodata not found
$
```

The default output stream for a >& operation is the standard output, and the default input stream is the standard error. If the preceding operation is written without using numbers, as shown in the next example, any error messages will be redirected into the standard output and saved in the same destination file for the standard output.

```
$ cat nodata >& mydata
```

Background: &

You execute a command in the background by placing an ampersand on the command line at the end of the command. When you do so, a user job number and a system process number are displayed. The user job number, placed in brackets, is the number by which the user references the job. The system process number is the number by which the system identifies the job. In the next example, the command to print the file **mydata** is placed in the background.

```
$ lpr mydata &
[1]   534
$
```

&& and ||

command && *command*
command || *command*

The logical commands perform logical operations on two Linux commands. In the case of the logical AND, **&&**, if both commands are successful, then the logical command is successful and returns an exit status of 0. For the logical OR, ||, if either command is successful, then the OR is successful and returns an exit status of 0. The logical commands allow you to use a logical operation as your test command in control structures.

Functions: (){}

function-name () {*commands*;}

You can define a function consisting of several commands placed between a set of enclosing braces. A function is specified by a pair of parentheses following the function name. This list is executed whenever the function name is specified as the name of a simple command. The exit status of a function is the exit status of the last command executed from within the function.

BASH Commands

A description of each BASH builtin command follows. The commands are listed alphabetically. In most cases, each description begins with the command's syntax.

Colon (:)

```
: [arguments]
```

The colon (:) allows you to list more than one command on the same command line, each separated by a colon. The exit code is zero.

source, .

```
. filename [arguments]
source filename [arguments]
```

The period (.), or **source**, reads and executes commands from a file in the current shell. It returns the exit status of the last command executed in that file. If the filename does not include a full path name, then the path names defined in **PATH** are used to locate the directory in which the filename resides.

CTRL-Z: Interruptions

You can interrupt a job and stop it with the CTRL-Z command. The job is not ended; it merely remains suspended until you wish to continue. When you're ready, you can continue with the job in either the foreground or the background using the **fg** or **bg** command. The **fg** command will restart an interrupted job in the foreground. The **bg** command will place the interrupted job in the background.

There will be times when you need to place a job that is currently running in the foreground into the background. However, you cannot move a currently running job directly into the background. You first need to interrupt it with CTRL-Z, and then place it in the background with the **bg** command. In the next example, the current command to list and redirect .c files is first interrupted with a CTRL-Z. Then that job is placed in the background.

```
$ cat *.c > myprogs
^Z
$ bg
```

Often, while in the Vi editor, you may make the mistake of entering a CTRL-Z instead of a SHIFT-ZZ to end your session. The CTRL-Z will interrupt the Vi editor and return you to the Linux prompt. The editing session has not ended; it has only been interrupted. You may not detect such a mistake until you try to log out. The system will not allow you to log out while an interrupted job remains. To log out, you must first restart the interrupted job with the **fg** command. In the case of the Vi editor interruption, the **fg** command will place you back in the Vi editor. Then a ZZ editor command will end the Vi editor job, and you can log out. In the next example, the **jobs** command shows that there is a stopped job. The **fg** command then brings the job to the foreground.

```
$ jobs
[1]  +  Stopped  vi mydata
$ fg %1
```

alias

alias [alias-name[=value] ...]

The **alias** command alone displays the list of defined aliases. To display the value of a particular alias, you can use its name alone as an argument. If you provided a name that has not been defined as an alias, then the command returns false; otherwise, it returns true. You can also use the **alias** command to define aliases, providing the name and the value separated by an equal (=) sign. A trailing space in value causes the next word to be checked for alias substitution when the alias is expanded.

at

With the **at** command, you can execute commands at a specified time. Instead of placing a job immediately in the background, you can specify a time when you want it executed. You can then log out and the system will keep track of what commands to execute and when to execute them.

The **at** command takes as its argument a time when you want commands executed. The time is a number specifying the hour followed by the keywords **am** or **pm**. You can also add a date. If no date is specified, today's date is assumed. The **at** command will then read in Linux commands from the standard input. You can enter these commands at the keyboard, ending the standard input with a CTRL-D. You can also enter the commands into a file, which you can then redirect through the standard input to the **at** command. In the next example, the user decides to execute a command at 4:00 A.M.

```
$ at 4am
lpr intro
^D
$
```

You have a great deal of leeway in specifying the time and date. The **at** command assumes a 24-hour sequence for the time unless modified by the keywords **am** or **pm**. You can specify minutes in an hour by separating the hour and minutes with a colon, for example, 6:30. The **at** command also recognizes a series of keywords that specify certain dates and times. The keyword **noon** specifies 12:00 P.M. You can use the keyword **midnight** instead of 12:00 A.M. In the next examples, the user executes commands using a minute specification and then the keyword **noon**.

```
$ at 8:15pm < latecmds
$ at noon < latecmds
```

The date can be specified as a day of the month or a day of the week. The day of the month consists of the number of the day and a keyword representing the month. Months can be represented by three-letter abbreviations; for example, January is written as Jan. The day of the month follows the month's name. If there is no name, then the current month is assumed. Feb 14 specifies the 14th of February; 21 by itself specifies the 21st day of the current month. In the next example, the user first executes commands on the 15th of this month and then on the 29th of October.

```
$ at 8:15pm  15 < latecmds
$ at noon Oct 29 < latecmds
```

bg [*jobspec*]

bg places a job in the background. If *jobspec* is not present, the shell's notion of the current job is used. The **bg** command returns 0 unless run when job control is disabled or, when run with job control enabled, if *jobspec* was not found or started without job control.

bind

```
bind [-m keymap] [-lvd] [-q name]
bind [-m keymap] -f filename
bind [-m keymap] keyseq:function-name
```

The **bind** command displays current readline key and function bindings, or binds a key sequence to a readline function or macro. The binding syntax accepted is identical to that of **.inputrc**, but each binding must be passed as a separate argument (for example, '"\C-x\C-r": re-read-init-file'). The return value is 0 unless an unrecognized option is given or an error occurred. Options, if supplied, have the following meanings:

Option	Description
-m *keymap*	Use *keymap* as the keymap to be affected by the subsequent bindings. Acceptable keymap names are **emacs**, **emacs-standard**, **emacs-meta**, **emacs-ctlx**, **vi**, **vi-move**, **vi-command**, and **vi- insert**. **vi** is equivalent to **vi-command**; **emacs** is equivalent to **emacs-standard**.
-l	List the names of all readline functions.
-v	List current function names and bindings.
-d	Dump function names and bindings in such a way that they can be reread.
-f *filename*	Read key bindings from *filename*.
-q *function*	Query about which keys invoke the named function.
keyseq:function-name	Determine keys that invoke the named function.

break

```
break [n]
```

break forces an exit from within a **for**, **while**, or **until** loop. The *n* argument, if present, specifies the number of nested levels to break out of. If *n* is greater than the number of enclosing loops, all enclosing loops are exited. **break** returns a value of 0 unless the shell is not executing a loop when break is executed.

builtin

```
builtin shell-builtin [arguments]
```

The **builtin** command executes the specified shell builtin, passing it arguments, and returning its exit status. This is useful when you wish to define a function whose name is the same as a shell builtin, but also need the functionality of the builtin within the function itself. The **cd** builtin is commonly redefined this way. The return status is false if *shell-builtin* is not a shell builtin command.

case

```
case variable in
    pattern)
        commands
        ;;
    pattern)
        commands
        ;;
    *)
        default commands
        ;;
    esac
```

The **case** structure chooses among several possible alternatives. The choice is made by comparing a value with several possible patterns. Each possible pattern is associated with a set of operations. If a match is found, the associated operations are performed. The **case** structure begins with the keyword **case**, an evaluation of a variable, and the keyword **in**. A set of patterns then follows. Each pattern is a regular expression terminated with a closing parenthesis. After the closing parenthesis, commands associated with this pattern are listed, followed by a double semicolon on a separate line, designating the end of those commands. After all the listed patterns, the keyword **esac** ends the **case** command.

A pattern can include any shell special characters. The shell special characters are the *, [,], ?, and I. You can specify a default pattern with a single * special character. The * special character matches on any pattern; so if all other patterns do not match, the * will. In this way, the default option is executed if no other options are chosen. The default is optional; you do not have to put it in.

A **case** structure is often used to implement menus. In the program **lschoice**, in the next example, the user is asked to enter a choice for listing files in different ways. Notice the default option that warns of invalid input.

lschoice

```
# Program to allow the user to select different ways of
#     listing files
echo   s. List Sizes
echo   l. List All File Information
echo   c. List C Files
echo -n "Please enter choice: "
read choice
case $choice in
    s)
        ls -s
        ;;
    l)
        ls -l
        ;;
    c)
        ls *.c
        ;;
    *)
        echo Invalid Option
    esac
```

```
$ lschoice
s. List Sizes
l. List All File Information
c. List C Files
Please enter choice: c
main.c    lib.c    file.c
$
```

cd

cd [*dir*]

Change the current directory to *dir*. The value of the variable **HOME** is the default directory. The variable **CDPATH** defines the search path for the directory containing *dir*. Alternative directory names are separated by a colon (:). A null directory name in **CDPATH** is the same as the current directory (i.e., .). If *dir* begins with a slash (/), then **CDPATH** is not used. An argument of - is equivalent to **$OLDPWD**. The return value is true if the directory was successfully changed; otherwise, it is false.

continue

```
continue [n]
```

Skip the remainder of the body of the current loop and reexecute it beginning the next iteration. Works for the **for**, **while**, or **until** loops. With the *n* argument, **continue** will begin at the *n*th enclosing loop. If *n* is greater than the number of enclosing loops, the last enclosing loop (the "top-level" loop) is resumed. **continue** returns 0 unless the shell is not executing a loop when **continue** is executed.

declare

```
declare [-frxi] [variable-name[=value]]
typeset [-frxi] [variable-name[=value]]
```

declare declares a variable, specifying the variable name and its initial value separated by an equal (=) sign. If there are no arguments, then the values of variables are displayed. Attributes for variables can be set using the following options:

Option	Description
-f	Use function names only.
-r	Make variables read-only.
-x	Mark variables for export to subsequent commands via the environment.
-i	Treat variables as integers; arithmetic evaluation is performed when the variable is assigned a value.

Using + instead of - turns off the attribute instead. If **declare** is used in a function, variables are declared as local variables (as the **local** command does). A 0 is returned unless an illegal option or illegal name is used, or an attempt is made to turn off read-only status for a read-only variable, or an attempt is made to display a nonexistent function with -**f**.

dirs

```
dirs [-l] [+/-n]
```

dirs displays the list of currently remembered directories. Directories are added to the list with the **pushd** command; the **popd** command moves back up through the list. The following options can be used with **dirs**:

Option	Function
+*n*	Display the *n*th entry counting from the left of the list shown by **dirs** when invoked without options, starting with zero.
-*n*	Display the *n*th entry counting from the right of the list shown by **dirs** when invoked without options, starting with zero.
-l	Produce a longer listing; the default listing format uses a tilde (~) to denote the home directory.

The return value is 0 unless an illegal option is supplied or *n* indexes beyond the end of the directory stack.

echo

```
echo string
echo variable
```

The **echo** command will send data to the standard output. The data is in the form of a string of characters. The **echo** command can output variable values as well as string constants. The return status is always 0.

Option	Function
-n	Suppress a newline at the end.
-e	Enable interpretation of the following escaped characters.
-E	Disable the interpretation of the following escaped characters.

Escaped Character	Description
\a	Alert (bell)
\b	Backspace
\c	Suppress trailing newline
\f	Form feed
\n	Newline
\r	Carriage return
\t	Horizontal tab
\v	Vertical tab
\\	Backslash
\nnn	The character whose ASCII code is nnn (octal)

elif

```
if Linux command
    then
            commands
elif Linux command
    then
            commands
        else
            commands
fi
```

The **elif** structure allows you to nest **if-then-else** operations. The **elif** structure stands for "else if." With **elif**, you can choose between several alternatives. The first alternative is specified with the **if** structure, followed by other alternatives, each specified by its own **elif** structure. The alternative to the last **elif** structure is specified with an **else**. If the test (a Linux command) for the first **if** structure fails, control will be passed to the next **elif** structure, and its test will be executed. If it fails, control is passed to the next **elif** and its test will be checked. This continues until a test is true. Then that **elif** has its commands executed, and control passes out of the **if** structure to the next command after the **fi** keyword.

elseif

```
echo Enter s to list file sizes,
echo Enter a to list dot files,
echo otherwise all file information is listed.
```

```
echo -n "Please enter option: "
read choice
if [ "$choice"=s ]
    then
        ls -s
elif [ "$choice"=a ]
    then
        ls -a
    else
        ls -l
fi
echo Good-bye

$ elseif
Enter s to list file sizes,
Enter a to list dot files,
otherwise all file information is listed.
Please enter option: s
total 2
    1 monday     2 today
Good-bye
$
```

enable

```
enable [-n] [-all] [command-name ...]
```

The **enable** command can enable and disable builtin shell commands. The **-n** option disables commands. With no arguments it displays a list of all enabled shell builtins. With only the **-n** option, a list of all disabled builtins is displayed. The **-all** (or **-a**) option displays all builtins, with indications of whether each one is enabled. **enable** returns 0 unless a name is not a shell builtin.

eval

```
eval [arguments ...]
```

eval reads and concatenates its arguments into a single command that is then read and executed by the shell. **eval** returns the exit status of that command. If there are no arguments or the arguments are null, **eval** returns 0.

exec

```
exec [[-] command [arguments]]
```

exec executes a command, replacing the current shell; no new process is created. You can specify arguments for the command. If **exec**'s first argument is -, the shell places a dash in the zeroth *argument* passed to *command*. If **exec** has no arguments, then any redirections take effect in the current shell, returning 0 as its exit status.

exit

```
exit [n]
```

exit causes the shell to exit. If *n* is provided, the shell exits with a status of *n*. Without *n*, the exit status is that of the last command executed. A trap on **exit** is executed before the shell terminates.

export

```
export [-nf] [name[=word] ...]
export -p
```

The named variables are marked for automatic export to the environment of subsequently executed shells and commands. You can also assign a value to a variable in the **export** command. With the **-f** option, the *names* refer to functions instead of variables. With the **-p** option or with no arguments, a list of all names that are exported in this shell is displayed. With the **-n** option, you can remove the export capability from a variable. An argument of -- disables option checking for the rest of the arguments. **export** returns an exit status of 0 unless an illegal option is used, one of the *names* is not a legal shell variable name, or **-f** is used with a *name* that is not a function.

When you execute a script file, you initiate a new process that has its own shell. Within this shell you can define variables, execute Linux commands, and even execute other scripts. If you execute another script from within the script currently running, the current script suspends execution, and control is transferred to the other script. All the commands in this other script are first executed before returning to continue with the suspended script. The process of executing one script from another operates much like a function or procedure call in programming languages. You can think of a script calling another script. The calling script waits until the called script finishes execution before continuing with its next command.

Any variable definitions that you place in a script will be defined within the script's shell and only known within that script's shell; they are local to their own shells. Suppose, however, you want to be able to define a variable within a script and use it in any scripts it may call. You cannot do this directly, but you can export a variable definition from one shell to another using the **export** command. When the **export** command is applied to a variable, it will instruct the system to define a copy of that variable for each new subshell generated. Each new subshell will have its own copy of the exported variable. In the next example, the **myname** variable is defined and exported.

```
$ myname="Charles"
$ export myname
```

It is a mistake to think of exported variables as global variables. A shell can never reference a variable outside of itself. Instead, a copy of the variable with its value is generated for the new shell. Exported variables export their values to a shell, not themselves. An exported variable operates to some extent like a scoped global parameter. It is copied to any shell derived from its own shell. Any shell script called directly or indirectly after the exported variable's shell will be given a copy of the exported variable with the initial value. It is important to remember that an exported variable will not be given to a process's parent shell.

fc

```
fc [-e ename] [-nlr] [first-event] [last-event]
fc -s [pattern=replacement] [event]
```

fc selects a set of events (commands you have recently executed) from the history list. The events can be specified as a string or as a number. (A negative number is used as an offset from the current event number.) If there is no *last-event* argument, the current event is used. If no arguments are used, the then *first-event* is set to –16. The **-n** option suppresses the event numbers. The **-r** option reverses the order of the events. The **-l** option displays events on the standard output. By default, the editor invoked on a file contains these history events. With the **-e** option, you can specify the editor to be used (*ename*). If *ename* is not given, the value of the **FCEDIT** variable is used, and the value of **EDITOR** if **FCEDIT** is not set. If neither variable is set, Vi is used. **fc** returns 0 unless an illegal option is encountered or *first-event* or *last-event* specify history lines out of range. If the **-e** option is supplied, the return value is the value of the last event executed, or failure if an error occurs with the temporary file of events.

With the **-s** option you can reexecute a specified history event. The *event* argument can be either a pattern or an event number. You can also replace patterns in the event using the equal (=) sign (*pattern=replacement*). **fc -s mv** executes an event beginning with **mv**. **fc -s** returns exit status of the event reexecuted.

fg

```
fg [jobspec]
```

Places a background job in the foreground, making it the current job. If *jobspec* is not present, the shell's notion of the current job is used. **fg** returns the value of the command placed into the foreground. It returns 0 if *jobspec* does not specify a valid job or if job control is disabled. *jobspec* can be a job control number as displayed by the **jobs** command.

In the next example, the second job is brought back into the foreground. You may not immediately receive a prompt again because the second command is now in the foreground and executing. When the command has finished executing, the prompt will appear, and you can execute another command.

```
$ fg %2
cat *.c > myprogs
$
```

for

```
for variable
    do
    commands
    done
```

Within a shell file the **for** structure without a specified list of values takes as its list of values the arguments specified on the command line when the shell file is invoked. The variable used in the **for** command is set automatically to each argument value in sequence. The first time through the loop, the variable is set to the value of the first argument. The second time, it is set to the value of the second argument.

The **for** structure without a specified list is equivalent to the list **$@**. **$@** is a special argument variable whose value is the list of command-line arguments. In the next example, a list of C program files is entered on the command line when the shell file **cbackuparg** is invoked. In **cbackuparg**, each argument is automatically referenced by a **for** loop. **backfile** is the variable used in the **for** loop. The first time through the loop, **$backfile** holds the value of the first argument, **$1**. The second time through, it holds the value of the second argument, **$2**.

cbackuparg

```
for backfile
do
     cp $backfile sourcebak/$backfile
     echo "$backfile"
done

$ cbackuparg  main.c  lib.c  io.c
main.c
lib.c
io.c
```

for-in

```
for variable in list of values
     do
     commands
     done
```

The **for-in** structure is designed to reference a list of values sequentially. It takes two operands—a *variable* and a *list of values*. Each value in the list is assigned, one by one, to the *variable* in the **for-in** structure. Like the **while** command, the **for-in** structure is a loop. Each time through the loop, the next value in the list is assigned to the *variable*. When the end of the list is reached, the loop stops. Like the **while** loop, the body of a **for-in** loop begins with the keyword **do** and ends with the keyword **done**.

In the **mylistfor** script, the user simply outputs a list of each item with today's date. The list of items makes up the list of values read by the **for-in** loop. Each item is consecutively assigned to the **grocery** variable.

mylistfor

```
tdate=`date +%D`
for grocery in milk cookies apples cheese
    do
    echo "$grocery      $tdate"
    done
```

```
$ mylistfor
milk      05/23/99
cookies   05/23/99
apples    05/23/99
cheese    05/23/99
$
```

The **for-in** loop is handy for managing files. You can use special characters to generate filenames for use as a list of values in the **for-in** loop. For example, the ***** special character, by itself, generates a list of all files and directories, and ***.c** lists files with the **.c** extension. The special character ***** placed in the **for-in** loop's value list will generate a list of values consisting of all the filenames in your current directory.

```
for myfiles in *
    do
```

The **cbackup** script makes a backup of each file and places it in a directory called **sourcebak**. Notice the use of the ***** special character to generate a list of all filenames with a **.c** extension.

cbackup

```
for backfile in *.c
    do
    cp $backfile sourcebak/$backfile
    echo $backfile
    done
```

```
$ cbackup
io.c
lib.c
main.c
$
```

getopts

getopts *optstring variable-name* [*arguments*]

getopts is used for detecting options to be used for a shell script. The *optstring* argument specifies a list of characters that can be used as valid options for the shell script. If the character is followed by a colon, the option is expected to have an argument, separated from it by a space. Each time it is executed, **getopts** places the next option in the shell variable *name* and the index of the next argument to be processed into the variable **OPTIND**. If an option requires an argument, **getopts** places that argument into the variable **OPTARG**. The shell does not reset **OPTIND** automatically; it must be manually reset between multiple calls to **getopts** within the same shell invocation, if a new set of parameters is to be used. **getopts** can report errors in two ways. If the first character of *optstring* is a colon, silent error reporting is used. In normal operation, diagnostic messages are printed when illegal options or missing option arguments are encountered. If the variable **OPTERR** is set to 0, no error message will be displayed, even if the first character of *optstring* is not a colon.

getopts normally parses the positional parameters; but if more arguments are given in *arguments*, **getopts** parses those instead. **getopts** returns true if an option, specified or unspecified, is found, or false if the end of options is encountered or an error occurs.

getopts is often used in a loop to check for options a user may have entered when invoking a script. The following loop allows the user to enter three possible options to a script: **t**, **r**, and **s**. **r** with its colon (:) following it, is expected to take an argument. In this example, if the user enters the **-a** option, the **ls** command displays all files in a long format. However, if the **-r** option is entered with a filename, then the filename argument is accessed from the **OPTARG** variable and the long format of just that file is displayed.

```
while getopts  tr:s  myoption
    do
    case $myoption in
            a)  ls -al
            r)  ls -l $OPTARG
            s)  ls -s
    esac
    done
```

hash

```
hash [-r] [name]
```

hash determines and remembers the full path name of a command. With the **-r** option, the shell forgets all remembered locations. With no arguments, information about all remembered commands is displayed. An argument of -- disables option checking for the rest of the arguments. The return status is true unless a name is not found or an illegal option is supplied.

help

```
help [pattern]
```

help displays information about commands. You can use a pattern to list help information on all commands matching the *pattern*.

history

```
history [number]
history -rwan [filename]
```

With no options, **history** displays the command history list with line numbers. Lines preceded by a * have been modified. A *number* used as an argument will list the last *number* of lines. If a nonoption argument is provided, it is used as the name of the history file; if not, the value of **HISTFILE** is used. The options for **history** are as follows:

Option	Description
-a	Add the history events entered since the beginning of the current BASH session to the history file.
-n	Read the history events not already read from the history file into the current history list.
-r	Read the events of the history file and use them as the current history.
-w	Replace the history file with the current history list.

history returns 0 unless an illegal option is encountered or an error occurs while reading or writing the history file.

if-then

```
if Linux command
    then
            commands
    else
            commands
fi
```

The **if** structure places a condition on commands. That condition is the exit status of a specific Linux command. If the command is successful, returning an exit status of 0, then the commands within the **if** structure are executed. If the exit status is anything other than 0, then the command has failed and the commands within the **if** structure are not executed.

The **if** command begins with the keyword **if** and is followed by a *Linux command* whose exit condition will be evaluated. This command is always executed. After the command, the keyword **then** goes on a line by itself. Any set of commands may then follow. The keyword **fi** ends the command. Often, you need to choose between two alternatives based on whether or not a Linux command is successful. The **else** keyword allows an **if** structure to choose between two alternatives. If the Linux command is successful, then those commands following the **then** keyword are executed. If the Linux command fails, then those commands following the **else** keyword are executed.

The **elsels** script in the next example executes the **ls** command to list files with two different possible options, either by size or with all file information. If the user enters an **s**, files are listed by size; otherwise, all file information is listed.

elsels

```
echo Enter s to list file sizes,
echo otherwise all file information is listed.
echo -n "Please enter option: "
read choice
if [ "$choice"=s ]
    then
            ls -s
    else
            ls -l
fi
echo Good-bye
```

```
$ elsels
Enter s to list file sizes,
otherwise all file information is listed.
Please enter option: s
total 2
     1 monday      2 today
Good-bye
$
```

The **if** structure is often used to check whether the user entered the appropriate number of arguments for a shell script. The special shell variable (#) contains the number of arguments the user entered. Using **$#** in a test operation allows you to check whether the user entered the correct number of arguments.

If an incorrect number of arguments has been entered, you may need to end the shell script. You can do this with the **exit** command, which ends the shell script and returns an exit condition, supplied as a number argument. An argument of 0 indicates that the shell script ended successfully. Any other argument, such as 1, indicates that an error occurred. In the next example, the **ifarg** script takes only one argument. If the user fails to enter an argument, or enters more than one argument, then the **if** test will be true, and the error message will be printed out and the script exited with an error value.

ifarg

```
if [ $# -ne 1 ]
    then
    echo Invalid number of arguments
    exit 1
fi
echo $1

$ ifarg

Invalid number of arguments
```

jobs

```
jobs [-lnp] [jobspec ...]
jobs -x command [arguments ...]
```

The **jobs** command lists active jobs. The -l option also displays process IDs, whereas the -**p** option lists only the process ID of the job's process group. The -**n** option displays only jobs that have changed status since last notified. If a particular job's number is provided as an argument (*jobspec*), then only information about that job is displayed. **jobs** returns 0 unless an illegal option is encountered or an illegal job specification is listed. With the -**x** option, **jobs** is used to reference processes in current jobs. Any job specification found in the *command* or *arguments* is replaced by the corresponding process group ID, and then the command with its arguments is executed.

Each entry in the resulting list will consist of the job number in brackets, whether it is stopped or running, and the name of the job. The plus (**+**) sign indicates the job currently being processed, and the hyphen (**-**) indicates the next job to be executed. In the next example, two commands have been placed in the background. The **jobs** command then lists those jobs, showing which one is currently being executed.

```
$ lpr intro &
[1]   547
$ cat *.c > myprogs &
[2]   548
$ jobs
[1]   +   Running   lpr intro
[2]   -   Running   cat *.c > myprogs
$
```

If you wish, you can place several commands at once in the background by entering the commands on the command line, separated by an ampersand, **&**. In this case, the **&** both separates commands on the command line and executes them in the background. In the next example, the first command to **sort** and redirect all files with a **.l** extension, is placed in the background. On the same command line, the second command, to print all files with a **.c** extension, is also placed in the background. Notice that the two commands each end with **&**. The **jobs** command then lists the **sort** and **lpr** commands as separate operations.

```
$ sort *.l > ldocs & lpr *.c &
[1]   534
[2]   567
$ jobs
```

```
[1]  +  Running  sort *.1 > ldocs
[2]  -  Running  lpr
$
```

kill

```
kill [-s sigspec | -sigspec] [pid | jobspec] ...
kill -l [signum]
```

kill is used to terminate a process or job. With the **-s** option you can specify a signal to be sent (*sigspec*). By default, the signal sent is to terminate a process. With the -l option, the command lists the signal names. For signal numbers (*signum*) provided with the -l option, the names of the corresponding signals are listed. An argument of -- disables option checking for the rest of the arguments. **kill** returns true if at least one signal was successfully sent, or false if an error occurs or an illegal option is encountered.

The **kill** command takes as its argument either the user job number (*jobspec*) or the system process number (*pid*). The user job number must be preceded by a percent sign, **%**. You can find out the job number from the **jobs** command. In the next example, the **jobs** command lists the background jobs; then job 2 is canceled.

```
$ jobs
[1]  +  Running  lpr intro
[2]  -  Running  cat *.c > myprogs
$ kill %2
$
```

let

```
let value1 operator value2
```

The **let** command is the BASH shell command for performing operations on arithmetic values. With **let** you can compare two values or perform arithmetic operations, such as addition or multiplication on them. Such operations are used often in shell programs to manage control structures or perform necessary calculations. The **let** command can be indicated either with the keyword **let** or with a set of double parentheses. The syntax consists of the keyword **let** followed by two numeric values separated by an arithmetic or relational operator.

You can use as your operator any of those listed earlier in this chapter in the "Arithmetic Operators" section. The **let** command automatically assumes that operators are arithmetic or relational. You do not have to quote shell-like operators. **let** also automatically evaluates any variables and converts their values to arithmetic values. This means that you can write your arithmetic operations as simple arithmetic expressions. In the next example, the **let** command multiplies the values 2 and 7. The result is output to the standard output and displayed.

```
$ let 2*7
14
```

If you want to have spaces between operands in the arithmetic expression, you must quote the expression. The **let** command expects one string.

```
$ let "2 * 7"
```

You can also include assignment operations in your **let** expression. In the next example, the result of the multiplication is assigned to **res**.

```
$ let "res=2 * 7"
$ echo $res
14
$
```

You can also use any of the relational operators to perform comparisons between numeric values, such as checking to see whether one value is less than another. Relational operations are often used to manage control structures, such as loops and conditions. In the next example, **helloprg** displays the word "hello" three times. It makes use of a **let** less-than-or-equal operation to manage the loop, **let "again <= 3 "**, and to increment the **again** variable, **let "again = again + 1"**. Notice that when again is incremented, it does not need to be evaluated. No preceding **$** is needed. **let** will automatically evaluate variables used in expressions.

helloprg

```
again=1
while let "again <= 3 "
            do
            echo $again Hello
```

```
            let "again=again + 1"
            done
```

$ **helloprg**
1 Hello
2 Hello
3 Hello

local

local [*variable-name*[=*value*] ...]

local is used to define local variables. The variable *named* is defined and assigned an initial *value* using the equal (=) sign. **local** is also used within functions to limit the scope of a variable to that function and the function's children. With no arguments, local displays a list of local variables. The **local** command can only be used within a function. It cannot be used directly in a shell script or interactive shell. The command returns 0 unless used outside a function or an illegal name is supplied.

logout

logout

This command is used to exit a login shell.

notify

notify *job-number*

After you execute any command in Linux, the system will tell you what background jobs, if you have any running, have been completed so far. The system will not interrupt any operation, such as editing, to notify you about a completed job. If you want to be notified immediately when a certain job ends, no matter what you are doing on the system, you can use the **notify** command to instruct the system to tell you. The **notify** command takes as its argument a job number. When that job is finished, the system will interrupt what you are doing to notify you that the job has ended. The next example tells the system to notify the user when job 2 has finished.

$ **notify %2**

popd

```
popd [+/-n]
```

popd removes directory entries from the directory list. With no arguments, it removes the top directory from the list, and performs a **cd** to the new top directory. +*n* removes the *n*th entry counting from the left of the list shown by **dirs**, starting with zero. **popd +0** removes the first entry. -*n* removes the *n*th entry counting from the right of the list shown by **dirs**, starting with zero. **popd -0** removes the last directory. **popd** returns false if directory list is empty, a directory entry specified does not exist, or the directory change fails.

ps

```
ps [-] [lujsvmaxScewhrnu] [txx] [O[+|-]k1[[+|-] k2...]]
[pids]
```

The **ps** command displays information on Linux processes. The next example lists the processes a user is running. The PID is the system process number, also known as the process ID. TTY is the terminal identifier. TIME is how long the process has taken so far (CPU). COMMAND is the name of the process.

```
$ ps
PID      TTY        TIME       COMMAND
523      tty24      0:05       sh
567      tty24      0:01       lpr
570      tty24      0:00       ps
```

The **ps** command has several options for different kinds of reports with varying detail. The options may or may not have a preceding -, as you wish.

Option	Function/Description
l	Long format.
u	User format: give user name and start time.
j	Jobs format: pgid sid.
s	Signal format.
v	vm format.
m	Display memory info.

Option	Function/Description
f	"Forest" family tree format for command line.
a	Show processes of other users also.
x	Show processes without terminals.
S	Include child CPU time and page faults info.
c	Command name from **task_struct**.
e	Show environment after command line and **+**.
w	Wide output: don't truncate command lines to fit on one line.
h	No header.
r	Run processes only.
n	Numeric output for **USER** and **WCHAN**.
t*device-name*	Show only processes with controlling tty terminal. (For the device name you can use either the full name of the device file or the device file with either **tty** or **cu** sliced off.)
O[+ | -]**k1**[,[+ | -]**k2**[,...]]	Sort processes according to a sequence of short keys (**k1, k2, ...**). (+ optional; - reverses direction of the sort on the key it precedes.)
pids	List only the specified processes. (The processes are comma delimited. They must follow immediately after the last option with no intervening space. For example, **ps -j3,7,6.**)

pushd

```
pushd [dir]
pushd +/-n
```

pushd adds a directory to the list of remembered directories. With no arguments, it exchanges the top two directories and returns 0, unless the directory list is empty.

Option	Description
+*n*	Rotate the list so that the *n*th directory (counting from the left of the list shown by **dirs**) is at the top.
-*n*	Rotate the stack so that the *n*th directory (counting from the right) is at the top.
dir	Add *dir* to the directory list at the top, making it the new current working directory.

pwd

pwd

pwd displays the path name of the current working directory. The path printed contains no symbolic links if the **-P** option to the **set** command is set. Returns 0 unless an error occurs while reading the path name of the current directory.

read

read [-r] [*variable* ...]

The **read** command reads in a value for a variable. It is used to allow a user to interactively input a value for a variable. The **read** command literally reads the next line in the standard input. Everything in the standard input up to the newline character is read in and assigned to a variable. If no variables are supplied, the line read is assigned to the special shell variable **REPLY**. **read** returns zero, unless an end-of-file character is encountered. With the **-r** option, a newline that has been quoted by a backslash is not ignored, and the backslash is taken as part of the line.

In shell programs, you can combine the **echo** command with the **read** command to prompt the user to enter a value and then read that value into a variable. In the script in the next example, the user is prompted to enter a value for the **greeting** variable. The **read** command then reads the value the user typed and assigns it to the **greeting** variable.

greetvar

```
echo Please enter a greeting:
read greeting
echo "The greeting you entered was $greeting"

$ greetvar
Please enter a greeting: hi
The greeting you entered was hi
$
```

When dealing with user input, you must consider the possibility that the user may enter shell special characters. Any special characters in a Linux command, whether within a script or not, will be evaluated unless quoted. If the value of a variable is a special character and the variable's value is referenced with a **$**, then the special character will be evaluated by the shell. However, placing the evaluated variable within quotes prevents any evaluation of special characters such as **$**. In the **greetvar** script, **$greeting** was placed within a quoted string, preventing evaluation of any special characters. However, if **$greeting** is not quoted, then any special characters it contains will be evaluated.

There are times when you want special characters evaluated. Suppose you want to retrieve the list of files beginning with characters the user enters. In this case, any special characters entered by the user need to be evaluated. In the **listfiles** script that follows, any special characters for generating file lists will be expanded. Notice that **$fref** is not quoted.

listfiles

```
echo Please enter a file reference:
read fref
echo The files you requested are: $fref
```

```
$ listfiles
Please enter a file reference: *.c
The files you requested are: calc.c lib.c main.c
```

readonly

```
readonly [-f] [variable ...]
readonly -p
```

readonly marks the named variables as read-only. Their values cannot be changed by subsequent assignments. The **-f** option will mark a function also as read-only, so it cannot be changed or redefined. With no arguments or with the **-p** option, a list of all read-only names is displayed. An argument of -- disables option checking for the rest of the arguments. **readonly** returns 0 if an invalid or undefined variable name or function is provided, or an invalid option is listed.

return

```
return [n]
```

Exit a function or shell script. If an argument (*n*) is provided, then that becomes the return value of the function. If there is no argument, then the return status is that of the last command executed. If used outside a function, but within a shell script, **return** stops execution of the script. If there is no argument specified as the return value, it returns the exit status of the last command executed in the script. If used outside a function and not in a script, then the return status is false.

select

```
select variable in list-of-items
do
      commands
done
```

The **select** command is used to display a simple menu of numbered items for the user to select. The *list of items* following **in** is displayed on the standard error, each preceded by a number. If **in** is omitted, then the values of positional parameters are used. After displaying the items, the **PS3** prompt is displayed, prompting the user to enter a number. The number is read from the standard input and matched to the number for each item in turn. If a corresponding value is found, then **select** assigns that word to the variable. If the user enters an empty line, then the menu is displayed again. If EOF is read, the command terminates. The exit status of **select** is the exit status of the last command executed or zero if no commands were executed.

```
select mychoice in Sizes Information Cfiles
   do
     case $mychoice in
        Sizes)
             ls -s
             ;;
        Information)
             ls -l
             ;;
        Cfiles)
             ls *.c
      esac
   done
```

set

```
set [--abefhkmnptuvxldCHP] [-o option name][arguments ...]
```

You use the **set** command to set various shell options or to list shell variables. Single options set general features. Specific features can be turned on using a **+o** followed by the option name. To turn them off you use **-o** and the option name. The options are off by default unless otherwise noted. The **set** command by itself with no options specified will list all currently defined shell variables. **set** is always true unless an illegal option is encountered.

You can also list these options when the BASH shell is invoked. The current set of options is listed in **$-**. After the option arguments are processed, any remaining arguments are assigned as values to the positional parameters (**$1**, **$2**, ... **$**n).

Option	Description
-a	Automatically mark variables that are modified or created for export to the environment of subsequent commands.
-b	Cause the status of terminated background jobs to be reported immediately, rather than before the next primary prompt.
-e	Exit immediately if a command exits with a nonzero status.
-f	Disable path name expansion.
-h	Locate and remember function commands as functions are defined. Function commands are normally looked up when the function is executed.
-k	All keyword arguments are placed in the environment for a command, not just those that precede the command name.
-m	Monitor mode. Job control is enabled. This option is on by default for interactive shells on systems that support it. Background processes run in a separate process group and a line containing the exit status is printed on each completion.
-n	Read commands but do not execute them. Used commonly to check a shell script for syntax errors. Ignored for interactive shells.

-o *option-name*   The *option-name* can be one of the following:

Option	Description	
	allexport	Same as **-a**.
	braceexpand	The shell performs brace expansion. This is on by default.
	emacs	Use an **emacs**-style command-line editing interface. This is enabled by default when the shell is interactive, unless the shell is started with the **-nolineediting** option.
	errexit	Same as **-e**.
	histexpand	Same as **-H**.
	ignoreeof	The effect is as if the shell command **IGNOREEOF=10** had been executed.
	interactive-comments	Allow a word beginning with # to cause that word and all remaining characters on that line to be ignored in an interactive shell.
	monitor	Same as **-m**.
	noclobber	Same as **-C**.
	noexec	Same as **-n**.
	noglob	Same as **-f**.
	nohash	Same as **-d**.
	notify	Same as **-b**.
	nounset	Same as **-u**.
	physical	Same as **-P**.
	posix	Change the behavior of BASH where the default operation differs from the Posix 1003.2 standard to match the standard.

Option	Description
	verbose Same as **-v**.
	vi Use a Vi-style command-line editing interface.
	XTRACE Same as **-x**. If no option name is supplied, the values of the current options are printed.
-p	Turn on privileged mode. (In this mode, the **$ENV** file is not processed, and shell functions are not inherited from the environment. This is enabled automatically on startup if the effective user (group) ID is not equal to the real user (group) ID. Turning this option off causes the effective user and group IDs to be set to the real user and group IDs.)
-t	Exit after reading and executing one command.
-u	Treat unset variables as an error when performing parameter expansion. (If expansion is attempted on an unset variable, the shell prints an error message and, if not interactive, exits with a nonzero status.)
-v	Print shell input lines as they are read.
-x	After expanding each simple command, display the expanded value of **PS4**, followed by the command and its expanded arguments.
-l	Save and restore the bindings of *name* in a **for** command.
-d	Disable the hashing of commands that are looked up for execution. (Normally, commands are remembered in a hash table, and once found, do not have to be looked up again.)

Option	Description
-C	The effect is as if the shell command **noclobber=** had been executed.
-H	Enable !-style history substitution. (This option is on by default when the shell is interactive.)
-P	If set, do not follow symbolic links when performing commands such as **cd** that change the current directory. Use the physical directory instead.
--	If no arguments follow this option, unset the positional parameters. Otherwise, set the positional parameters to the *arguments*, even if some of them begin with a -.
-	Signal the end of options, causing all remaining *arguments* to be assigned to the positional parameters. (The **-x** and **-v** options are turned off. If there are no *arguments*, the positional parameters remain unchanged.)

shift

```
shift [n]
```

If an argument n is provided, **shift** renames the positional parameters so that parameter $n+1$ is **$1**, $n+2$ is **$2**, etc. Parameters n and less are unset. If n is 0, no parameters are changed. If there is no argument, n is assumed to be 1. The argument must be nonnegative. **shift** returns 0 unless the argument is less than 0 or greater than the number of positional parameters.

suspend

```
suspend [-f]
```

This command suspends a shell's execution of this shell until it receives a SIGCONT signal. If you execute this command in the login shell, then you should use the **-f** option to suppress the shell's complaint; just suspend anyway. **suspend** returns 0 unless the shell is a login shell and **-f** is not supplied, or if job control is not enabled.

test

```
test value -option value
test string=string
```

Often you may need to perform a test that compares two values. There is a Linux command called **test** that can perform such a comparison of values. The **test** command will compare two values and return as its exit status a 0 if the comparison is successful.

With the **test** command, you can compare integers or strings, and even perform logical operations. The command consists of the keyword **test** followed by the *values* being compared, separated by an *option* that specifies what kind of comparison is taking place. The *option* can be thought of as the operator, but is written, like other options, with a minus sign and letter codes. For example, **-eq** is the option that represents the equality comparison. However, there are two string operations that actually use an operator instead of an option. When you compare two strings for equality you use the equal (**=**) sign. For inequality you use **!=**.

In the next example, the user compares two integer values to see if they are equal. In this case, you need to use the equality option, **-eq**. The exit status of the **test** command is examined to find out the result of the test operation. The shell special variable **$?** holds the exit status of the most recently executed Linux command.

```
$ num=5
$ test $num -eq 10
$ echo $?
1
```

Instead of using the keyword **test** for the **test** command, you can use enclosing brackets. The command **test $greeting="hi"** can be written as

```
$ [ $greeting="hi" ]
```

Similarly, the **test** command **test $num -eq 10** can be written as

```
$ [ $num -eq 10 ]
```

The brackets themselves must be surrounded by white spaces: a space, tab, or hard return. Without the spaces it would be invalid.

The **test** command is used extensively as the Linux command in the test component of control structures. Be sure to keep in mind the different options used for strings and integers. Do not confuse string comparisons and integer comparisons. To compare two strings for equality, you use the equal (**=**) sign; to compare two integers, you use the option -**eq**.

Option	Returns
-b	True if file exists and is block special.
-c	True if file exists and is character special.
-d	True if file exists and is a directory.
-e	True if file exists.
-f	True if file exists and is a regular file.
-g	True if file exists and is set-group-id.
-k	True if file has its "sticky" bit set.
-L	True if file exists and is a symbolic link.
-p	True if file exists and is a named pipe.
-r	True if file exists and is readable.
-s	True if file exists and has a size greater than zero.
-S	True if file exists and is a socket.
-t	True if file is opened on a terminal.
-u	True if file exists and its set-user-id bit is set.
-w	True if file exists and is writable.
-x	True if file exists and is executable.
-O	True if file exists and is owned by the effective user ID.
-G	True if file exists and is owned by the effective group ID.
-nt	True if *file1* is newer (according to modification date) than *file2*.
-ot	True if *file1* is older than *file2*.
-ef	True if *file1* and *file2* have the same device and inode numbers.
-z	True if the length of file is zero.
-n	True if the length of file is nonzero.
=	True if the strings are equal.
!=	True if the strings are not equal.

!	True if test is false.
-a	True if both test1 AND test2 are true.
-o	True if either test1 OR test2 is true.

**Relational
Operations**

-eq	Equal
-ne	Not equal
-lt	Less than
-le	Less than or equal
-gt	Greater than
-ge	Greater than or equal

trap

```
trap [-l] [argument] [sigspec]
```

Specifies that a certain command listed here as the argument is to
be read and executed when the shell receives a system signal as
specified by *sigspec*. The signal can be either a signal name
defined in **<signal.h>**, or a signal number. If *sigspec* is EXIT (0),
the command *argument* is executed on exit from the shell.
If no command argument is listed for the signal, then the signal
is reset.

The **trap** command alone, with no arguments, displays the list of
commands associated with each signal number. With the -l
option, it displays the list of signal names and their corresponding
numbers. An argument of -- disables option checking for the rest
of the arguments. Signals ignored on entry to the shell cannot be
trapped or reset. Trapped signals are reset to their original values
in a child process when it is created. **trap** returns false if either
the trap name or number is invalid.

type

```
type [-all] [-type | -path] name [name ...]
```

With no options, **type** indicates how each name would be
interpreted if used as a command name. If the **-type** option is
used, **type** prints a phrase that is one of alias, keyword, function,
builtin, or file if *name* is an alias, shell-reserved word, function,
builtin, or disk file, respectively. If the name is not found, then

nothing is printed, and an exit status of false is returned. If the
-path option is used, **type** returns either the name of the disk file
that would be executed if *name* were specified as a command
name, or nothing, if **-type** would not return the file. If a command
is hashed, **-path** prints the hashed value, not necessarily the file
that appears first in **PATH**. If the **-all** option is used, **type** prints all
of the places that contain an executable named *name*. This
includes aliases and functions, if and only if the **-path** option is
not also used. The table of hashed commands is not consulted
when using **-all**. **type** accepts **-a**, **-t**, and **-p** in place of **-all**, **-type**,
and **-path**, respectively. An argument of -- disables option
checking for the rest of the arguments. **type** returns true if any of
the arguments are found; false if none are found.

umask

umask [-S] [*mode*]

umask specifies the user file-creation mask. With no arguments or
with the **-S** option, **umask** displays the value of the file-creation
mask. The **-S** option displays the mask in symbolic form. With the
mode argument, the file-creation mask is set to that mode. The
mode can be either an octal number or a symbolic specifier, as
used by **chmod** in setting file permissions. An argument of --
disables option checking for the rest of the arguments. **umask**
returns 0 if the mode was successfully changed or if no mode
argument was supplied, and false otherwise.

unalias

unalias [-a] [*alias-name* ...]

unalias removes aliases that have been defined. With the **-a**
option, you can remove all defined aliases. **unalias** returns true
unless an *alias-name* provided is not a defined alias.

unset

unset [-fv] [*variable* ...]

unset is used to undefine shell variables. You can list a series of
variable names as arguments, removing them all at once. With the
-f option, you can remove defined functions. An argument of --

disables option checking for the rest of the arguments. Certain
system shell variables, such as **PATH**, **IFS**, **PPID**, **PS1**, **PS2**, **UID**,
and **EUID**, cannot be unset. If **RANDOM**, **SECONDS**, **LINENO**, or
HISTCMD are unset, they lose their special properties, even if
they are later redefined. **unset** returns true, unless a variable
name does not exist or cannot be removed.

wait

```
wait [n]
```

The shell waits for the specified process to complete and return
its termination status. The argument *n* can be a process ID or a
job specification. If a job specification is used, then all the
processes that are part of that job are waited for. If no argument is
used, then all current child processes are waited for, and **wait**
then returns zero. **wait** returns the exit status of the last process
or job waited for. If the argument specifies an invalid or
nonexistent process or job, **wait** returns 127.

while

```
while Linux command
    do
         commands
    done
```

The **while** loop repeats commands. A **while** loop begins with the
keyword **while** and is followed by a *Linux command*. The
keyword **do** follows on the next line. The end of the loop is
specified by the keyword **done**.

The Linux command used in **while** structures is often a test
command indicated by enclosing brackets. In the **myname** script,
in the next example, the user is asked to enter a name. The name
is then printed out. The loop is controlled by testing the value of
the variable **again** using the bracket form of the **test** command.

myname

```
again=yes
while [ "$again" = yes ]
do
    echo -n "Please enter a name: "
    read name
```

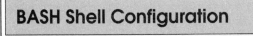

```
        echo "The name you entered is $name"
        echo -n "Do you wish to continue? "
        read again
done
echo Good-bye

$ myname
Please enter a name: George
The name you entered is George
Do you wish to continue? yes
Please enter a name: Robert
The name you entered is Robert
Do you wish to continue? no
Good-bye
```

BASH Shell Configuration

The BASH shell has a set of configuration files used to configure your system when you log in, log out, or whenever you enter a new BASH shell.

The BASH Shell Login Initialization File: .bash_profile

The **.bash_profile** file is the BASH shell's login initialization file. It is a script file that is automatically executed whenever a user logs in. The file contains shell commands that define special environment variables used to manage your shell. They may be either redefinitions of system-defined special variables or definitions of user-defined special variables. For example, when you log in, your user shell needs to know what directories hold Linux commands. It will reference the **PATH** variable in order to find the path names for these directories. However, the **PATH** variable must first be assigned those path names. In the **.bash_profile** file there is an assignment operation that does just this. Since it is in the **.bash_profile** file, the assignment is executed automatically when the user logs in.

Special variables also need to be exported, using the **export** command, in order to make them accessible to any subshells you may enter. You can export several variables in one **export**

command by listing them as arguments. Usually at the end of the
.bash_profile file there is an **export** command with a list of all the
variables defined in the file. If a variable is missing from this list,
you may not be able to access it. Notice the **export** command at
the end of the .bash_profile file in the example described next.

A copy of the standard .bash_profile file provided for you when
your account is created is listed in the next example. Notice how
PATH is assigned itself and the value of **$HOME**. Both **PATH** and
HOME are system special variables that the system has already
defined. **PATH** holds the path names of directories searched for
any command that you enter, and **HOME** holds the path name of
your home directory. The assignment **PATH=$PATH:$HOME/bin**
has the effect of redefining **PATH** to include your **bin** directory
within your home directory—so your **bin** directory will also be
searched for any commands, including ones you create yourself,
such as scripts and programs. Notice that **PATH** is then exported
so that it can be accessed by any subshells. Should you want to
have your home directory searched also, you can use the Vi or
Emacs editor to modify this line in your **.bash_profile** file to
PATH=$PATH:$HOME/bin:$HOME, adding **:$HOME** at the end.
In fact, you can change this entry to add as many directories as
you want searched.

.bash_profile

```
# .bash_profile

# Get the aliases and functions
if [ -f ~/.bashrc ]; then
    . ~/.bashrc
fi

# User-specific environment and startup programs

PATH=$PATH:$HOME/bin
ENV=$HOME/.bashrc
USERNAME=""

export USERNAME ENV PATH
```

Your Linux system also has its own profile file that it executes
whenever any user logs in. This system initialization file is simply
called **.profile** and is found in the **/etc** directory, **/etc/profile**. It
contains special variable definitions that the system needs to
provide for each user. A copy of the system **.profile** file follows.

Notice how **PATH** is redefined to include the **/usr/X11R6/bin** directory. This is the directory that holds the X-Window commands that you execute when using the Caldera Desktop. **HISTFILE** is also redefined to include a larger number of history events.

/etc/profile

```
# /etc/profile

# Systemwide environment and startup programs
# Functions and aliases go in /etc/bashrc

PATH="$PATH:/usr/X11R6/bin"
PS1="[\u@\h \W]\\$ "

ulimit -c 1000000
umask 002

HOSTNAME=`/bin/hostname`
HISTSIZE=1000
HISTFILESIZE=1000
# Default page for the arena browser
WWW_HOME=file:/usr/doc/calderadoc-0.80-1/Caldera_Info
# Default path for CRiSPlite
CRPATH=/usr/lib/CRiSPlite/macros

export PATH PS1 HOSTNAME HISTSIZE HISTFILESIZE
WWW_HOME CRPATH

if [ "$TERM"=console ]
then
    MINICOM="-l -m -con -tmc" ; export MINICOM
fi
```

Your **.bash_profile** initialization file is a text file that can be edited with a text editor like any other text file. You can easily add new directories to your **PATH** by editing .bash_profile and using editing commands to insert a new directory path name in the list of directory path names assigned to the **PATH** variable. You can even add new variable definitions. If you do so, be sure, however, to include the new variable's name in the **export** command's argument list. For example, if your .bash_profile file does not have any definition of the **EXINIT** variable, you can edit the file and add a new line that assigns a value to **EXINIT**. The definition **EXINIT='set nu ai'** will configure the Vi editor with line numbering and indentation. You then need to add **EXINIT** to the **export** command's argument list. When the **.bash_profile** file executes again, the **EXINIT** variable will be set to the command **set nu ai**. When the Vi editor is invoked, the command in the **EXINIT** variable will be executed, setting the line number and auto-indent options automatically.

In the following example, the user's **.bash_profile** has been modified to include definitions of **EXINIT** and redefinitions of **CDPATH**, **PS1**, and **HISTSIZE**. The redefinition of **HISTSIZE** reduces the number of history events saved, from 1000, defined in the system **.profile** file, to 30. The redefinition of the **PS1** special variable changes the prompt to include the path name of the current working directory. Any changes that you make to special variables within your **.bash_profile** file will override those made earlier by the system's **.profile** file. All these special variables are then exported with the **export** command.

.bash_profile

```
# .bash_profile

# Get the aliases and functions
if [ -f ~/.bashrc ]; then
    . ~/.bashrc
fi

# User-specific environment and startup programs

PATH=$PATH:$HOME/bin:$HOME
ENV=$HOME/.bashrc
USERNAME=""
CDPATH=$CDPATH:$HOME/bin:$HOME
HISTSIZE=30
EXINIT='set nu ai'
PS1="\w \$"

export USERNAME ENV PATH CDPATH HISTSIZE EXINIT PS1
```

Though **.bash_profile** is executed each time you log in, it is not automatically reexecuted after you make changes to it. The **.bash_profile** file is an initialization file that is only executed when you log in. If you want to take advantage of any changes you make to it without having to log out and log in again, you can reexecute **.bash_profile** with the dot (.) command. **.bash_profile** is a shell script and, like any shell script, can be executed with the **.** command.

```
$ . .bash_profile
```

The BASH Shell Initialization File: .bashrc

The **.bashrc** file is an initialization file that is executed each time you enter the BASH shell or generate any subshells. If the BASH shell is your login shell, **.bashrc** is executed along with your **.bash_login** file when you log in. If you enter the BASH shell from another shell, the **.bashrc** file is automatically executed, and the variable and alias definitions it contains will be defined.

The **.bashrc** shell initialization file is actually executed each time you generate a shell, such as when you run a shell script. In other words, each time a subshell is created, the **.bashrc** file is executed. This has the effect of exporting any local variables or aliases that you have defined in the **.bashrc** shell initialization file. The **.bashrc** file usually contains the definition of aliases and any feature variables used to turn on shell features. Aliases and feature variables are locally defined within the shell. But the **.bashrc** file will define them in every shell. For this reason, the **.bashrc** file usually holds such aliases as those defined for the **rm**, **cp**, and **mv** commands. The next example is a **.bashrc** file with many of the standard definitions.

.bashrc

```
# Source global definitions
if [ -f /etc/bashrc ]; then
    . /etc/bashrc
fi
set  -o ignoreeof
set  -o noclobber

alias rm 'rm -i'
alias mv 'mv -i'
alias cp 'cp -I'
```

Linux systems usually contain a system **.bashrc** file that is executed for all users. This may contain certain global aliases and features needed by all users whenever they enter a BASH shell. This is located in the **/etc** directory, **/etc/.bashrc**. A user's own **.bashrc** file, located in the home directory, will contain commands to execute this system **.bashrc** file. The **. /etc/bashrc** command in the previous example of **.bashrc** does just that.

You can add any commands or definitions of your own to your **.bashrc** file. If you have made changes to **.bashrc** and you want them to take effect during your current login session, you need to reexecute the file with the **source** command:

```
$ source .bashrc
```

The BASH Shell Logout Initialization File: .bash_logout

The **.bash_logout** file is also an initialization file, which is executed when the user logs out. It is designed to perform any operations you want done whenever you log out. Instead of variable definitions, the **.bash_logout** file usually contains shell commands that form a kind of shutdown procedure—actions you always want taken before you log out. One common logout command is to clear the screen and then issue a farewell message.

As with **.bash_profile**, you can add your own shell commands to **.bash_logout**. In fact, the **.bash_logout** file is not automatically set up for you when your account is first created. You need to create it yourself, using the Vi or Emacs editor. You could then add a farewell message or other operations. In the next example, the user has a **clear** and an **echo** command in the **.bash_logout** file. When the user logs out, the **clear** command will clear the screen, and then the **echo** command will display the message "Good-bye for now".

.bash_logout

```
clear
echo "Good-bye for now"
```

BASH Shell Configuration Variables

The BASH shell has a set of configuration variables that are used to configure your shell. You can modify these variables to configure your shell to your own needs. Some variables are set up by the system and are not to be changed. Others are set up with initial values that you can change to ones you want. Still others need to be defined by the user.

Shell Special Variables	Variable Contents
System-Determined:	
HOME	Path name for user's home directory.
LOGNAME	Login name.

Shell Special Variables	Variable Contents
User	Login name.
TZ	Time zone used by system.

Redefinable Special Variables:

SHELL	Path name of program for type of shell you are using.
PATH	List of path names for directories searched for executable commands.
PS1	Primary shell prompt.
PS2	Secondary shell prompt.
PS3	Prompt for the **select** command.
PS4	The value of this prompt is expanded and the value is displayed before each command BASH displays during an execution trace. The first character of **PS4** is replicated multiple times, as necessary, to indicate multiple levels of indirection. The default is +.
IFS	Interfield delimiter symbol.
MAIL	Name of mail file checked by mail utility for received messages.
MAILCHECK	Interval for checking for received mail.

User-Defined Special Variables:

MAILPATH	List of mail files to be checked by mail for received messages.
TERM	Terminal name.
MAILWARNING	If set, and a file in which BASH is checking for mail has been accessed since the last time it was checked, the message "The mail in mailfile has been read" is displayed.
CDPATH	Path names for directories searched by **cd** command for subdirectories.

Shell Special Variables	Variable Contents
EXINIT	Initialization commands for Ex/Vi editor.
PWD	The current working directory.
OLDPWD	The previous working directory, as set by the **cd** command.
REPLY	Set to the line of input read by the **read** builtin command when no arguments are supplied.
UID	Expands to the user ID of the current user, initialized at shell startup.
EUID	Expands to the effective user ID of the current user, initialized at shell startup.
BASH	The full path name of BASH.
BASHVERSION	The version number of BASH.
SHLVL	Incremented by one each time an instance of BASH is started.
RANDOM	Generates a random integer when referenced. The sequence of random numbers may be initialized by assigning a value to **RANDOM**.
HISTCMD	Index in the history list of the current command.
HISTSIZE	The number of commands remembered by the history command. The default value is 500.
OPTARG	The value of the last option argument processed by the **getopts** builtin command.
OPTIND	The index of the next argument to be processed by the **getopts** builtin command.
HOSTTYPE	Automatically set to a string that uniquely describes the type of machine on which BASH is executing.
HOSTFILE	Complete host name of the system. In the same format as **/etc/hosts**.

Shell Special Variables	Variable Contents
OSTYPE	Description of the operating system on which BASH is executing.
ENV	Filename containing commands to initialize the shell, as in **.bashrc** or **.tcshrc**. The value of **ENV** is subjected to parameter expansion, command substitution, and arithmetic expansion before being interpreted as a path name.
HISTFILESIZE	The maximum number of lines contained in the history file. When this variable is assigned a value, the history file is truncated, if necessary, to contain no more than that number of lines. The default value is 500.
OPTERR	If set to the value 1, BASH displays error messages generated by the **getopts** builtin command. **OPTERR** is initialized to 1 each time the shell is invoked or a shell script is executed.
PROMPTCOMMAND	Holds the command to be executed prior to displaying a primary prompt.
TMOUT	The number of seconds to wait for input after the primary prompt. BASH terminates after waiting for that number of seconds if input does not arrive.
FCEDIT	The default editor for the **fc** command.
FIGNORE	A colon-separated list of suffixes to ignore when performing filename completion.
INPUTRC	The filename for the readline startup file, overriding the default of ~/**.inputrc**.

BASH Shell Features	Function
$ set [- | +]o *feature*	Turn shell features on and off with the **set** command; set a feature on with **-o** and turn it off with **+o**. **$ set -o noclobber** *set noclobber on* **$ set +o noclobber** *set noclobber off*
notify	If set, report terminated background jobs immediately, rather than waiting until it displays the next primary prompt.
globdotfilenames	Include filenames beginning with a period (.) in the results of path name expansion.
commandorientedhistory	Save all lines of a multiple-line command in the same history entry. This allows easy reediting of multiple-line commands.
nolinks	Do not follow symbolic links when executing commands that change the current working directory; use the physical directory structure instead. (By default, BASH follows the logical chain of directories when performing commands, such as **cd**, that change the current directory.)
noexitonfailedexec	Do not allow a noninteractive shell to exit if it cannot execute the file specified in the **exec** command. Do not allow an interactive shell to exit if **exec** fails.
cdablevars	Assume that an argument to the **cd** command that is not a directory is the name of a variable whose value is the directory to change to.
ignoreeof	Disable CTRL-D logout.
noclobber	Do not overwrite files through redirection.
noglob	Disable special characters used for filename expansion: *****, **?**, **~**, **[**, and **]**.

Chapter 2
TCSH Shell Programming

The TCSH shell differs from other shells in that its control structures conform more to a programming language format. For example, the test condition for a TCSH shell's control structure is an expression, not a Linux command, that evaluates to true or false. A TCSH shell expression uses the same operators as those found in the C programming language. You can perform a variety of assignment, arithmetic, relational, and bitwise operations. The TCSH shell also allows you to declare numeric variables that can easily be used in such operations.

TCSH Shell Variables, Scripts, and Arguments

You can define variables in a shell and assign values to them, as well as reference script arguments. You can also define environment variables that operate much like BASH shell exported variables. However, the TCSH shell differs in the way it defines variables and the type of variables you can define. The TCSH shell defines its variables using the TCSH shell commands **set**, @, and **setenv**. The TCSH shell also allows you to define numeric variables and arrays. The @ command defines a numeric variable on which you perform arithmetic operations. Parentheses and brackets allow you to define and reference arrays.

Scripts also operate in much the same way, but with several crucial differences. A TCSH shell script must begin with a sharp (or pound) sign (#) in the first column of the first line. Also, though prompts can be output using the **echo** command, there is no **read** command to handle input. Instead, you need to redirect the standard input to a variable.

Script Input and Output: $<

You can easily define and use variables within a shell script. As in the example coming up, you can place Linux commands, such as the assignment operation and **echo**, in a file using a text editor. You can then make the file executable and invoke it on the command line as another command. Remember that to add the execute permission, you use the **chmod** command with a **u+x** permission or the 700 absolute permission. Within a script, you can use the **echo** command to output data. However, input must be read into a variable by redirecting the standard input. There is no comparable version of the Linux **read** command in the TCSH shell.

The TCSH shell examines the first character of a file to determine whether or not it is a TCSH shell script. Remember that all TCSH shell scripts must have a # character as the first character on the first line. This identifies the file as a TCSH shell script. Notice the # character at the beginning of the **greet** script. The # character placed anywhere in the file other than the first character of the first line, operates as a common character.

greet

```
#
# Script to output hello greeting
set greeting = "hello"
echo The value of greeting is $greeting
```

```
> chmod u+x greet
> greet
The value of greeting is hello
```

The **set** command combined with the redirection operation, **$<**, will read whatever the user enters into the standard input. The next example reads user input into the **greeting** variable.

```
> set greeting = $<
```

You can place the prompt on the same line as the input using the **echo** command. The TCSH shell uses a special option for **echo**, the **-n** option, which eliminates the newline character at the end of the output string. The cursor remains on the same line at the end of the output string:

```
> echo -n Please enter a greeting:
```

If you wish to include a space at the end of your prompt, you
need to place the output string within double quotes, including
the space:

```
> echo -n "Please enter a greeting: "
```

The **greetpt** script, shown next, contains a TCSH shell version of a
prompt remaining on the same line as the input.

greetpt

```
#
echo -n "Please enter a greeting: "
set greeting = $</
echo "The greeting you entered was $greeting"

> greetpt
Please enter a greeting: hello
The greeting you entered was hello
>
```

Operators

The TCSH shell has a standard set of assignment, arithmetic,
and relational operators (see the following table) as found in
most programming environments, as well as operators for shell
functions such as redirection and background operations.

Assignment Operators	Function/Description
=	Assignment.
+=	Add to expression and then assign.
-=	Subtract from expression and then assign.
*=	Multiply with expression and then assign.
/=	Divide into expression and then assign.
%=	Modulo operation with expression and assignment.

Assignment Operators	Function
++	Increment variable.
--	Decrement variable.
Arithmetic Operators	**Description**
-	Minus unary operator
+	Addition
-	Subtraction
*	Multiplication
/	Division
%	Modulo
Relational Operators	**Description**
>	Greater than
<	Less than
>=	Greater than or equal
<=	Less than or equal
!=	Not equal
==	Equal

Redirection and Pipes: <, <<, >, |

The TCSH shell also supports standard input and output
redirection operations and pipes as described in Chapter 1. To
overwrite an existing file with redirection you need to use >!
instead of just > alone, if the **noclobber** feature is set.

Control Structures

As in other shells, the TCSH shell has a set of control structures
that let you control the execution of commands in a script. There
are loop and conditional control structures with which you can
repeat Linux commands or make decisions on which commands
you want to execute. The **while** and **if** control structures are
general-purpose control structures, performing iterations and
making decisions using a variety of different tests. The **switch**
and **foreach** control structures are more specialized operations.
The **switch** structure is a restricted form of the **if** condition; it
checks to see if a value is equal to one of a set of possible values.
The **foreach** structure is a limited type of loop that runs through a

list of values, assigning a new value to a variable with each iteration. The following table lists the different control structures:

Conditional Control Structures:

if-then, else, switch	Function

if(*expression*) **then**
commands
endif
	If the *expression* is true, execute the *commands*. (You can specify more than one Unix command.)

if(*expression*) **then**
commands
else
commands
endif
	If the *expression* is true, execute the *commands* following **then**. If the *expression* is false, execute the *commands* following **else**.

switch(*string*) **case** *pattern*: *commands* **breaksw** **default:** *commands* **endsw**	Allow a choice among several alternative commands, comparing the string to different specified patterns.

Loop Control Structures:

while and foreach	Function
while(*expression*) *commands* **end**	Execute *commands* as long as the *expression* is true.
foreach *variable* (*argument-list*) *commands* **end**	Iterate the loop for as many arguments as there are in the *argument-list*. (Each time through the loop, the *variable* is set to the next argument in the list; it operates like **for-in** in the Bourne shell.)

The TCSH shell differs from other shells in that its control structures conform more to a programming language format. The test condition for a TCSH shell control structure is an expression that evaluates to true or false. One key difference between BASH shell and TCSH shell control structures is that TCSH shell structures cannot redirect or pipe their output. They are strictly control structures, controlling the execution of commands.

Test Expressions: ()

The **if** and **while** control structures use an expression as their test. A true test is any expression that results in a nonzero value. A false test is any expression that results in a 0 value. In the TCSH shell, relational and equality expressions can be easily used as test expressions, because they result in 1 if true and 0 if false. There are many possible operators that you can use in an expression. The test expression can also be arithmetic or a string comparison, but strings can only be compared for equality or inequality.

Unlike the BASH shell, you must enclose the TCSH shell **if** and **while** test expressions within parentheses. The next example shows a simple test expression testing to see if two strings are equal.

```
if ( $greeting == "hi" ) then
    echo Informal Greeting
endif
```

The TCSH shell has a separate set of operators for testing strings against other strings or against regular expressions. The == and != operators test for the equality and inequality of strings. The =~ and !~ operators test a string against a glob pattern used for filename substitution to see if a pattern match is successful or not. The regular expression can contain any of the shell's special characters. In the next example, any value of greeting that begins with an uppercase or lowercase *h* will match the glob pattern, **[Hh]***.

```
if ( $greeting =~ [Hh]* ) then
    echo Informal Greeting
endif
```

Glob patterns use the *****, **?**, and **[]** special characters. The ***** matches any string of characters, including the null string. The **?** matches any single character. The **[]** matches any of the characters enclosed with it. A range of characters is specified by the two boundaries of the range separated by a hyphen (-). **[b-k]** matches on any characters between and including **b** through **k**. (For example, it would match on **c** or **f** or any others in the range.) If you include a ^ with the **[]** as the first character, then it negates the following characters matching on anything other than those. **[^agm]** would match on any character other than **a**, **g**, and **m**, and **[^a-zA-Z]** would match on anything other than an alphabetic character such as a punctuation mark or a number. You can also use ^ to negate the entire glob pattern as in **^he***, for strings that do not begin with **he**.

Like the BASH shell, the TCSH shell also has several special operators that test the status of files. Many of these operators are the same in both shells. In the next example, the **if** command tests to see if the file **mydata** is readable.

```
if ( -r mydata ) then
    echo Informal Greeting
endif
```

The following table lists the operators for test expressions:

String Comparisons	Function
==	Test strings for equality and return true if successful.
!=	Test for not-equal strings. Return true if strings are not equal.
=~	Compare string to a pattern to test if equal. The pattern can be any regular expression.
!~	Compare string to a pattern to test if not equal. The pattern can be any regular expression.
File Tests	**Function**
-e	Test to see if the file exists.
-r	Test to see if the file is readable.
-w	Test to see if the file can be written to (modified).
-x	Test to see if the file is executable.
-d	Test to see if the filename is a directory name.
-f	Test to see if the file is an ordinary file.
-o	Test to see if the file is owned by the user.
-z	Test to see if a file is empty.
Logical Operators	**Description**
&&	Logical AND.
| |	Logical OR.
!	Logical NOT.

TCSH Commands

A listing of the TCSH commands follows, arranged alphabetically.
In most cases, the description for each command begins with its
syntax.

Numeric Variables: @

In the TCSH shell, you can declare numeric variables using the @
command instead of the **set** command. You can then perform
arithmetic, relational, and bitwise operations on such variables. In
this respect, the TCSH shell is similar to programming languages.
Numeric and string variables are two very different types of
objects, managed in very different ways. You cannot use the **set**
command on a numeric variable. The @ command consists of the
keyword @, the variable name, an assignment operator, and an
expression. The next example declares the numeric variable **num**
and assigns the value 10 to it.

```
> @ num = 10
```

Many different assignment operators are available for you to use,
such as increments and arithmetic assignment operators. They
are the same as those used in the Unix programming utility **awk**
and in the C programming language. The expression can be any
arithmetic, relational, or bitwise expression, and you can create
complex expressions using parentheses. The operands in an
expression should be separated from the operator by spaces; for
example, 10*5 is not a valid expression and should be written
with spaces, 10 * 5. You can also use a numeric variable as an
operand in an expression. In the next example, the variable **count**
is declared as numeric and used in an arithmetic expression.
Notice that **count** is evaluated with a **$** operator so that the value
of **count**, 3, is used in the expression. The "Operators" section,
earlier in this chapter, provides a list of numeric operators.

```
> @ count = 3
> @ num = 2 * ($count + 10)
> echo $num
```

26

alias

alias [*name* [*command*]]

You use the **alias** command to create another name for a command. The alias operates like a macro that expands to the command it represents. The alias does not literally replace the name of the command; it simply gives another name to that command.

An **alias** command begins with the keyword **alias** and the new *name* for the command, followed by the command that the alias will reference. In the next example, the **ls** command is aliased with the name **list**, which becomes another name for the **ls** command.

```
> alias list ls
> ls
mydata intro
> list
mydata intro
>
```

Should the command you are aliasing have options, you will need to enclose the command and the options within single quotes. An aliased command that has spaces in its name will need quotation marks as well. In the next example, **ls** with the -l option is given the alias **longl**:

```
> alias longl 'ls -l'
> ls -l
-rw-r--r--  1  chris weather 207 Feb  20  11:55    mydata
> longl
-rw-r--r--  1  chris weather 207 Feb  20  11:55    mydata
>
```

You can also use the name of a command as an alias. In the case of the **rm**, **cp**, and **mv** commands, the -i option should always be used to ensure that an existing file is not overwritten. Instead of constantly being careful to use the -i option each time you use one of these commands, you can alias the command name to include the option. In the next examples, the **rm**, **cp**, and **mv** commands have been aliased to include the -i option.

```
> alias rm 'rm -i'
> alias mv 'mv -i'
> alias cp 'cp -i'
```

The **alias** command, by itself, provides a list of all aliases in effect and their commands. An alias can be removed with the **unalias** command.

```
> alias
lss    ls -s
list   ls
rm     rm -i
> unalias lss
> alias
list   ls
rm     rm -I
```

argv

When a shell script is invoked, all the words on the command line are parsed and placed in elements of an array called **argv**; **argv[0]** will hold the command name. Beginning with **argv[1]** and on, each element will hold an argument entered on the command line. In the case of shell scripts, **argv[0]** will always contain the name of the shell script. Just as with any array element, you can access the contents of an argument array element by preceding it with a $ operator. **$argv[1]** accesses the contents of the first element in the **argv** array—the first argument. If more than one argument is entered, they can be referenced with each corresponding element in the **argv** array. In the next example, the **myargs** script prints out four arguments. Four arguments are then entered on the command line.

myargs

```
#
echo "The first argument is: $argv[1]"
echo "The second argument is: $argv[2]"
echo "The third argument is: $argv[3]"
echo "The fourth argument is: $argv[4]"

> myargs Hello Hi yo "How are you"
The first argument is: Hello
The second argument is: Hi
The third argument is: yo
The fourth argument is: How are you
>
```

An **argv** element can be abbreviated to the number of the element preceded by a **$** sign. **$argv[1]** can be written as **$1**. This makes for shell scripts whose argument references are very similar to BASH and ZSH shell argument references. A special argument variable **argv[*]** references all the arguments in the command line. **$argv[*]** can be abbreviated as **$***. Notice that this is the same name used in the BASH shell to reference all arguments.

The **#argv** argument identifier contains the number of arguments entered on the command line. This is useful for specifying the required number of arguments to run a script. The **$#argv** variable can be checked to see if the correct number have been entered on the command line.

The **arglist** script in the next example shows the use of both the **$argv[*]** and **$#argv** special argument variables. The user first displays the number of arguments, using **#argv**, and then uses **argv[*]** to display the list of arguments entered.

arglist

```
#
echo "The number of arguments entered is $#argv"
echo "The list of arguments is: $argv[*]"
```

```
> arglist Hello hi yo
The number of arguments entered is 3
The list of arguments is: Hello hi yo
```

The following table lists the **argv** variables:

Command-Line Arguments	Description
$argv[0] or **$0**	Name of the Linux command.
$argv[n] or **$n**	The nth command-line argument beginning from 1, **$1-$n**. You can use **set** to change them.
$argv[*] or **$***	All the command-line arguments beginning from 1. You can use **set** to change them.
$#argv or **$#**	The count of the command-line arguments.

bg

```
bg [%job ...]
```

bg puts the specified *jobs* (or, without arguments, the current job) into the background, continuing each if it is stopped.

The *job* argument is a job reference using a job number or one of the following strings: ', %, +, or -. For a number, place the job number after the %, as in **%2** for job 2. Using only the job reference on the command line will imply the use of the **fg** command. (For example, **%2** will place job 2 in the foreground. Conversely, **%2&** will place it in the background, implying the **bg** command.) Instead of a job number, you can use an unambiguous string. (For example, **%lp** would reference a print job, provided it is the only print job.) With a preceding question mark (**?**), you can reference a job that contains a string, not just one that begins with a string. (For example, **%?myfile** references any job that contains the string **myfile**.) You can use the **%+**, **%**, and **%%** operators to reference the current job, and **%-** to reference the previous job.

break

```
break
```

This command breaks out of the nearest enclosing **foreach** or **while**. Remaining commands on the same line are executed. Multiple breaks are implemented by listing several breaks on the same line.

breaksw

breaksw allows you to break from a switch, resuming after the **endsw**.

builtins

builtins lists the names of all builtin commands.

cd

```
cd [-p] [-l] [-n|-v] [name]
```

If a directory name is given, this command changes the shell's working directory to *name*. If no *name* is included, the working directory changes to the user's home directory. A - used for the *name* references the previous working directory. If the *name* given is not a subdirectory, or the full path name is not given or referenced with ./ or ../ for current and parent directories, then the directories listed in the **cdpath** shell variable are checked for that directory name. If this fails, then the *name* is checked to see if it is a shell variable that holds a directory path name.

With the **-p** option included, Linux displays the directory list as it does **dirs**. The **-l**, **-n**, and **-v** options are the same as those used in the **dirs** command and imply the use of **-p**: **-l** displays full path names for subdirectories, **-v** displays directories on separate lines, and **-n** wraps directory names on the right margin.

continue

This command continues execution of the nearest enclosing **while** or **foreach**. The rest of the commands on the current line are executed.

dirs

```
dirs [-l] [-n|-v]
dirs -S|-L [filename]
dirs -c
```

With no arguments, the **dirs** command displays the directory list. The beginning of the list is to the left and the first directory is the current directory. With the -l option, all subdirectories of the user's home directory are expanded with the home directories path name. The -n option wraps entries before they reach the edge of the screen. The -v option displays entries one on each line and numbered. With the -c option, the directory list is cleared.

With the -S option, you can save the directory list to a file as a series of **cd** and **pushd** commands. With the -L option, such a list can be read in from a specified file that holds **cd** and **pushd** commands that were saved by a -S option. If no *filename* is given in either case, a file assigned to the **dirsfile** shell variable is used. If **dirsfile** is unset, then ~/.cshdirs is used. The login shells do the equivalent of **dirs -L** on startup and, if **savedirs** is set, **dirs -S** before exiting. Because only ~/.tcshrc is normally sourced before ~/.cshdirs, **dirsfile** should be set in ~/.tcshrc rather than ~/.login.

echo

```
echo [-n] word ...
```

echo writes each *word* to the shell's standard output, separated by spaces and terminated with a newline character. The **echostyle** shell variable can be set to emulate the options and escape sequences of the BSD and/or System V versions of **echo**.

eval

```
eval argument ...
```

eval treats the *arguments* as input to the shell and executes the resulting command(s) in the context of the current shell. This is usually used to execute commands generated as the result of command or variable substitution, since parsing occurs before these substitutions.

exec

```
exec command
```

exec executes the specified *command* in place of the current shell.

exit

```
exit [expression]
```

The shell exits either with the value of the specified *expression* or, if no *expression* is included, with the value of the status variable.

fg

```
fg [%job ...]
```

fg brings the specified *jobs* (or, without arguments, the current job) into the foreground, continuing each if it is stopped.

The *job* argument is a job reference using a job number or one of the following strings: ', %, +, or -. For a number, place the job number after the %, as in **%2** for job 2. Using only the job reference on the command line will imply the use of the **fg** command. (For example, **%2** will place job 2 in the foreground. Conversely, **%2&** will place it in the background, implying the **bg** command.) Instead of a job number, you can use an unambiguous string. (For example, **%lp** would reference a print job, provided it is the only print job.) With a preceding question mark (**?**), you can reference a job that contains a string, not just one that begins with a string. (For example, **%?myfile** references any job that contains the string **myfile**.) You can use the **%+**, **%**, and **%%** operators to reference the current job, and **%-** to reference the previous job.

foreach

```
foreach variable ( list of values )
    commands
end
```

The **foreach** structure is designed to sequentially reference a list of values. It is very similar to the BASH shell's **for-in** structure. The **foreach** structure takes two operands—a *variable* and a *list of values* enclosed in parentheses. Each value in the list is assigned to the *variable* in the **foreach** structure. Like the **while** structure, the **foreach** structure is a loop. Each time through the loop, the next value in the list is assigned to the *variable*. When the end of the list is reached, the loop stops. Like the **while** loop, the body of a **foreach** loop ends with the keyword **end**.

The **mylist** script in the next example simply outputs a line consisting of the item name and today's date for each item read by the **foreach** loop. Each item in the list is consecutively assigned to the variable **grocery**.

mylist

```
#
set tdate=`date '+%D'`
foreach grocery ( milk cookies apples cheese )
    echo "$grocery     $tdate"
end
```

```
> mylist
milk       05/23/99
cookies    05/23/99
apples     05/23/99
cheese     05/23/99
>
```

The **foreach** loop is useful for managing files. In the **foreach** structure, you can use shell special characters in a pattern to generate a list of filenames for use as your list of values. This generated list of filenames then becomes the list referenced by the **foreach** structure. An asterisk by itself generates a list of all files and directories. ***.c** lists files with the **.c** extension. These are usually C source code files. The next example makes a backup of each file and places the backup in a directory called **sourcebak**. The pattern ***.c** generates a list of filenames that the **foreach** structure can operate on.

cbackup

```
#
foreach backfile ( *.c )
    cp $backfile sourcebak/$backfile
    echo $backfile
end
```

```
> cbackup
io.c
lib.c
main.c
```

The **foreach** structure without a specified list of values takes as its list of values the command-line arguments. The arguments specified on the command line when the shell file is invoked become a list of values referenced by the **foreach** structure. The variable used in the **foreach** structure is set automatically to each argument value in sequence. The first time through the loop, the variable is set to the value of the first argument. The second time, it is set to the value of the second argument, and so on.

In the **mylistarg** script in the next example, there is no list of values specified in the **foreach** loop. Instead, the **foreach** loop consecutively reads the values of command-line arguments into the grocery variable. When all the arguments have been read, the loop ends.

mylistarg

```
#
set tdate = `date '+%D'`
foreach grocery ( $argv[*] )
    echo "$grocery     $tdate"
end
```

```
> mylistarg milk cookies apples cheese
milk       05/23/99
cookies    05/23/99
apples     05/23/99
cheese     05/23/99
>
```

You can explicitly reference the command-line argument by using the **argv[*]** special argument variable. In the next example, a list of C program files is entered on the command line when the shell script **cbackuparg** is invoked. In the **foreach** loop, **argv[*]** references all the arguments on the command line. Each argument will be consecutively assigned to the variable **backfile** in the **foreach** loop. The first time through the loop, **$backfile** is the same as **$argv[1]**. The second time through, it is the same as **$argv[2]**. The variable **argnum** is used to reference each argument. Both the argument and the value of **backfile** are displayed to show that they are the same.

cbackuparg

```
#
@ argnum = 1
foreach backfile ($argv[*])
    cp $backfile sourcebak/$backfile
    echo "$backfile $argv[$argnum]"
    @ argnum = $argnum + 1
end

> cbackuparg  main.c  lib.c  io.c
main.c main.c
lib.c lib.c
io.c io.c
```

history

```
history [-hr] [n]
history -S|-L|-M [filename]
history -c
```

With no options, **history** displays the command history list with line numbers. A number used as an argument will list that last number of lines. If a nonoption argument is provided, it is used as the name of the history file; if not, the value of **histfile** is used.

With the **-h** option, the history list is printed without leading numbers and with timestamps in comment form. With **-r** option, the list is reversed, starting with the most recent. With the **-c** option, the history list is cleared.

With the **-S** option, you can save the history list to a file. If the first word of the **savehist** shell variable is set to a number, the history will be saved up to that maximum number of lines. If the second word of **savehist** is set to 'merge', the history list is merged with the existing history file instead of replacing it (if there is one) and is sorted by timestamp.

With the **-L** option, the shell reads a history list from a saved history list file and appends it to the current history list. The **-M** option also reads a history list but merges it and sorts it with the current history list. If no filename is given with either of these options, then the filename assigned to the **histfile** shell variable is used. If **histfile** is unset, ~/**.history** is used.

hup

```
hup [command]
```

With a *command* argument included, **hup** runs the *command* such that it will exit on a hang-up signal and arranges for the shell to send it a hang-up signal when the shell exits. Note that commands may set their own response to hang-ups, overriding **hup**. Without an argument (allowed only in a shell script), **hup** causes the shell to exit on a hang-up for the remainder of the script.

if-then

```
if ( expression ) then
    commands
endif
```

The **if-then** structure places a condition on several Linux commands. That condition is an *expression*. If the *expression* results in a value other than 0, then the *expression* is true, and the commands within the **if** structure are executed. If the *expression* results in a 0 value, then the *expression* is false, and the commands within the **if** structure are not executed.

The **if-then** structure begins with the keyword **if** and is followed by an *expression* enclosed in parentheses. The keyword **then** follows right after the *expression*. You can specify any number of Linux commands on the following lines. The keyword **endif** ends the **if** command. Notice that, whereas in the BASH shell the **then** keyword is on a line of its own, in the TCSH shell, **then** is on the same line as the test *expression*.

The **ifls** script shown next allows you to list files by size. If you enter an **s** at the prompt, each file in the current directory is listed, followed by the number of blocks it uses. If the user enters anything else, the **if** test fails and the script does nothing.

ifls
```
#
echo -n "Please enter option: "
set option = $<
if ($option == "s") then
        echo Listing files by size
        ls -s
endif
```

```
> ifls
Please enter option: s
Listing files by size
total 2
    1 monday      2 today
>
```

if-then-else

```
if ( expression ) then
        commands
    else
        commands
endif
```

Often, you need to choose between two alternatives based on whether or not an *expression* is true. The **else** keyword allows an **if** structure to choose between two alternatives. If the *expression* is true, then those *commands* immediately following the test *expression* are executed. If the *expression* is false, those *commands* following the **else** keyword are executed.

The **elsels** script in the next example executes the **ls** command to list files with two different possible options, either by size or with all file information. If the user enters an **s**, files are listed by size; otherwise, all file information is listed. Notice how the syntax differs from the BASH shell version of the **elsels** script.

elsels

```
#
echo Enter s to list file sizes,
echo otherwise all file information is listed.
echo -n "Please enter option: "
set option = $<
if ($option == "s") then
        ls -s
    else
        ls -l
endif
echo Good-bye
```

```
> elsels
Enter s to list file sizes,
otherwise all file information is listed.
Please enter option: s
total 2
    1 monday     2 today
Good-bye
>
```

jobs

```
jobs [-l]
```

jobs lists the active jobs. With -**l**, it lists process IDs in addition to the normal information.

kill

```
kill [-signal] %job|pid ...
kill -l
```

kill is used to terminate a process or job. With the -**signal** option, you can specify a signal to be sent. By default, the signal sent is SIGTERM. With the -**l** option, the command lists the signal names.

For signal numbers provided with the -l option, the names of the corresponding signals are listed.

logout

This command terminates a login shell. It is especially useful if **ignoreeof** is set.

nice

```
nice [+number] [command]
```

nice sets the scheduling priority for the shell to *number*, or to 4 if no *number* is included. With a *command* specified, **nice** runs the *command* at the appropriate priority. The greater the *number*, the less CPU time the process gets.

nohup

```
nohup [command]
```

With no *command* argument, **nohup** instructs the shell to ignore any hang-up signals. With a *command*, it executes the *command* and ignores any hang-up signals for it.

notify

```
notify [%job ...]
```

After you execute any command in Linux, the system will tell you what background jobs, if you have any running, have been completed so far. The system will not interrupt any operation, such as editing, to notify you about a completed job. If you want to be notified immediately when a certain job ends, no matter what you are doing on the system, you can use the **notify** command to instruct the system to tell you. The **notify** command takes as its argument a job number. When that job is finished, the system will interrupt what you are doing to notify you that the job has ended. The following example tells the system to notify the user when job 2 has finished.

```
> notify %2
```

onintr

```
onintr [-|label]
```

onintr controls the action of the shell on interrupts. Without arguments, it restores the default action of the shell on interrupts, which is to terminate shell scripts or to return to the terminal command input level. With - (the hyphen argument), it causes all interrupts to be ignored. With *label*, the command causes the shell to execute a **goto** label when an interrupt is received or when a child process terminates because it was interrupted.

popd

```
popd [-p] [-l] [-n|-v] [+n]
```

popd removes directory entries from the directory list. With no arguments, **popd** removes the top directory from the list. +*n* removes the *n*th entry from the left of the list.

popd then displays the final directory list. The **pushdsilent** shell variable can be set to suppress this, and the -**p** option can be given to override **pushdsilent**.

printenv

```
printenv [name]
```

printenv displays the names and values of all environment variables or, with a *name* argument, the value of the environment variable *name*.

pushd

```
pushd [-p] [-l] [-n|-v] [name|+n]
```

pushd adds a directory to the list of remembered directories and then displays the directory list. With no arguments, **pushd** exchanges the top two directories and returns 0, unless the directory list is empty.

+*n* rotates the list so that the *n*th directory (counting from the left of the list shown by **dirs**) is at the top. If **dextract** is set, however,

pushd +n extracts the nth directory, pushes it onto the top of the stack, and changes to it.

-n rotates the stack so that the nth directory (counting from the right) is at the top. **dir** adds **dir** to the directory list at the top, making it the new current working directory.

If **pushdtohome** is set, **pushd** without arguments does **pushd ~**, like **cd**.

If **dunique** is set, **pushd** removes any instances of the name from the stack before pushing it onto the stack.

The **pushdsilent** shell variable can be set to suppress display of the directory list, and the **-p** option can then be used to override **pushdsilent**.

repeat

```
repeat count command
```

repeat repeats a command the specified (count) number of times.

set

```
set
set name ...
set name = value ...
set name = (wordlist) ...
set name[index] = word ...
set -r
set -r name ...
set -r name = value ...
set -r name = (wordlist) ...
```

With no arguments, **set** displays the values of all shell variables. Variables that contain more than a single word print as a parenthesized word list. With just a name argument, **set** defines a variable and assigns it the null string. With a name and a value separated by the = sign, it defines the variable and assigns to it that value. To assign a wordlist as the value for the name variable, encase the words in the list within parentheses as the value assigned. To assign a value to an element in an array, specify the element's index using enclosing brackets. The element must already exist.

The **-r** option is used to reference read-only variables. With the **-r** option alone, **set** lists the read-only variables. Used with a variable *name*, it makes that variable a read-only variable. Used with an assigned *value*, it initializes that variable with the *value* and makes it a read-only variable that cannot be changed.

In the TCSH shell, you need to first declare a variable before you can use it. You declare a variable with the **set** command followed by the variable's name. A variable name may be any set of alphabetic characters, including the underscore. The name may also include a number, but the number cannot be the first character in the name. A name may not have any other type of character, such as an exclamation point, ampersand, or even a space. Such symbols are reserved by the shell for its own use. A name may not include more than one word since the shell parses its command line on the space. The space is a delimiter between the different elements of the command line. The next example declares the variable **greeting**. You can later undefine the variable with the **unset** command.

```
> set greeting
```

You also use the **set** command to assign a value to a variable. You type in the keyword **set**, the variable name, the assignment operator (=), and then the value assigned. Any set of characters can be assigned to a variable. In the next example, the variable **greeting** is assigned the string "hello".

```
> set greeting = "hello"
```

In the TCSH shell assignment operation, you need to either place spaces on both sides of the assignment operator or have no spaces at all. The assignment operation

```
> set greeting ="hello"
```

will fail because there is a space before the assignment operator, but not after.

You can obtain a list of all the defined variables by using the **set** command without any arguments. The next example uses **set** to display a list of all defined variables and their values.

```
> set
greeting hello
poet   Virgil
```

As in the BASH shell, the dollar sign, **$**, is a special operator that evaluates a shell variable. Evaluation retrieves a variable's value—usually a set of characters. This set of characters then replaces the variable name. In effect, wherever a **$** is placed before a variable name, the shell replaces the variable name with the value of the variable. In the next example, the shell variable **greeting** is evaluated and its contents, "hello", are then used as the argument for an **echo** command. The **echo** command prints a set of characters on the screen.

```
> echo $greeting
hello
```

setenv

setenv [*name* [*value*]]

setenv is used to define an environment variable with a specified value. With no *value*, **setenv** sets the *name* variable to the null string. With no arguments, it displays the names and values of all environment variables.

The TCSH shell has two types of variables: local variables and environment variables. A local variable is local to the shell it was declared in; an environment variable operates like a scoped global variable. It is known to any subshells, but not to any parent shells. An environment variable is defined with the **setenv** command. You assign a value to an environment variable using the **setenv** command, the variable name, and the value assigned. There is no assignment operator. In the next example, the greeting environment variable is assigned the value "hello".

```
> setenv greeting hello
```

Whenever a shell script is called, it generates its own shell. If a shell script is executed from another shell script, it will have its own shell separate from that of the first script. There are now two shells, the parent shell belonging to the first script and a subshell, which is the new shell generated when the second script was executed. When a script is executed from within another script, its shell is a subshell of the first script's shell. The original script's shell is a parent shell.

Each shell has its own set of variables. The subshell cannot reference local variables in the parent shell, but it can reference environment variables. Any environment variables declared in the parent shell can be referenced by any subshells.

shift

```
shift [variable]
```

Without arguments, this command shifts **argv** one value to the left, discarding the original value of **argv[1]** and replacing it with the value of **argv[2]**, and so on. It is an error for **argv** not to be set or to have less than one word as its value. With a *variable* as an argument whose value is a list or array, the command shifts values of that list or array to the left.

source

```
source [-h] name [arguments ...]
```

source reads and executes commands in *name*, usually a shell script (commands are not placed on the history list). Any *arguments* are placed in **argv**. With the **-h** option, commands are placed on the history list instead of being executed.

stop

```
stop %job|pid ...
```

stop stops the specified *job*s or processes that are executing in the background. You can reference a *job* with a number or string. There is no default job; saying just **stop** does not stop the current job.

switch

```
switch (test-string)
    case pattern:
            commands
breaksw
    case pattern:
            commands
            breaksw
    default:
            commands
```

```
        breaksw
endsw
```

The **switch** structure chooses among several possible alternatives. It is very similar to the BASH shell's **case** structure. A choice is made by comparing a string with several possible patterns, and each possible pattern is associated with a set of commands. If a match is found, the associated commands are performed. The **switch** structure begins with the keyword **switch** and a *test string* within parentheses. The string is often derived from a variable evaluation. A set of patterns then follows. Each *pattern* is preceded with the keyword **case** and terminated with a colon. *Commands* associated with the choice are listed after the colon, and the *commands* are terminated with the keyword **breaksw**. After all the listed patterns, the keyword **endsw** ends the **switch** structure.

Each pattern will be matched against the test string until a match is found. If no match is found, the default option is executed. The default choice is represented with the keyword **default**. The **default** is optional; you do not have to put it in. However, it is helpful for notifying the user of test strings with no match.

A **switch** structure is often used to implement menus. In the program **lschoice**, in the next example, the user is asked to enter an option for listing files in different ways. Notice the **default** option that warns of invalid input.

lschoice

```
#
echo s. List Sizes
echo l. List All File Information
echo c. List C Files
echo -n "Please enter choice: "
set choice = $<
switch ($choice)
    case s:
        ls -s
        breaksw
    case l:
        ls -l
        breaksw
    case c:
        ls *.c
        breaksw
```

```
        default:
            echo Invalid Option
            breaksw
        endsw

> lschoice
s. List Sizes
l. List All File Information
c. List C Files
Please enter choice: c
io.c    lib.c    main.c
>
```

time

```
time [command]
```

With no argument, **time** displays a time summary for the current shell. With a simple *command* as its argument, it executes the *command* and displays a time summary for it.

umask

```
umask [value]
```

umask specifies the user file-creation mask. The *value* of the mask is specified in octal.

unalias

```
unalias pattern
```

unalias removes all aliases whose names match the *pattern*.

unset

```
unset pattern
```

unset undefines a shell variable. The name can be a *pattern* that matches several variables, in which case all are removed. (Avoid **unset** *, as it will remove all shell variables.)

unsetenv

unsetenv *pattern*

unsetenv undefines an environment variable. The name can be a *pattern* that matches several variables, in which case all are removed. (Avoid **unsetenv ***, as it will remove all environment variables.)

wait

wait instructs the shell to wait for all background jobs to finish. In an interactive shell, you can interrupt a wait operation and remaining jobs will be displayed.

where

where *command*

where reports all known instances of *command*, including aliases, builtins, and executables in the path.

which

which *command*

The **which** command displays the particular *command* that will be executed by the shell.

while

```
while ( expression )
    commands
end
```

The **while** loop repeats commands. A **while** loop begins with the keyword **while** and is followed by an *expression* enclosed in parentheses. The end of the loop is specified by the keyword **end**.

The **while** loop can easily be combined with a **switch** structure to drive a menu. In the next example, notice that the menu contains a **quit** option that will set the value of **again** to **no** and stop the loop.

lschoicew

```
#
set again = yes
while ($again == yes)
echo "1. List Sizes"
echo "2. List All File Information"
echo "3. List C Files"
echo "4. Quit"
echo -n "Please enter choice: "
set choice = $<
switch ($choice)
    case 1:
        ls -s
        breaksw
    case 2:
        ls -l
        breaksw
    case 3:
        ls *.c
        breaksw
    case 4:
        set again = no
        echo Good-bye
        breaksw
    default:
        echo Invalid Option
    endsw
end
```

```
> lschoicew
1. List Sizes
2. List All File Information
3. List C Files
4. Quit
Please enter choice: 3
main.c    lib.c    file.c
1. List Sizes
2. List All File Information
3. List C Files
4. Quit
Please enter choice: 4
Good-bye
>
```

> # TCSH Configuration

2

The TCSH shell lets you configure your own shell using shell configuration variables and features. You can set features on and off with the **set** command. The TCSH shell also has configuration files for login, logout, and whenever you enter a TCSH shell.

TCSH Shell Features

The TCSH shell has several features that allow you to control how different shell operations work. The TCSH shell's features include those in the PDSKH shell as well as many of its own. For example, the TCSH shell has a **noclobber** option to prevent redirection from overwriting files. Some of the more commonly used features are **echo**, **noclobber**, **ignoreeof**, and **noglob**. The TCSH shell features are turned on and off by defining and undefining a variable associated with that feature. A variable is named for each feature; for example, the **noclobber** feature is turned on by defining the **noclobber** variable. You use the **set** command to define a variable and the **unset** command to undefine a variable. To turn on the **noclobber** feature, you issue the command **set noclobber**. To turn it off, you use the command **unset noclobber**.

```
set feature-variable
unset feature-variable
```

These variables are also sometimes referred to as *toggles* since they are used to turn features on and off.

echo
Setting **echo** enables a feature that displays a command before it is executed. The command **set echo** turns the echo feature on, and the command **unset echo** turns it off.

ignoreeof
Setting **ignoreeof** enables a feature that prevents users from logging out of the user shell with a CTRL-D. It is designed to prevent accidental logouts. With this feature turned off, you can log out by pressing CTRL-D. However, CTRL-D is also used to end user input entered directly into the standard input. It is used often for the **mail** program or for utilities such as **cat**. You could easily

enter an extra CTRL-D in such circumstances and accidentally log
yourself out. The **ignoreeof** feature prevents such accidental
logouts. When it is set, you have to explicitly log out, using the
logout command:

```
> set ignoreeof
> ^D
Use logout to logout
>
```

noclobber

Setting **noclobber** enables a feature that safeguards existing files
from redirected output. With the **noclobber** feature, if you redirect
output to a file that already exists, the file will not be overwritten
with the standard output; the original file will be preserved. There
may be situations in which you use a name that you have already
given to an existing file as the name for the file to hold the
redirected output. The **noclobber** feature prevents you from
accidentally overwriting your original file:

```
> set noclobber
> cat preface > myfile
myfile: file exists
>
```

There may be times when you want to overwrite a file with
redirected output. In this case, you can place an exclamation point
after the redirection operator. This will override the **noclobber**
feature, replacing the contents of the file with the standard output:

```
> cat preface >! myfile
```

noglob

Setting **noglob** enables a feature that disables special characters
in the user shell. The characters *****, **?**, **[,]**, and **~** will no longer
expand to matched filenames. This feature is helpful if, for some
reason, you have special characters as part of a filename. In the
next example, the user needs to reference a file that ends with the
? character: **answers?**. First, the user turns off special characters,
using the **noglob** option. Now the question mark on the command
line is taken as part of the filename, not as a special character,
and the user can reference the **answers?** file.

```
> set noglob
> ls answers?
answers?
```

The following table lists several commonly used TCSH shell features:

Feature	Function
set	Turn on shell features.
unset	Turn off shell features.
echo	Display each command before executing it.
ignoreeof	Disable CTRL-D logout.
noclobber	Do not overwrite files through redirection.
noglob	Disable special characters used for filename expansion: *, ?, ~, [, and].
notify	Notify the user immediately when a background job is completed.
verbose	Display command after a history command reference.

TCSH Shell Variables

As in the BASH shell, you can use special shell variables in the TCSH shell to configure your system. Some are defined initially by your system, and you can later redefine them with a new value. There are others that you must initially define yourself. One of the more commonly used special variables is the **prompt** variable that allows you to create your own command-line prompts. Another is the **history** variable with which you determine how many history events you want to keep track of.

In the TCSH shell, many special variables have names and functions similar to those in the BASH or ZSH shells. Some are in uppercase, but most are written in lowercase. The **EXINIT** and **TERM** variables retain their uppercase form. However, **history** and **cdpath** are written in lowercase. Other special variables may perform similar functions, but have very different implementations. For example, the **mail** variable holds the same information as the BASH shell's **MAIL**, **MAILPATH**, and **MAILCHECK** variables together.

prompt, prompt2, prompt3

The **prompt**, **prompt2**, and **prompt3** variables hold the prompts for your command line. You can configure your prompt to be any symbol or string that you want. To have your command line display a different symbol as a prompt, you simply use the **set** command to assign that symbol to the prompt variable. In the next example, the user assigns a + sign to the **prompt** variable, making it the new prompt.

```
> set prompt = "+"
+
```

You can use a predefined set of codes to make configuring your prompt easier. With them, you can make the time, your user name, or your directory path name a part of your prompt. You can even have your prompt display the history event number of the current command you are about to enter. Each code is preceded by a % symbol. For example, %/ represents the current working directory; **%t**, the time; and **%n**, your user name. **%!** will display the next history event number. In the next example, the user adds the current working directory to the prompt.

```
> set prompt = "%/ >"
/home/dylan >
```

The next example incorporates both the time and the history event number with a new prompt.

```
> set prompt = "%t %! $"
```

Here is a list of the codes:

Code	Description
%/	Current working directory
%h, %!, !	Current history number
%t	Time of day
%n	User name
%d	Day of the week
%w	Current month
%y	Current year

The **prompt2** variable is used in special cases when a command may take several lines to input. **prompt2** is displayed for the added lines needed for entering the command. **prompt3** is the prompt used if the spell check feature is activated.

cdpath

The **cdpath** variable holds the path names of directories to be searched for specified subdirectories referenced with the **cd** command. These path names form an array just like the array of path names assigned to the TCSH shell **path** variable. Notice the space between the path names.

```
> set cdpath = (/usr/chris/reports /usr/chris/letters)
```

history and savehist

As you learned earlier, the **history** variable can be used to determine the number of history events you want saved. You simply assign to it the maximum number of events that **history** should record. When the maximum is reached, the count starts over again from 1. The **savehist** variable, however, holds the number of events that will be saved in the **.history** file when you log out. When you log in again, these events will become the initial history list.

In the next example, up to 20 events will be recorded in your history list while you are logged in. However, only the last 5 will be saved in the **.history** file when you log out. Upon logging in again, your history list will consist of your last 5 commands from the previous session.

```
> set history = 20
> set savehist = 5
```

mail

In the TCSH shell, the **mail** variable combines the features of the **MAIL**, **MAILCHECK**, and **MAILPATH** variables in the BASH and ZSH shells. The value of the TCSH shell **mail** variable is an array whose elements contain both the time interval for checking for mail and the directory path names for mailbox files to be checked. To assign values to these elements, you assign an array of values to the **mail** variable. The array of new values is specified with a list of words separated by spaces and enclosed in parentheses. The first value is a number that sets the number of seconds to wait before checking for mail again. This value is comparable to that held by the BASH shell's **MAILCHECK** variable. The remaining values consist of the directory path names of mailbox files that are to be checked for your mail. Notice that these values combine the functions of the BASH and ZSH shells' **MAIL** and **MAIL-PATH** variables.

In the next example, the **mail** variable is set to check for mail every 20 minutes (1200 seconds), and the mailbox file checked is in **usr/mail/chris**. The first value in the array assigned to **mail** is 1200, and the second value in the array is the path name of the mailbox file to be checked.

```
> set mail ( 1200 /usr/mail/chris )
```

You can, just as easily, add more mailbox file path names to the **mail** array. In the next example, two mailboxes are designated. Notice the spaces surrounding each element.

```
> set mail ( 1200 /usr/mail/chris /home/mail/chris )
```

The following table lists several commonly used shell configuration variables:

Variable	Description
home	Path name for user's home directory.
user	Login name.
cwd	Path name of current working directory.
shell	Path name of program for login shell.
path	List of path names for directories searched for executable commands.
prompt	Primary shell prompt.
mail	Name of mail file checked by **mail** utility for received messages.
cdpath	Path names for directories searched by **cd** command for subdirectories.
history	Number of commands in your history list.
savehist	Number of commands in your history list that you save for the next login session. Commands are saved in a file named **.history**.
EXINIT	Initialization commands for Ex/Vi editor.
TERM	Terminal name.

TCSH Shell Initialization Files

The TCSH shell has three initialization files: **.login**, **.tcshrc**, and **.logout**. The files are named for the operations they execute. The

.login file is a login initialization file that executes each time you
log in. The **.tcshrc** file is a shell initialization file that executes
each time you enter the TCSH shell, either from logging in or by
explicitly changing to the TCSH shell from another shell with the
tcsh command. The **.logout** file executes each time you log out.

2

.login

The TCSH shell has its own login initialization file called the
.login file that contains shell commands and special variable
definitions used to configure your shell. The **.login** file
corresponds to the **.profile** file used in the BASH and ZSH shells.

A **.login** file contains **setenv** commands that assign values to
special environment variables, such as **TERM**. You can change
these assigned values by editing the **.login** file with any of the
standard editors. You can also add new values. Remember,
however, that in the TCSH shell, the command for assigning a
value to an environment variable is **setenv**. In the next example,
the **EXINIT** variable is defined and it is assigned the Vi editor's
line numbering and autoindent options.

```
> setenv EXINIT 'set nu ai'
```

Be careful when editing your **.login** file. Inadvertent editing
changes could cause variables to be set incorrectly or not at all. It
is wise to make a backup of your **.login** file before editing it.

If you have made changes to your **.login** file and you want the
changes to take effect during your current login session, you will
need to reexecute the file. You do so using the **source** command.
The **source** command will actually execute any initialization file,
including the **.tcshrc** and **.logout** files. In the next example, the
user reexecutes the **.login** file.

```
> source .login
```

.tcshrc

The **.tcshrc** initialization file is executed each time you enter the
TCSH shell or generate any subshells. If the TCSH shell is your
login shell, then the **.tcshrc** file is executed along with your **.login**
file when you log in. If you enter the TCSH shell from another
shell, the **.tcshrc** file is automatically executed, and the variable
and alias definitions it contains will be defined.

The **.tcshrc** shell initialization file is actually executed each time
you generate a shell, such as when you run a shell script. In other

words, each time a subshell is created, the **.tcshrc** file is executed. This allows you to define local variables in the **.tcshrc** initialization file and have them, in a sense, exported to any subshells. Even though such user-defined special variables as **history** are local, they will be defined for each subshell generated. In this way, **history** is set for each subshell. However, each subshell has its own local **history** variable. You could even change the local **history** variable in one subshell without affecting any of those in other subshells. Defining special variables in the shell initialization file allows you to treat them like BASH shell exported variables. An exported variable in a BASH or ZSH shell only passes a copy of itself to any subshell. Changing the copy does not affect the original definition.

The **.tcshrc** file also contains the definition of aliases and any feature variables used to turn on shell features. Aliases and feature variables are locally defined within the shell. But the **.tcshrc** file will define them in every shell. For this reason, **.tcshrc** usually holds such aliases as those defined for the **rm**, **cp**, and **mv** commands. The next example is a **.tcshrc** file with many of the standard definitions.

.tcshrc

```
#
set shell = /usr/bin/csh
set path = $PATH (/bin /usr/bin . )
set cdpath = (/home/chris/reports /home/chris/letters)

set prompt = "! $cwd >"
set history = 20

set ignoreeof
set noclobber

alias rm 'rm -i'
alias mv 'mv -i'
alias cp 'cm -i'
```

Local variables, unlike environment variables, are defined with the **set** command. Any local variables that you define in **.tcshrc** should use the **set** command. Any variables defined with **setenv** as environment variables, such as **TERM**, should be placed in the **.login** file. The next example shows the kinds of definitions found in the **.tcshrc** file. Notice that the **history** and **noclobber** variables are defined using the **set** command.

```
set history = 20
set noclobber
```

You can edit any of the values assigned to these variables. However, when editing the path names assigned to **path** or **cdpath**, bear in mind that these path names are contained in an array. Each element in an array is separated by a space. If you add a new path name, you need to be sure that there is a space separating it from the other path names.

If you have made changes to **.tcshrc** and you want them to take effect during your current login session, remember to reexecute the **.tcshrc** file with the **source** command:

```
> source .tcshrc
```

.logout

The **.logout** file is also an initialization file, but it is executed when the user logs out. It is designed to perform any operations you want done whenever you log out. Instead of variable definitions, the **.logout** file usually contains shell commands that form a shutdown procedure. For example, one common logout command is the one to check for any active background jobs; another is to clear the screen and then issue a farewell message.

As with **.login**, you can add your own shell commands to the **.logout** file. Using the Vi editor, you could change the farewell message or add other operations. In the next example, the user has a **clear** and an **echo** command in the **.logout** file. When the user logs out, the **clear** command will clear the screen, and **echo** will display the message "Good-bye for now".

.logout

```
#
clear
echo "Good-bye for now"
```

Chapter 3
Z-Shell Programming

The Z shell has programming-language-like capabilities that allow you to create complex shell programs. It is very similar to the BASH shell in many respects. At the same time, it is possible to use C-programming-like syntax for many control structures. Certain basic features, such as variable definition and assignment, as well as redirection and pipes, operate the same as in the BASH shell.

Shell Scripts: Commands and Comments

You define a script and place commands and comments in it much as you would a BASH shell script. (For a more detailed explanation, see this heading in Chapter 1.) If you put a **#!/bin/zsh** at the beginning of the first line of the **hello** script, you could execute it directly from the TCSH shell. The script will first change to the Z shell, execute its commands, and then return to the TCSH shell (or whatever type of shell it was executed from). In the next example, the **hello** script includes the **#!/bin/zsh** command. The user then executes the script while in the TCSH shell.

hello

```
#!/bin/zsh
# The hello script says hello
echo "Hello, how are you"

$ hello
Hello, how are you
```

Control Structures

The Z shell has many of the same control structures as the BASH shell, though there are a few additional ones. The Z-shell loops are

while, for and **for-in, repeat, select,** and **foreach.** There are several condition structures: **if, switch,** and **case.**

Control Structures: AND, OR, and NOT	Function
command **&&** *command*	The logical AND condition returns a true 0 value if both *commands* return a true 0 value; if one *command* returns a nonzero value, then the AND condition is false and also returns a nonzero value.
command I I *command*	The logical OR condition returns a true 0 value if one or the other *command* returns a true 0 value; if both *commands* return a nonzero value, then the OR condition is false and also returns a nonzero value.
! *command*	The logical NOT condition inverts the return value of the *command.*

Loop Control Structures: while, until, for, for-in, select	Function
while *command* **do** *command* **done**	**while** executes an action as long as its test *command* is true.
until *command* **do** *command* **done**	**until** executes an action as long as its test *command* is false.
for *variable* **in** *list-values* **do** *command* **done**	**for-in** is designed for use with lists of values; the *variable* operand is consecutively assigned the values in the list.
for *variable* **do** *command* **done**	**for** is designed for reference script arguments; the *variable* operand is consecutively assigned each argument value.

Loop Control Structures: while, until, for, for-in, select	Function
select *string* **in** *item-list* **do** *command* **done**	**select** creates a menu based on the items in the *item-list*; then it executes the *command*; the *command* is usually a **case**.

3

Condition Control Structures: if, else, elif, case	Function
if *command* **then** *command* **fi**	**if** executes an action if its test *command* is true.

if *command* **then**
    command
else
    command
fi
	if-else executes an action if the exit status of its test *command* is true; if false, then the **else** action is executed.

if *command* **then**
    command
elif *command* **then**
    command
else
    command
fi
	elif allows you to nest **if** structures, enabling selection among several alternatives; at the first true **if** structure, its *commands* are executed and control leaves the entire **elif** structure.

case *string* **in** *pattern*) *command*;; **esac**	**case** matches the string value to any of several *patterns*; if a *pattern* is matched, its associated *commands* are executed.

Jobs: Background, Kills, and Interruptions

The Z shell has the same job-control features as the BASH shell. The commands are much the same. You can run a job in the background while you execute other commands. You can also cancel commands before they have finished executing. You can even interrupt a command, starting it up again later from where you left off.

Operators

The Z-shell has a standard set of arithmetic, relational, and assignment operators, as found in most programming environments, and operators for shell functions such as redirection and background operations.

Definition and Evaluation of Variables: =, $

A variable is defined in a shell when you first use the variable's name. A variable name may be any set of alphabetic characters, including the underscore. The name may also include a number, but the number cannot be the first character in the name. A name may not have any other type of character, such as an exclamation point, ampersand, or even a space. Such symbols are reserved by a shell for its own use. A name may not include more than one word, because a shell uses spaces to parse commands, delimiting command names and arguments.

You assign a value to a variable with the assignment operator. You type the variable name, the assignment operator, **=**, and then the value assigned. Note that you cannot place any spaces around the assignment operator. Any set of characters can be assigned to a variable. In the next example, the **greeting** variable is assigned the string "Hello".

```
$ greeting="Hello"
```

Once you have assigned a value to a variable, you can then use that variable to reference the value. Often you use the values of variables as arguments for a command. You can reference the value of a variable using the variable name preceded by the **$** operator. The dollar sign is a special operator that uses a variable name to reference a variable's value, in effect, evaluating the variable. Evaluation retrieves a variable's value—a set of characters. This set of characters then replaces the variable name on the command line. Thus, wherever a **$** is placed before the variable name, the variable name is replaced with the value of the variable.

Here: <<

The Z shell also supports the Here operator, <<, just as the BASH shell does. (For a more detailed explanation, see this heading in Chapter 1.)

Double Quotes, Single Quotes, and Backslashes: "", ", \

Double quotes, single quotes, and backslashes operate the same as described in the BASH shell, for quoting strings and single characters. (For a more detailed explanation, see this heading Chapter 1.)

Back Quotes: ``` `` ```

Back quotes operate the same as described in the BASH shell, executing enclosed commands on a line and returning its value. (For a more detailed explanation, see this heading in Chapter 1.)

Positional Parameters: $

Like Linux commands, a shell script can take arguments. When you invoke a script, you can enter arguments on the command line after the script name. These arguments can then be referenced within the script using positional parameters. To reference a positional parameter, you use the **$** operator and the number of its position on the command line. Arguments on the command line are sequentially numbered from 1. The first argument is referenced with the positional parameter **$1**, the second argument with **$2**, and so on. The argument **$0** will contain the name of the shell script, the first word on the command line. (For a more detailed explanation, see this heading in Chapter 1.)

A set of special variables allows you to reference different aspects of command-line arguments, such as the number of arguments or all the arguments together: **$***, **$@**, **$#**. The **$#** argument contains the number of arguments entered on the command line. This is useful when you need to specify a fixed number of arguments for a script. The variable **$*** references all the arguments in the command line. A command line may have more than nine arguments. The **$@** also references all the arguments on the command line, but allows you to separately quote each one. The difference between **$*** and **$@** is not clear until you use them to reference arguments using the **for-in** control structure.

Positional Parameters	Description
$0	Name of Linux command.
$n	The nth command-line argument beginning from **1**, **$1-$n**; you can use **set** to change it.
$*	All the command-line arguments beginning from 1; you can use **set** to change them.
$@	The command-line arguments individually quoted.
$#	The count of the command-line arguments.

Process Variables	Description
$$	The PID number, or *process ID*, of the current process.
$!	The PID number of the most recent background job.
$?	The exit status of the last Linux command executed.

Arithmetic Operators

Arithmetic expressions use nearly the same syntax, precedence, and associativity of expressions in C. The table of operators shown here is grouped by equal-precedence operators, with the groups listed in order of decreasing precedence. Precedence can be overridden by using nested parentheses.

Operator	Description
+, -, !, ~, ++, --	Unary plus/minus, logical NOT, complement, increment, and decrement
&	Logical AND
^	Logical XOR
|	Logical OR
*, /, %, **	Multiplication, division, remainder, and exponentiation

Operator	Description
+, -	Addition, subtraction
<<, >>	Logical shift left, shift right
<, >, <=, >=	Comparison
==, !=	Equality and inequality
&&	Boolean AND
| |, ^^	Boolean OR, XOR
?, :	Ternary operator
=, +=, -=, *=, /=, %=, &=, ^=, |=, <<=, >>=, &&=, | |=, ^^=, **=	Assignment

3

You can use shell variables as operands. Constants beginning with a **0** are interpreted as octal numbers; a preceding **x** denotes a hexadecimal number. The #\ operator placed before a character gives the ASCII value of that character.

Conditional Expressions

A test command is used with conditional operators to test the attributes of files and to compare strings. You can use enclosing double brackets to evaluate the conditional expression, as in **[[$myname > "justin"]]**. If true, then **[[ ]]** returns 0.

```
[[ expression ]]
```

Option	Returns
-a file	True if file exists.
-b file	True if file exists and is a block special file.
-c file	True if file exists and is a character special file.
-d file	True if file exists and is a directory.
-e file	True if file exists.
-f file	True if file exists and is an ordinary file.
-g file	True if file exists and has its setgid bit set.
-h file	True if file exists and is a symbolic link.
-k file	True if file exists and has its sticky bit set.
-n string	True if length of string is nonzero.
-o option	True if named option is on.
-p file	True if file exists and is a fifo special file or a pipe.

Option	Returns
-r *file*	True if *file* exists and is readable.
-s *file*	True if *file* exists and has size greater than zero.
-t *fd*	True if file descriptor number *fd* is open and is associated with a terminal device.
-u *file*	True if *file* exists and has its setuid bit set.
-w *file*	True if *file* exists and is writable.
-x *file*	True if *file* exists and is executable. If *file* exists and is a directory, then that directory can be searched by the current process.
-z *string*	True if length of *string* is zero.
-L *file*	True if *file* exists and is a symbolic link.
-O *file*	True if *file* exists and is owned by the effective user ID of this process.
-G *file*	True if *file* exists and its group matches the effective group ID of this process.
-S *file*	True if *file* exists and is a socket.
file1 **-nt** *file2*	True if *file1* exists and is newer than *file2*.
file1 **-ot** *file2*	True if *file1* exists and is older than *file2*.
file1 **-ef** *file2*	True if *file1* and *file2* exist and refer to the same file.
string **=** *pattern*	True if *string* matches *pattern*.
string **!=** *pattern*	True if *string* does not match *pattern*.
string1 **<** *string2*	True if *string1* comes before *string2* based on the ASCII value of their characters.
string1 **>** *string2*	True if *string1* comes after *string2* based on the ASCII value of their characters.
exp1 **-eq** *exp2*	True if *exp1* is equal to *exp2*.
exp1 **-ne** *exp2*	True if *exp1* is not equal to *exp2*.
exp1 **-lt** *exp2*	True if *exp1* is less than *exp2*.
exp1 **-gt** *exp2*	True if *exp1* is greater than *exp2*.
exp1 **-le** *exp2*	True if *exp1* is less than or equal to *exp2*.
exp1 **-ge** *exp2*	True if *exp1* is greater than or equal to *exp2*.
(*exp* **)**	True if *exp* is true.
! *exp*	True if *exp* is false.
exp1 **&&** *exp2*	True if *exp1* and *exp2* are both true.
exp1 **I I** *exp2*	True if either *exp1* or *exp2* is true.

Redirection and Pipes: <, <<, >, |

The ZSH shell also supports standard input and output redirection operations and pipes as described in the BASH chapter. (For a detailed explanation, see Chapter 1.) To overwrite an existing file with redirection, you need to use >! instead of just > alone, if the noclobber feature is set.

3

Background: &

You execute a command in the background by placing an ampersand on the command line at the end of the command. When you do so, a user job number and a system process number are displayed. The user job number, placed in brackets, is the number by which the user references the job. The system process number is the number by which the system identifies the job. In the next example, the command to print the file **mydata** is placed in the background.

```
$ lpr mydata &
[1]   534
$
```

Z-Shell Commands

A description of each Z-shell builtin command follows. The commands are listed alphabetically. Each description begins with the command's syntax.

Colon (:)

```
: [arguments]
```

The colon allows you to list more than one command on the same command line, each separated by a :. The exit code is 0.

Period (.)

```
. filename [arguments]
```

The period reads and executes commands from a file in the current shell. It returns the exit status of the last command executed in that file. If the filename does not include a full path name, then the path names defined in **PATH** are used to locate the directory in which the filename resides. If **PATHDIRS** is set, the shell looks in the components of **PATH** to find the directory containing the file.

Double Parentheses: (( ))

`((expression))`

This is an alternative form of the **let** command, enclosing an arithmetic expression between two double parentheses. After a **((,** all the characters until a matching **))** are treated as a quoted expression.

Double Brackets: [[ ]]

`[[expression]]`

Enclosing double brackets evaluate the conditional *expression* and return a 0 exit status if it is true.

CTRL-Z: Interruptions

You can interrupt a job and stop it with the CTRL-Z command. This places the job to the side until it is restarted. The job is not ended; it merely remains suspended until you wish to continue. When you're ready, you can continue with the job in either the foreground or the background using the **fg** or **bg** command. The **fg** command will restart an interrupted job in the foreground. The **bg** command will place the interrupted job in the background. (For a more detailed explanation, see this heading in Chapter 1.)

alias

`alias [-grm] [name[=value] ...]`

The **alias** command alone displays the list of defined aliases. To display the value of a particular alias, you can use its name alone as an argument. If you provided a name that has not been defined as an alias, then the command returns false; otherwise, it returns true. You can also use the **alias** command to define aliases, providing the *name* and the *value* separated by an = symbol.

The **-g** option defines a global alias. If only the **-g** or the **-r** option is used, only global or regular aliases are listed. With the **-m** option, the arguments can be patterns, displaying the aliases matching these patterns.

bg

bg [*jobsref*]

bg places a job in the background. If *jobsref* is not present, the shell's notion of the current job is used. The command returns 0 unless run when job control is disabled or, when run with job control enabled, if *jobsref* was not found or started without job control.

break

break [*n*]

break forces an exit from within a **for**, **while**, or **until** loop. The *n* argument, if present, specifies the number of nested levels to break out of. If *n* is greater than the number of enclosing loops, all enclosing loops are exited. **break** returns a value of 0 unless the shell is not executing a loop when **break** is executed.

builtin

builtin *shell-builtin* [*arguments*]

builtin executes the specified *shell-builtin*, passing it *arguments*, and returns its exit status. This is useful when you wish to define a function whose name is the same as a shell builtin, but need the functionality of the builtin within the function itself. The **cd** builtin is commonly redefined this way. The return status is false if *shell-builtin* is not a shell builtin command.

case

case *variable* in
    pattern)

```
        commands
        ;;
    pattern)
        commands
        ;;
    *)
        default commands
        ;;
    esac
```

The **case** structure chooses among several possible alternatives. The choice is made by comparing a value with several possible patterns. Each possible pattern is associated with a set of operations. If a match is found, the associated operations are performed. The **case** structure begins with the keyword **case**, an evaluation of a variable, and the keyword **in**. A set of patterns then follows. Each pattern is a regular expression terminated with a closing parenthesis. After the closing parenthesis, commands associated with this pattern are listed, followed by a double semicolon on a separate line, designating the end of those commands. After all the listed patterns, the keyword **esac** ends the **case** command.

A pattern can include any shell special characters. The shell special characters are the *, [,], ?, and |. You can specify a default pattern with a single * special character. The * special character matches on any pattern—if all other patterns do not match, the * will. In this way, the default option is executed if no other options are chosen. The default is optional. You do not have to put it in.

cd

```
cd [dir]
cd
cd ±n
```

cd changes the current directory to *dir*. The variable **HOME** is the default directory. If the directory is not specified by a full path name beginning with a slash (/) or dot (.), then the list of directories in the variable **CDPATH** is searched for the directory containing that directory. With the - argument, **cd** changes to the directory held in **$OLDPWD**. The **cd** command with no arguments changes to the home directory. An argument of - is equivalent to **$OLDPWD**. The return value is true if the directory was successfully changed; false otherwise. **cd** with a +*n* or -*n* is the same as **popd**, changing to directories in the remembered directory list.

continue

```
continue [n]
```

continue skips the remainder of the body of the current loop and reexecutes it beginning the next iteration. It works for the **for**, **while**, and **until** loops. With the *n* argument, **continue** will begin at the *n*th enclosing loop. If *n* is greater than the number of enclosing loops, the last enclosing loop (the "top-level" loop) is resumed. **continue** returns 0 unless the shell is not executing a loop when the command is executed.

declare

```
declare [±LRZfilrtuxm [n]] [name[=value] ...]
```

declare is used to define shell variables and set attributes for them (same as **typeset**). When used within a function, it creates a shell variable that will be unset when the function finishes. If the **ALLEXPORT** variable is set, the shell variable will be exported, unless another shell variable of that name already exists. Attributes are specified with the following options. With just an option and no arguments, **declare** lists the variables that have been given that option. With no option or arguments, **declare** lists all defined variables. With the **-m** option, arguments are taken to be patterns, selecting any variables the patterns match.

Option	Function
-L	Left justify and remove leading blanks from the value specified.
-R	Right justify and fill with leading blanks. (The *n* argument can be used to specify the width of the field; otherwise, the width of the first value assigned is used.)
-Z	Right justify and fill with leading zeros if the first nonblank character is a digit and the **-L** option is not set. (The *n* argument can be used to specify the width of the field; otherwise, the width of the first value assigned is used.)

Option	Function
-f	Specify that the *name* arguments refer to functions, not variables. (There is a -t (tracing) and a -u (marked for autoloading) option for this option.)
-i	Use an internal integer representation. (With an *n* argument, *n* defines the output arithmetic base; otherwise, the base is determined by first assignment.)
-l	Convert to lowercase.
-r	Mark the defined variables (*name* arguments) read-only.
-t	Tag the *named* variables.
-u	Convert to uppercase.
-x	Automatically export to the subsequent shell environments.

dirs

```
dirs [-v] [arguments ...]
```

dirs displays the list of currently remembered directories. Directories are added to the list with the **pushd** command. **-v** numbers the directory entries. If directory *arguments* are listed, load them into the directory stack.

echo

```
echo [-n] [arguments ...]
```

The **echo** command will send data to the standard output. The data is in the form of a string of characters. The **echo** command can output variable values as well as string constants. The return status is always 0. The **-n** option suppresses a newline at the end. **echo** supports a set of escape characters for outputting nonprinting characters such as newline and form feed. The following table lists the escape characters.

Escaped Character	Description
\a	Alert (bell)
\b	Backspace

Escaped Character	Description
\c	Suppress trailing newline
\f	Form feed
\n	Newline
\r	Carriage return
\t	Horizontal tab
\v	Vertical tab
\\	Backslash
\0*nn*	The character whose ASCII code is *nn* (octal)
\x*nn*	The character whose ASCII code is *nn* (hexadecimal)

elif

```
if Linux command
    then
            commands
elif Linux command
    then
            commands
    else
            commands
fi
```

The **elif** structure allows you to nest **if-then-else** operations. The **elif** structure stands for "else if." With **elif**, you can choose between several alternatives. The first alternative is specified with the **if** structure, followed by other alternatives, each specified by its own **elif** structure. The alternative to the last **elif** structure is specified with an **else**. If the test (a *Linux command*) for the first **if** structure fails, control will be passed to the next **elif** structure, and its test will be executed. If it fails, control is passed to the next **elif** and its test checked. This continues until a test is true. Then that **elif** has its commands executed and control passes out of the **if** structure to the next command after the **fi** keyword.

If the **CSH_JUNKIE_PAREN** option is set, you can use a C program format with parentheses for the test expression and braces for the body of the loop. No **then** or **fi** keywords are needed. The parentheses surrounding the expression can be omitted if it consists of a single conditional expression.

```
if ( ) {
        } elif ( ) {
        } ... else {
        }
```

enable

```
enable [-m] [name ...]
```

enable is used to enable and disable builtin shell commands. With the **-m** option, arguments can be patterns. With no arguments it displays a list of all enabled shell builtins.

eval

```
eval [arguments ...]
```

eval reads *arguments* as shell input and executes the command they constitute.

exec

```
exec [[-] command [arguments]]
```

exec executes a *command*, replacing the current shell. No new process is created. You can specify *arguments* for the *command*. If **exec**'s first argument is -, the shell places a dash in the zeroth argument passed to *command*. If **exec** has no *arguments*, then any redirections take effect in the current shell, returning 0 as its exit status.

exit

```
exit [n]
```

exit causes you to exit the shell with the exit code specified by *n*. If none is specified, the command uses the exit code from the last command executed.

export

```
export [name[=value] ...]
```

The specified variables are marked for automatic export to the environment of subsequently executed shells and commands.

fc

```
fc   [-e ename] [-nlrdDfEm] [old=new ...] [first[last]]
fc -ARWI [filename]
```

fc selects a range of commands from the history list with a *first* and *last* event reference. The references for the *first* and *last* events may be specified as numbers or as strings. You can use a negative number to offset to the current history event number. You can also specify substitution to be performed on the selected commands (*old=new*). With the -**l** option, resulting commands are displayed in the standard output. With the -**m** option, the first argument is treated as a pattern and only events that match the pattern will be displayed. Without these options, the editor is invoked on a file containing these history events. With the -**e** option you can specify the editor to be used. If *ename* is "-", no editor is invoked. When editing is complete, the edited commands are executed. If the first event is not specified, it will be set to −1 (the most recent event), or to −16 if the -**l** option is used. If the last event is not specified, it will be set to the first event, or to −1 if the -**l** option is used. The -**r** option reverses the order of the commands, and the -**n** option suppresses command numbers when displaying events. With the -**d** option, timestamps are displayed for each command, and with the -**f** option, full time-date stamps are displayed. With the -**E** option, the dates are displayed as in the format *dd.mm.yyyy*. With the -**D** option, **fc** displays elapsed times.

fc -R reads the history from the specified file, **fc -W** writes the history out to the specified file, and **fc -A** appends the history out to the specified file. **fc -AI** (**-WI**) appends (writes) only those events that are new since the last incremental append (write) to the history file.

fg

```
fg [jobsref]
```

fg places a background job in the foreground, making it the current job. If *jobsref* is not present, the shell's notion of the current job is used. **fg** returns the value of the command placed into the foreground. It returns 0 if *jobsref* does not specify a valid job or job control is disabled. *jobsref* can be a job control number, as displayed by the **jobs** command.

In the next example, the second job is brought back into the foreground. You may not immediately receive a prompt again because the second command is now in the foreground and executing. When the command has finished executing, the prompt will appear and you can execute another command.

```
$ fg %2
cat *.c > myprogs
$
```

for

```
for variable
    do
        commands
    done
```

The **for** structure, without a specified list of values, takes as its list of values the command-line arguments. The arguments specified on the command line when the shell file is invoked become a list of values referenced by the **for** command. The *variable* used in the **for** command is set automatically to each argument value in sequence. The first time through the loop, the *variable* is set to the value of the first argument. The second time, it is set to the value of the second argument.

The **for** structure without a specified list is equivalent to the list **$@**. **$@** is a special argument variable whose value is the list of command-line arguments. In the next example, a list of C program files is entered on the command line when the shell file **cbackuparg** is invoked. In **cbackuparg**, each argument is automatically referenced by a **for** loop. **backfile** is the variable used in the **for** loop. The first time through the loop, **$backfile** holds the value of the first argument, **$1**. The second time through, it holds the value of the second argument, **$2**.

cbackuparg

```
for backfile
do
    cp $backfile sourcebak/$backfile
    echo "$backfile"
done
```

```
$ cbackuparg  main.c  lib.c  io.c
main.c
lib.c
io.c
```

for-in

```
for variable in list of values
    do
        commands
    done
```

The **for-in** structure is designed to reference a list of values sequentially. It takes two operands—a *variable* and a *list of values*. Each value in the list is assigned, one by one, to the *variable* in the **for-in** structure. Like the **while** command, the **for-in** structure is a loop. Each time through the loop, the next value in the list is assigned to the *variable*. When the end of the list is reached, the loop stops. Like the **while** loop, the body of a **for-in** loop begins with the keyword **do** and ends with the keyword **done**.

If the **CSH_JUNKIE_PAREN** option is set, you can use C programming style syntax. Either of the following is valid.

```
for variable in list of values
            {
            commands
            }

for  ( ... ) {
            commands
            }
```

foreach

```
foreach variable (list of values)
        commands
end
```

The **foreach** structure is designed to sequentially reference a list of values. It is very similar to the **for-in** structure. The **foreach** structure takes two operands—a *variable* and a *list of values* enclosed in parentheses. Each value in the list is assigned to the variable in the **foreach** structure. Like the **while** structure, the **foreach** structure is a loop. Each time through the loop, the next value in the list is assigned to the variable. When the end of the list is reached, the loop stops. Like the **while** loop, the body of a **foreach** loop ends with the keyword **end**.

In the **mylist** script, in the next example, the user simply outputs a list of each item with today's date. The list of items makes up the list of values read by the **foreach** loop. Each item is consecutively assigned to the variable **grocery**.

mylist

```
#
set tdate=`date '+%D'`
foreach grocery ( milk cookies apples cheese )
    echo "$grocery     $tdate"
end
```

```
$ mylist
milk       05/23/99
cookies    05/23/99
apples     05/23/99
cheese     05/23/99
$
```

The **foreach** loop is useful for managing files. In the **foreach** structure, you can use shell special characters in a pattern to generate a list of filenames for use as your list of values. This generated list of filenames then becomes the list referenced by the **foreach** structure. An asterisk by itself generates a list of all files and directories. ***.c** lists files with the .c extension. These are usually C source-code files. The next example makes a backup of each file and places the backup in a directory called **sourcebak**. The pattern ***.c** generates a list of filenames that the **foreach** structure can operate on.

cbackup

```
#
foreach backfile ( *.c )
    cp $backfile sourcebak/$backfile
    echo $backfile
end
```

```
$ cbackup
io.c
lib.c
main.c
```

The **foreach** structure, without a specified list of values, takes as its list of values the command-line arguments. The arguments specified on the command line when the shell file was invoked become a list of values referenced by the **foreach** structure. The variable used in the **foreach** structure is set automatically to each argument value in sequence. The first time through the loop, the variable is set to the value of the first argument. The second time, it is set to the value of the second argument, and so on.

function

```
function name {commands}
```

function is used to define a function. Use the keyword **function** followed by the name you want to give to the function, and then the commands that you want to make up the function, enclosed within braces. These commands are executed whenever the function name is specified as the name of a command. The exit status of a function is the exit status of the last command.

```
function func_name
    {
        commands
    }
```

Alternatively, you can define a function using a set of enclosing parentheses after the name instead of the keyword **function**, giving it a style similar to C programs.

```
func_name ()
    {
        commands
    }
```

The Z shell has several special function names that you can use to define functions and that will be automatically executed at certain times by the shell. For example, if you define a function called **chpwd**, then the commands you defined in that function will be executed whenever the current directory is changed.

Function Name	Execution Time
chpwd	Executed whenever the current working directory is changed.
precmd	Executed before each prompt.
periodic	If the option **PERIOD** is set, this function is executed every **PERIOD** number of seconds, just before a prompt.
TRAPxxx	Executed whenever the shell receives a signal SIGxxx, where xxx is a signal name as specified for the **kill** builtin. This signal number will be passed as the first parameter to the function.
TRAPZERR	Executed whenever a command has a nonzero exit status.
TRAPDEBUG	Executed after each command.
TRAPEXIT	Executed when the shell exits, or, if defined with a function, when that function ends.

functions

```
functions [±tum] [name ...]
```

functions is used to set attributes for shell functions. It is equivalent to the **typeset -f** command. With no option or arguments, **functions** lists all defined functions. With the -**m** option, arguments are taken to be patterns, selecting any functions that match the patterns. The -**t** option turns on tracing for this function, and the -**u** option marks the function for autoloading.

getopts

```
getopts optstring name [arguments]
```

getopts is used for detecting options to be used for a shell script. The *optstring* argument specifies a list of characters that can be used as valid options for the shell script. If the character is followed by a colon, the option is expected to have an argument separated from it by white space. Each time it is executed, **getopts** places the next option in the shell variable *name,* and the index of the next argument to be processed into the variable

OPTIND. If an option requires an argument, **getopts** places that argument into the variable **OPTARG**. The shell does not reset **OPTIND** automatically; it must be manually reset between multiple calls to **getopts** within the same shell invocation if a new set of parameters is to be used. **getopts** can report errors in two ways. If the first character of *optstring* is a colon, silent error reporting is used. In normal operation, diagnostic messages are printed when illegal options or missing option arguments are encountered. If the variable **OPTERR** is set to 0, no error message will be displayed, even if the first character of *optstring* is not a colon.

3

getopts normally parses the positional parameters, but if more arguments are given in *arguments*, **getopts** parses those instead. **getopts** returns true if an option, specified or unspecified, is found. It returns false if the end of options is encountered or an error occurs.

getopts is often used in a loop to check for options a user may have entered when invoking a script. The following loop allows the user to enter three possible options to a script: **t**, **r**, and **s**. With a colon (:) following it, **r** is expected to take an argument. In this example, if the user enters a -**a** option, then the **ls** command displays all files in a long format. However, if the -**r** option is entered with a filename, then the filename argument is accessed from the **OPTARG** variable and the long format of just that file is displayed.

```
while getopts  tr:s  myoption
    do
    case $myoption in
        a)   ls -al
        r)   ls -l $OPTARG
        s)   ls -s
    esac
done
```

hash

hash *name path*

hash places the specified *name* in the command hash table, associating it with the specified *path*. When the command is executed, the shell will use the files specified in the associated path.

history

```
history [-nrdDfEm] [first[last]]
```

history is the same command as **fc -l**. It displays a range of history events as designated by the *first* and *last* arguments. See the **fc** discussion earlier in this chapter for an explanation of the options.

if-then

```
if Linux command
    then
        commands
    else
        commands
fi
```

The **if** structure places a condition on commands. That condition is the exit status of a specific *Linux command*. If that command is successful, returning an exit status of 0, then the commands within the **if** structure are executed. If the exit status is anything other than 0, then the command has failed and the commands within the **if** structure are not executed. If an **else** segment is present, then the *commands* following the **else** keyword are executed.

The **if** command begins with the keyword **if** and is followed by a *Linux command* whose exit condition will be evaluated. This command is always executed. After the command, the keyword **then** goes on a line by itself. Any set of commands may then follow. The keyword **fi** ends the command. Often, you need to choose between two alternatives based on whether or not a Linux command is successful. The **else** keyword allows an **if** structure to choose between two alternatives. If the Linux command is successful, then those commands following the **then** keyword are executed. If the Linux command fails, then those commands following the **else** keyword are executed.

integer

```
integer [±lrtux] [name[=]value ...]
```

integer is used to define a shell variable and set its attribute to integer, as does the **typeset -i** command. See **typeset** for an explanation of the options.

jobs

```
jobs [-lprs] [jobsref ...]
```

The **jobs** command lists active jobs. The -l option also displays process IDs, whereas the -**p** option lists only the process ID of the job's process group. The -**r** option displays only running jobs, and the -**s** option lists stopped jobs. The *jobref* argument may be a number or a string. For a number, place the job number after the % operator, as in **%2** for job 2.

kill

```
kill [-s sigspec] [jobsref ...]
kill -l
```

kill is used to terminate a process or job. With the -**s** option you can specify a signal to be sent. By default, the signal sent is to terminate a process. With the -**l** option, the command lists the signal names. The *jobref* argument may be a number or a string. For a number, place the job number after the % operator, as in **%2** for job 2.

let

```
let value1 operator value2
```

The **let** command is the BASH shell command for performing operations on arithmetic values. With **let**, you can compare two values or perform arithmetic operations, such as addition or multiplication, on them. Such operations are used often in shell programs to manage control structures or perform necessary calculations. The **let** command can be indicated either with the keyword **let** or with a set of double parentheses. The syntax consists of the keyword **let** followed by two numeric *values* separated by an arithmetic or relational *operator*.

You can use as your operator any of those listed in the "Arithmetic Operators" section, earlier in this chapter. The **let** command automatically assumes that operators are arithmetic or relational. You do not have to quote shell-like operators. **let** also automatically evaluates any variables and converts their values to arithmetic values. This means that you can write your arithmetic operations as simple arithmetic expressions. In the next example, the **let** command multiplies the values 2 and 7. The result is output to the standard output and displayed.

```
$ let 2*7
14
```

If you want to have spaces between operands in the arithmetic expression, you must quote the expression. The **let** command expects one string.

```
$ let "2 * 7"
```

You can also include assignment operations in your **let** expression. In the next example, the result of the multiplication is assigned to **res**.

```
$ let "res = 2 * 7"
$ echo $res
14
$
```

local

```
local [±LRZilrtu [n]] [name[=]value ...]
```

local locally defines a shell variable within a function, using the same options as the **typeset** command, except for the typeset **-x** and **-f** options. See the description of the **typeset** command, later in this chapter, for details.

logout

```
logout
```

logout exits a login shell.

notify

notify *job-number*

After you execute any command in Linux, the system will tell you what background jobs, if you have any running, have been completed so far. The system will not interrupt any operation, such as editing, to notify you about a completed job. If you want to be notified immediately when a certain job ends, no matter what you are doing on the system, you can use the **notify** command to instruct the system to tell you. The **notify** command takes as its argument a job number. When that job has finished, the system will interrupt what you are doing to notify you that the job has ended. The next example tells the system to notify the user when job 2 has finished.

$ **notify %2**

popd

popd [±*n*]

popd removes directory entries from the directory list. With no arguments, it removes the top directory from the list, and performs a **cd** to the new top directory. +*n* removes the *n*th entry counting from the left of the list shown by **dirs**, starting with zero. **popd +0** removes the first entry. -*n* removes the *n*th entry counting from the right of the list shown by **dirs**, starting with zero. **popd -0** removes the last directory. **popd** returns false if the directory list is empty, a directory entry specified does not exist, or the directory change fails. If the **PUSHD_MINUS** option is set, the meanings of + and - in this context are swapped.

print

print [-RnrslzpNDPoOic] [-un] [*argument* ...]

With no options, **print** operates like the **echo** command, outputting strings and variables (*arguments*) to the standard output as text. **print** recognizes the following additional escape characters. **\M-x** metafies the character **x** (sets the highest bit), **\C-x** produces a control character, and **\E** is a synonym for **\e**. If a character is not in an escape sequence, \ escapes it and it is not printed.

Option	Function
-r	Ignore the escape conventions of **echo**.
-R	Ignore the escape conventions of **echo** and print all subsequent arguments and options.
-s	Place the results in the history list instead of on the standard output.
-n	Suppress the newline normally added to the end of the output.
-l	Output the arguments on separate lines, instead of separated by spaces.
-N	Output the arguments separated and terminated by nulls.
-o	Output the arguments sorted in ascending order.
-O	Output the arguments sorted in descending order.
-i	If used with **-o** or **-O**, ignore case when sorting.
-c	Output the arguments in columns.
-u	Output the arguments to a file descriptor.
-p	Output the arguments to the input of the coprocess.
-z	Place the arguments onto the editing buffer stack, separated by spaces; escape sequences are not recognized.
-D	Take arguments as directory names, substituting prefixes with ~ expressions, as appropriate.
-P	Recognize the same escape sequences as those used in the **PROMPT** variable.

ps

```
ps [-] [lujsvmaxScewhrnu] [txx] [O[+|-]k1[[+|-]k2...]]
[pids]
```

The **ps** command displays information on Linux processes. (For a more detailed explanation, see the **ps** command in Chapter 1.)

pushd

```
pushd [dir]
pushd old new
pushd ±n
```

pushd adds a directory to the list of remembered directories and changes to that directory. With no arguments, it exchanges the top two directories and changes to the second one. If the option **PUSHD_SILENT** is not set, the directory stack will be printed after a **pushd** is performed. If *old* and *new* arguments are specified, then occurrences of the *old* string in the current directory are replaced with the *new* string and that resulting directory is changed to.

With the numeric argument, *n*, you can reference entries in the directory list. +*n* rotates the list so that the *n*th directory (counting from the left of the list shown by **dirs**) is at the top. -*n* rotates the stack so that the *n*th directory (counting from the right) is at the top. *dir* adds the specified directory to the directory list at the top, making it the new current working directory.

pwd

```
pwd
```

pwd displays the path name of the current working directory. It returns 0 unless an error occurs while reading the path name of the current directory.

read

```
read [-rzpqAclneE] [-k [num ]] [-un] [name?prompt]
[variables ...]
```

read reads one line of input and separates the line into fields using the separator characters listed in the **IFS** variable. The **?** option is used to specify a *prompt* for the standard error in interactive shells. The exit status is 0 unless an end-of-file character is encountered.

Option	Function/Description
-r	Raw mode; a \ at the end of a line does not signify line continuation.
-q	Read only one character and set to **y** if this character was **y** or **Y** and to **n** otherwise. (Return value is 0 if the character was **y** or **Y**.)
-k	Read only the number of characters specified by the *num* argument, or 1 if no *num* argument is specified.
-z	Read from the editor buffer stack, using each field as an argument.
-E	Display the words read after the whole line is read.
-e	Display the words read after the whole line is read, but do not assign to the parameters.
-A	Take the first argument as the *name* of an array and assign all words to it.
-c	Read the words of the current command. (Allowed only if called inside a function used for completion.)
-l	Assign the whole line as a scalar. (Allowed only if called inside a function used for completion.)
-n	With the -l option, give the number of the word the cursor is on and the index of the character the cursor is on, respectively. If -l is omitted, use **REPLY** for scalars and **reply** for arrays.
-u	Read input from the file descriptor as specified by the *n* argument.
-p	Reap input from the coprocess. If the first argument contains a **?**, use the remainder of this word as a standard error when the shell is interactive.

readonly

```
readonly [name[=value]]
```

readonly marks the listed variables as read-only, defines them if they are not already defined, and assigns an initial value if one is specified.

repeat

```
repeat Linux command
    do
        commands
    done
```

The **repeat** loop repeats commands. A **repeat** loop begins with the
keyword **repeat** and is followed by a *Linux command*. The *Linux
command* is treated as an arithmetic expression, returning a
number that is used as the number of times to repeat the loop.
The keyword **do** follows on the next line. The end of the loop is
specified by the keyword **done**.

3

return

```
return [n]
```

return exits a function or shell script. If an argument is provided,
then it becomes the return value of that function. If there is no
argument, then the return status is that of the last command
executed. If used outside a function but within a shell script,
return stops execution of the script. If there is no argument
specified as the return value, it returns the exit status of the last
command executed in the script. If used outside a function and
not in a script, then the return status is false.

select

```
select variable in list-of-items
    do
        commands
    done
```

The **select** command is used to display a simple menu of
numbered items for the user to select. The list of items following
in is displayed on the standard error, each preceded by a number.
If **in** is omitted, then the values of positional parameters are
used. After displaying the items, the **PS3** prompt is displayed,
prompting the user to enter a number. The number is read from
the standard input and matched to the number for each item in
turn. If a corresponding value is found, then **select** assigns that

word to the variable. If the user enters an empty line, then the menu is displayed again. If EOF is read, the command terminates. The exit status of **select** is the exit status of the last command executed, or 0 if no commands were executed. The following example shows the use of the **select** command to provide three different choices for listing files.

```
select mychoice in Sizes Information Cfiles
    do
        case $mychoice in
        Sizes)
            ls -s
            ;;
        Information)
            ls -l
            ;;
        Cfiles)
            ls *.c
        esac
    done
```

set

```
set [±o option-name ...] [-A [name]] [argument ...]
```

set is used to set the options for the shell, to set the positional parameters, and to declare arrays. Options may be specified by name using the -**o** option. With the -**A** option, an array is defined using the arguments entered. The -**A** option with no arguments will display all arrays. With neither the -**o** or -**A** option, arguments are used to set the positional parameters. With no arguments, the names and values of all shell variables are printed on the standard output. With just the + argument, the names of all variables are printed.

setopt

```
setopt [±options] [name ...]
```

setopt is used to set Z-shell options. You can set options either with the option *name* or option abbreviation. With no arguments, **setopt** lists currently set options. Case is important for option names, but underscores are ignored. With the -**m** option, you can specify a pattern, setting all options that match this pattern.

shift

```
shift [n] [name ...]
```

If an argument *n* is provided, **shift** renames the positional parameters so that parameter *n*+1 is **$1**, *n*+2 is **$2**, etc. Parameters *n* and less are unset. If *n* is 0, no parameters are changed. If there is no argument, *n* is assumed to be 1. The argument must be nonnegative. If you specify the name of a shell array, then elements of that array are shifted.

suspend

```
suspend [-f]
```

This command suspends a shell's execution of this shell until it receives a SIGCONT signal. If you execute this command in the login shell, then you should use the **-f** option to suppress the shell's complaint; just suspend anyway.

test

```
test value -option value
test string = string
```

The **test** command is included in the Z shell for compatibility. Usually the **[[ ]]** command is used to evaluate expressions. Both can use the same set of operators. The **[[ ]]** command works with expressions much like the **test** command. The **test** command will compare two values and return as its exit status a 0 if the comparison is successful. With the **test** command, you can compare integers, strings, and even perform logical operations. The command consists of the keyword **test** followed by the values being compared, separated by an option that specifies what kind of comparison is taking place. The option can be thought of as the operator, but is written, like other options, with a minus sign and letter codes. For example, **-eq** is the option that represents the equality comparison. However, there are two string operations that actually use an operator instead of an option. When you compare two strings for equality, you use the equal sign, **=**. For inequality you use **!=**. For a listing of the different options, see the **test** command in Chapter 1.

In the following example, the user compares two integer values to see if they are equal. In this case, you need to use the equality option, **-eq**. The exit status of the **test** command is examined to find out the result of the test operation. The shell special variable **$?** holds the exit status of the most recently executed Linux command.

```
$ num=5
$ test $num -eq 10
$ echo $?
1
```

Instead of using the keyword **test** for the **test** command, you can use enclosing brackets. The command **test $greeting = "hi"** can be written as

```
$ [[ $greeting = "hi" ]]
```

Similarly, the **test** command **test $num -eq 10** can be written as

```
$ [[ $num -eq 10 ]]
```

The brackets themselves must be surrounded by white spaces: a space, tab, or hard return. Without the spaces, it would be invalid.

trap

```
trap [argument] [sigspec]
```

trap specifies that a certain command listed here as the argument is to be read and executed when the shell receives a system signal as specified by *sigspec*. The signal can be either a signal name defined in **<signal.h>**, or a signal number. If *sigspec* is EXIT (0), the command *argument* is executed on exit from the shell. If no command *argument* is listed for the signal, then the signal is reset.

The **trap** command alone, with no arguments, displays the list of commands associated with each signal number. With an argument and a signal number, it specifies the command to be executed when that signal occurs. The signal can be either a number or a name. The - argument resets all signals to their default values. If the argument is the null string, the signal specified in the signal argument is ignored by the shell.

If the signal argument is ZERR, then the command argument will
be executed after each command with a nonzero exit status. If it is
DEBUT, then it is executed after each command. If the signal
argument is 0 or EXIT and executed within a function, then the
command is executed when that function ends. If it is 0 or EXIT
outside a function, then the command executes when the
shell terminates.

type

```
type
```

type displays a detailed report on how each argument would be
interpreted if used as a command name.

typeset

```
typeset [±LRZfilrtuxm [n]] [name[=value] ...]
```

typeset is used to determine attributes for shell variables. When
used within a function, it creates a shell variable that will be
unset when the function finishes. If the **ALLEXPORT** variable is
set, the shell variable will be exported, unless another shell
variable of that name already exists. Attributes are specified with
the following options. With just an option and no arguments,
typeset lists the variables that have been given that option. With
no option or arguments, **typeset** lists all defined variables. With
the **-m** option, arguments are taken to be patterns, selecting any
variables that match the patterns.

Option	Function
-L	Left justify and remove leading blanks from the *value* specified.
-R	Right justify and fill with leading blanks. (The *n* argument can be used to specify the width of the field; otherwise, the width of the first *value* assigned is used.)
-Z	Right justify and fill with leading zeros if the first nonblank character is a digit and the **-L** option is not set. (The *n* argument can be used to specify the width of the field; otherwise, the width of the first *value* assigned is used.)

Option	Function
-f	Specify that the *name* arguments refer to functions, not variables. (There is a **-t** (tracing) and a **-u** (marked for autoloading) option for this option.)
-i	Use an internal integer representation. (With an *n* argument, *n* defines the output arithmetic base; otherwise, the base is determined by the first assignment.)
-l	Convert to lowercase.
-r	Mark the defined variables (*name* arguments) read-only.
-t	Tag the *named* variables.
-u	Convert to uppercase.
-x	Automatically export to the subsequent shell environments.

umask

```
umask [mask]
```

umask specifies the user file-creation mask. With no arguments, **umask** displays the value of the file-creation mask. The mode can be either an octal number or a symbolic specifier as used by **chmod** in setting file permissions.

unalias

```
unalias [-m] [name ...]
```

unalias removes aliases that have been defined. With the -m option, the *name* argument is taken to be a pattern.

unfunction

```
unfunction [-m] function-name ...
```

unfunction removes the specified function definition. With the -m option, arguments are taken to be patterns.

unset

unset [-m] [*name* ...]

unset is used to undefine shell variables. You can list a series of variable names as arguments, removing them all at once. With the -**m** option, arguments are taken to be patterns.

3

until

until *Linux command*
    do
            commands
    done

The **until** loop repeats commands. An **until** loop begins with the keyword **until** and is followed by a *Linux command*. The keyword **do** follows on the next line. The end of the loop is specified by the keyword **done**. **until** continues execution while it returns false. When the *Linux command* that it uses for a test returns true, the loop stops execution.

wait

wait [*jobref*]

The shell waits for the specified process to complete and return its termination status. The argument *jobref* can be a process ID or a job specification. If a job specification is used, then all the processes that are part of that job are waited for. If no argument is used, then all current child processes are waited for and **wait** then returns 0. **wait** returns the exit status of the last process or job waited for.

whence

whence [-acpvm] *name*...

whence indicates how each argument would be interpreted if used as a command name.

Option	Function
-v	Produce a detailed report.
-p	Perform a path search for the argument even if it is a shell function, alias, or reserved word.
-c	Display the results in a C-shell format.
-a	Search for all occurrences of the command throughout the command path.
-m	Allow arguments to be patterns, retrieving any commands that match these patterns.

which

```
which name
```

which performs a search for a command called *name* and displays the result showing the path name (same as **whence -c**).

while

```
while Linux command
    do
        commands
    done
```

The **while** loop repeats commands. A **while** loop begins with the keyword **while** and is followed by a *Linux command*. The keyword **do** follows on the next line. The end of the loop is specified by the keyword **done**.

The Linux command used in **while** structures is often a test command indicated by enclosing brackets. In the **myname** script, in the next example, you are asked to enter a name. The name is then printed out. The loop is controlled by testing the value of the variable again using the bracket form of the **test** command.

myname

```
again=yes
while [ "$again" = yes ]
    do
        echo -n "Please enter a name: "
        read name
        echo "The name you entered is $name"
```

```
        echo -n "Do you wish to continue? "
        read again
done
        echo Good-bye
```

```
$ myname
Please enter a name: George
The name you entered is George
Do you wish to continue? yes
Please enter a name: Robert
The name you entered is Robert
Do you wish to continue? no
Good-bye
```

If the **CSH_JUNKIE_PAREN** option is set, you can use the C programming–style syntax with parentheses for the test, and braces for the body of the loop.

```
while ( ) {
}
```

ZSH-Shell Configuration

The Z shell has several initialization files, many configuration variables, and a variety of shell options. The initialization files are similar to those in both the BASH and TCSH shells with one of its own called **.zshenv**. Shell configuration variables are also much the same as those found in the BASH and TCSH shells. The Z shell has an extensive set of options for configuring many aspects of your shell.

ZSH Initialization Files

The system first reads commands in the system's **/etc/zshenv** Z-shell initialization file (with the **-f** or **NO_RCS** option, all other initialization files are skipped). Then the user's .zshenv file is read. This and other user initialization files (see the following list) can be either in the user's home directory or in the directory assigned to the **ZDOTDIR** variable. If the shell being started up is a login shell, then the **/etc/zprofile** file is read, followed by the user's **.zprofile** file. If the shell is also interactive, then the **/etc/zshrc** file is read along with the user's **.zshrc** file. If the shell is then a login shell, then **/etc/zlogin** and the user's **.zlogin** file are read.

```
$ZDOTDIR/.zshenv
$ZDOTDIR/.zprofile
$ZDOTDIR/.zshrc
$ZDOTDIR/.zlogin
$ZDOTDIR/.zlogout
/tmp/zsh*
/etc/zshenv
/etc/zprofile
/etc/zshrc
/etc/zlogin
```

Shell Configuration Variables

The following configuration variables can be used to apply different settings such as the shell prompt or history file:

Variable	Description
ARGV0	If exported, its value is used as **argv[0]** of external commands.
BAUD	The baud rate of the current connection.
cdpath (CDPATH)	An array (colon-separated list) of directories specifying the search path for the **cd** command.
COLUMNS	The number of columns for this terminal session.
DIRSTACKSIZE	The maximum size of the directory list.
FCEDIT	The default editor for the **fc** builtin.
fignore (FIGNORE)	An array (colon-separated list) containing the suffixes of files to be ignored during filename completion.
fpath (FPATH)	An array (colon-separated list) of directories specifying the search path for function definitions.
HISTCHARS	Three characters used by the shell's history and lexical analysis mechanism. The first character signals the start of a history substitution (default !). The second character signals the start of a quick history substitution (default ^). The third character is the comment character (default #).

Variable	Description
HISTFILE	The file to save the history in.
HISTSIZE	The maximum size of the history list.
HOME	The default argument for the **cd** command.
IFS	Internal field separators. The defaults are space, tab, and newline.
KEYTIMEOUT	The time the shell waits, in hundredths of seconds, for another key to be pressed.
LINES	The number of lines for this terminal session.
MAIL	If this parameter is set and **mailpath** is not set, the shell looks for mail in the specified file. The default is the user's system mailbox.
MAILCHECK	The interval in seconds between checks for new mail.
mailpath (**MAILPATH**)	An array (colon-separated list) of filenames to check for new mail.
NULLCMD	The default command used if a redirection is specified with no command.
PROMPT	The primary prompt string, displayed before a command is read. The default is **%m%#**.
PROMPT2	The secondary prompt, printed when the shell needs more information to complete a command. The default is **>**.
PROMPT3	Selection prompt used within a select loop. The default is **?#**.
PROMPT4	The execution trace prompt. The default is **+**.
READNULLCMD	The default command used if a single input redirection is specified with no command. The default is **more**.
RPROMPT RPS1	This prompt is displayed on the right-hand side of the screen when the primary prompt is being displayed on the left.
SAVEHIST	The maximum number of history events to save in the history file.
SPROMPT	The prompt used for spelling correction. The sequence **%R** expands to the string, which presumably needs spelling correction, and **%r** expands to the proposed correction.

3

Variable	Description
TMOUT	If nonzero, the shell will terminate if a command is not entered within the specified number of seconds after issuing a prompt.
TMPPREFIX	The path name prefix used for temporary files.
WORDCHARS	The nonalphanumeric characters considered part of a word by the line editor.
ZDOTDIR	The directory to search for Z-shell startup files, instead of **$HOME**.

Shell Options

Many options have abbreviated versions listed here in parentheses after the option name. You can use these abbreviated versions on the command line to set the options. Shell options can be set using the **set** or **setopt** command. **set +o** *option-name* will set the options, and **set -o** *option-name* will unset it.

Option	Function
ALL_EXPORT (-a)	Automatically export subsequently defined variables.
ALWAYS_TO_END	If a completion with the cursor in the word was started and it results in only one match, place the cursor at the end of the word.
APPEND_HISTORY	Append the session's history list to the history file, rather than overwriting it.
AUTO_CD (-J)	If a command is not in the hash table and there exists an executable directory by that name, perform the **cd** command to that directory.
AUTO_LIST (-9)	Automatically list choices on an ambiguous completion.
AUTO_NAME_DIRS	Immediately make any parameter that is set to the absolute name of a directory a name for that directory in the usual form **~param**.
AUTO_PUSHD (-N)	Make **cd** act like **pushd**.

Option	Function
AUTO_REMOVE_SLASH	When the last character resulting from a completion is a slash and the next character typed is a word delimiter, remove the slash.
AUTO_RESUME (-W)	Treat single-word simple commands without redirection as candidates for resumption of an existing job.
BG_NICE (-6)	Run all background jobs at a lower priority (default).
BRACE_CCL	Allow brace expansions.
CDABLE_VARS (-T)	If the argument to a **cd** command (or an implied **cd** with the **AUTO_CD**) is not a directory and does not begin with a slash, try to expand the expression as if it were preceded by a ~.
CHASE_LINKS (-w)	Resolve symbolic links to their true values.
COMPLETE_ALIASES	If set, do not internally substitute aliases on the command before completion is attempted.
COMPLETE_INWORD	If unset, set the cursor to the end of the word if completion is started; otherwise, keep it there and do completion from both ends.
CORRECT (-0)	Try to correct the spelling of commands.
CORRECT_ALL (-O)	Try to correct the spelling of all arguments in a line.
CSH_JUNKIE_HISTORY	Always refer a history reference without an event specifier to the previous command.
CSH_JUNKIE_LOOPS	Allow loop bodies to take the form **; end** instead of **do ; done**.
CSH_JUNKIE_PAREN	Allow **for**, **if**, and **while** loops where the argument list is given in parentheses. (Otherwise, the parentheses will be treated as specifying a subshell.)

Option	Function
CSH_JUNKIE_QUOTES	Complain if a quoted expression runs off the end of a line; prevent quoted expressions from containing unescaped newlines.
CSH_NULL_GLOB	If a pattern for filename generation has no matches, delete the pattern from the argument list; do not report an error unless all the patterns in a command have no matches. (Overrides **NULL_GLOB**.)
ERR_EXIT (-e)	If a command has a nonzero exit status, execute the ZERR trap, if set, and exit. (Disabled when running initialization scripts.)
EXTENDED_GLOB	Treat the #, ~, and ∧ characters as part of patterns for filename generation, etc.
EXTENDED_HISTORY	Save beginning and ending timestamps to the history file.
GLOB_DOTS (-4)	Do not require a leading dot (.) in a filename to be matched explicitly.
GLOB_SUBST	Make any characters resulting from variable and command substitution eligible for filename generation.
HIST_IGNORE_DUPS (-h)	Do not enter a command line into the history list if it is a duplicate of the previous event.
HIST_IGNORE_SPACE (-g)	Do not enter command lines into the history list if any command on the line begins with a blank.
HIST_LIT (-j)	Use literal versions of the history lines in the editor.
HIST_NO_STORE	Do not save the history command in history when invoked.
HIST_VERIFY	Do not immediately execute a line that has history substitution; first reload the line into the editing buffer.
IGNORE_BRACES (-I)	Do not perform brace expansion.
IGNORE_EOF (-7)	Do not exit on end-of-file character.
INTERACTIVE (-i)	Make an interactive shell.

Option	Function
INTERACTIVE_ COMMENTS (-k)	Allow comments in interactive shells.
KSH_OPTION_PRINT	Alter the way option settings are printed.
LOGIN (-l)	Make a login shell.
LONG_LIST_JOBS (-R)	List jobs in the long format by default.
MAGIC_EQUAL_SUBST	Perform file expansion on all unquoted arguments of the form *identifier* = *expression*. Perform file expansion on *expression* as if it were a parameter assignment, but do not otherwise treat the arguments specially.
MAIL_WARNING (-U)	Print a warning message if a mail file has been accessed since the shell was last checked.
MARK_DIRS (-8)	Append a trailing slash (/) to all directory names resulting from filename generation (*globbing*).
MONITOR (-m)	Allow job control (set by default in interactive shells).
NO_BAD_PATTERN (-2)	If a pattern for filename generation is badly formed, leave it unchanged in the argument list instead of printing an error.
NO_BANG_HIST (-K)	Do not perform textual history substitution. Do not treat the ! character specially.
NO_BEEP (-B)	Turn off beep.
NO_CLOBBER (-1)	Prevent > redirection from truncating existing files; use >! instead. Also prevent >> from creating files; use >>! instead.
NO_EQUALS	Do not perform = filename substitution.
NO_EXEC (-n)	Read commands and check them for syntax errors, but do not execute them.
NO_GLOB (-F)	Disable filename generation.

3

Option	Function
NO_HIST_CLOBBER	Do not add exclamation marks to output redirections in the history.
NO_HUP	Do not send the HUP signal to running jobs when the shell exits.
NO_LIST_BEEP	Do not beep on an ambiguous completion.
NO_NOMATCH (-3)	If a pattern for filename generation has no matches, leave it unchanged in the argument list instead of displaying an error. This also applies to file expansion of an initial ~ or =.
NO_PROMPT_CR (-V)	Do not print a carriage return just before printing a prompt in the line editor.
NO_RCS (-f)	Source only the **/etc/zshenv** file. Do not source the **.zshenv**, **/etc/zprofile**, **.zprofile**, **/etc/zshrc**, **.zshrc**, **/etc/zlogin**, **.zlogin**, or **.zlogout** file.
NO_SHORT_LOOPS	Disallow the short forms of **for**, **select**, **if**, and **function** constructs.
NOTIFY (-5)	Report the status of background jobs immediately, rather than waiting until a prompt is displayed.
NO_UNSET (-u)	Treat unset parameters as errors when substituting.
NULL_GLOB (-G)	If a pattern for filename generation has no matches, delete the pattern from the argument list instead of reporting an error. (Overrides **NONOMATCH**.)
NUMERIC_GLOB_SORT	If numeric filenames are matched by a filename generation pattern, sort the filenames numerically rather than lexicographically.
OVER_STRIKE	Start up the line editor in overstrike mode.
PATH_DIRS (-Q)	Perform a path search even on command names with slashes in them.
PRINT_EXIT_VALUE (-C)	Print the exit value of programs with a nonzero exit status.

Option	Function
PROMPT_SUBST	Expand expressions in prompts.
PUSHD_IGNORE_DUPS	Do not push multiple copies of the same directory onto the directory list.
PUSHD_SILENT (-E)	Do not print the directory list after **pushd** or **popd**.
PUSHD_TO_HOME (-D)	Have **pushd** with no arguments act like **pushd $HOME**.
RC_EXPAND_PARAM (-P)	Expand an array variable.
REC_EXACT (-S)	In completion, recognize exact matches even if they are ambiguous.
RM_STAR_SILENT (-H)	Do not query the user before executing **rm *** or **rm path/***.
SHIN_STDIN (-s)	Read commands from the standard input.
SINGLE_LINE_ZLE (-M)	Use single-line command-line editing instead of multiline.
SUN_KEYBOARD_ HACK (-L)	If a line ends with a back quote and there is an odd number of back quotes on the line, ignore the trailing back quote. (This is useful on some keyboards where the ENTER key is too small and the back quote key lies annoyingly close to it.)

3

Chapter 4
Compilers and Libraries: gcc, g++, and gdb

An application is an executable program created by a programmer using one of several programming languages. Linux provides several utilities with which a programmer can control development of an application. Foremost among these is the **gcc** utility, which invokes the compiler for the C and C++ programming languages, generating an executable version of a program. Most Linux applications are written in the C or C++ programming languages.

Application development often makes extensive use of libraries. You can create your own libraries or choose from specialized libraries. You can use libraries that have been set up for specific operations, such as the X-Window library for programming X-Window displays, or the **gdbm** library, which gives you database access to files. Libraries have become more flexible than they were and can now be shared or loaded dynamically.

Other utilities allow you to better manage the development of your applications. The **gdb** symbolic debuggers help you locate run-time errors. **indent**, **cproto**, and **??** help you prepare your source code. **autoconf** and **rpm** help you package your software for distribution. There are also compilers for all of the major programming languages, including Pascal, Lisp, Ada, Fortran, Basic, and Modula-2.

Getting Information: info

Though there are **man** pages for all the compilers and their tools, much more detailed information is available through the GNU info system. These are files located in the **/usr/info** directory that contain detailed descriptions and examples for various GNU tools. They are the equivalent of a compact online manual. There are **info** documents for the **gcc** compiler, the C and C++ libraries, the **autoconf** utility, and even **indent**. Other applications may have their own local directories with **info** files, such as the directory **/usr/TeX/info**, which holds **info** files for LaTeX.

You invoke the main menu of an **info** document by entering the command **info**.

```
$ info
```

You then use the SPACEBAR to page down the menu. When you find a topic you want, press the M key. This opens up a line at the bottom of the screen where you can type in the name of the menu item. On pressing ENTER, that document is displayed. Pressing B pages you back to the beginning, and U takes you up to the previous menu. The command **info info** will bring up a tutorial on how to use **info**.

The C Compiler: gcc

There is a special relationship between the Unix operating system and the C programming language. The C programming language was developed specifically as a tool for programming the Unix operating system, and the code for the Unix operating system is actually written in C. Linux has the same kind of special relationship with C. Most Linux systems include the GNU version of the C compiler, **gcc**. The C programming language is a very complex language with many different features. This section briefly describes the basic components of the C programming language and uses them to construct a useful programming example. With an example program we can then examine the different ways you can compile C programs.

A C program is made up of a set of function definitions that contain variable declarations and statements. Program execution always begins with a function named **main**. The program then progresses from one function to another through function calls. For example, the **printf** function is an often-called function that outputs data.

The definition of a C function consists of a header and a body. The header contains the return value of the function, the function name, and function argument variables encased in parentheses. If there is no return value or no argument variables for the function, then the keyword **void** is used instead. The body of the function consists of variable declarations and statements enclosed in opening and closing braces.

You create a C program by first making a source code file. The source code file is a text file that you can create using any standard editor such as Vi, Emacs, or Crisplite. You simply type in the function definitions and then compile the source code file.

In addition to the function definition, a C program usually contains what is called a *preprocessor* command. When you compile your C program, the source code is first read by a preprocessor utility, which then generates a modified version of the program that the C compiler will work on. The preprocessor performs a word-processing-like operation, generating an edited form of the source code file. Preprocessor commands in the source code file act as editing commands, instructing the preprocessor on what changes to make. All preprocessing commands begin with a sharp (#) sign. **#include <stdio.h>** is a preprocessor command. In the next example, the **#include** preprocessing command performs a file insert, merging the contents of the **stdio.h** file with the **greet.c** source code file, to generate a version of a C program that includes the contents of **stdio.h**.

The **stdio.h** file stands for standard input/output. It contains references to input/output functions contained in C program libraries. When a final executable version of the following **greet.c** program is made, it will be linked to precompiled libraries that will contain the object code for the **printf** function. You need the references in **stdio.h** in order to ensure a correct connection.

greet.c

```
#include <stdio.h>
void main(void)
    {
    printf("Hello, how are you\n");
    }
```

You invoke the GNU C compiler on your Linux system with the **gcc** command. The **gcc** command, in turn, calls four other components. The first is the *preprocessor*. A C program contains special preprocessor commands that modify the code before it is sent to the compiler. The second component is the *compiler* itself. The compiler will process the code and generate an assembly code version of the program. The third component is the *assembler*. The assembler will use the assembly code version of the program to generate an object code version. The fourth component is the *linker*. The linker uses the program's object code to generate an executable file. The default name of this executable file is **a.out**. Normally, you should give the executable file a name of your own choosing. The **-o** option takes a filename as its argument. This filename will be the name of the executable file instead of the default, **a.out**.

gcc takes as possible arguments the source code, object code, and assembly code files, as well as several options. **gcc** recognizes a file by its extension.

Extension	Description
.c	C source code files
.o	Object code files
.s	Assembly code files
.C	C++ files
.cpp	C++ files

In the next example, the **gcc** command compiles the program **greet.c**. The user names the executable file **greet**. The executable file is run by entering it at the Linux prompt as if it were a command.

```
$ gcc greet.c -o greet
$ greet
Hello, how are you
```

The **gcc** utility has many options that can stop the compiling process at any component. These are **-P** for the preprocessor, **-S** for the assembler, and **-c** for the compiler. The **-P** option generates a copy of the source code after the preprocessor has worked on it. This preprocessor version of the source code file is saved in a file with the **.P** extension. For example, the preprocessor version of the **greet.c** file would be saved in a file called **greet.P**. The **-S** option generates an assembly code version of the program. The assembly code version is saved in a file with the **.s** extension. The assembly code version of the **greet.c** file would be saved in a file called **greet.s**. The **-c** option generates only an object code file, not an executable one. The object code version is saved in a file with the **.o** extension. The object code version of the **greet.c** file would be saved in a file called **greet.o**. In the next example, the user generates an assembly code version and then an object code version of the program.

```
$ gcc -S greet.c
$ gcc -c greet.c
$ ls
greet.c greet.o greet.s
```

Option	Function
-S	Output only assembly code. (Assembly code versions of compiled files have the extension **.s**. The example will generate a file called **greet.s**.)
-P	Output result of preprocessor.
-c	Create object code file only. (Object code versions of compiled files have the extension **.o**.)
-g	Prepare compiled program for use with symbolic debugger.
-o *filename*	Name executable file *filename*. (Default is **a.out**.)
-O	Optimize compilation.
-l *filename*	Link system library by name of *filename*. (The *filename* is preceded by **lib** and has an extension of **.a**. Neither is included on the **gcc** command line. The -l option must always be placed after source code and object code filenames on the command line.)

4

Source, Object, and Executable Files

You can organize your C program into many different source code files. This allows you to manage a very large program more easily by cutting the program into several smaller source code files. Each source code file could contain functions designed to concentrate on a specific task. In a database program, you could have functions that perform input placed in one file and functions that perform searching placed in another. By convention, the **main** function is usually placed in a file by itself, sometimes called **main.c**.

In the **bookrec** program that follows, the **bookinput** and **printbook** functions are placed in a source code file called **io.c**, since they both handle input and output operations. The **main** function is placed in **main.c** and calls the **bookinput** and **printbook** functions. **main.c** also contains function declarations for those functions. A function declaration is a reference to a function, detailing its name, arguments, and return value. A function declaration is used by the compiler and linker to correctly connect functions used in one source code file, but defined in another.

bookrec

main.c
```
void bookinput(char[], float*);
```

```
void printbook(char[], float);

void main(void)
    {
    char title[20];
    float price;

    bookinput(title, &price);
    printbook(title, price);
    }
```

io.c
```
#include <stdio.h>

void bookinput(char title[], float *price)
  {
  printf("Please enter book record : ");
  scanf("%s%f", title, price);
  }

void printbook(char title[], float price)
  {
  printf("The book record is: %s %f\n",title,price);
  }
```

With multiple file programs, you need to keep in mind the difference between the C compiler and the linker. The purpose of a C compiler is to generate object code, whereas the purpose of a linker is to build an executable file using object code files. The C compiler will individually compile each source code file, generating a separate object code file for each one. These object code files will have the extension **.o** instead of **.c**. For the **bookrec** program, the compiler will generate object code for the **main.c** file and place it in a new file, **main.o**. The same will happen for the **io.c** file. Its object code file will be **io.o**. There are now four files: **main.c, io.c, main.o,** and **io.o**. At this point, the compiler has finished its work. It has generated the object code for the source code files. But there is still no runable program. The linker will then combine the object code files into one executable file that you can run.

You compile and link multiple file programs using the same **gcc** command. Simply list the source code filenames as arguments on

the command line. In the next example, the user compiles the
bookrec program by invoking **gcc** with the source code files that
make it up. The -**o** option specifies that the executable file will be
called **bookrec**.

```
$ gcc main.c io.c -o bookrec
```

You can then run the program using the name of the executable
file, in this case **bookrec**.

```
$ bookrec
Please enter a book record : Raven 2.50
The book record is : Raven 2.50
```

You can use the **gcc** utility to perform just a link operation by only
listing object code files as its arguments. An object code file has a
.**o** extension. In the next example, the user just performs a link
operation. No compiling takes place. Of course, this operation
assumes that the object code files have been previously
generated.

```
$ gcc main.o io.o
```

As you develop and debug your program, you will be making
changes to source code files and then recompiling your program to
see how it runs. If you have a very large program made up of
many source code files, it would be very inefficient to recompile
all of them if you only made changes to just a few of them. Those
to which you made no changes do not need to be recompiled, just
linked. You can direct the **gcc** utility to do just that, by mixing
source code and object code files as arguments on the command
line. Source code files have a .**c** extension, and object code files
have a .**o** extension. **gcc** will compile the source code files you
specify on the command line, and will link the resulting object
code files with the .**o** files listed on the command line. This has
the advantage of letting you compile only those files where
changes have been made. If changes were made in **main.c**, but
not in **io.c**, **io.c** would not have to be recompiled. You would then
specify the source code file **main.c** and the object code file **io.o** on
the command line. In the next example, **io.o** will not be compiled,
whereas **main.c** will be compiled.

```
$ gcc main.c io.o -o bookrec
```

ELF and a.out Binary Formats

There are two possible formats for binary files, such as executable programs. The first is the **a.out** format, which is the original format used on Unix systems, as well as early Linux systems. The term *a.out* comes from the default name given to an executable file by the Unix C compiler. As shared libraries came into use, difficulties arose with the **a.out** format. Adapting an **a.out** format for use as a shared library is a very complex operation. For this reason, a new format was introduced for Unix System 5, Release 4, and for Solaris. It is called the Executable and Linking Format (ELF). Its design allowed for the easy implementation of shared libraries.

The ELF format has been adopted as the standard format for Linux systems. All binary files generated by the **gcc** compiler are in ELF format (even though the default name for the executable file is still **a.out**). Older programs that may still be in the **a.out** format will still run on a system supporting ELF.

C++ and Objective C: g++

The **gcc** utility is also a C++ compiler. It can read and compile any C++ program. However, it will not automatically link with the C++ Class library. You would have to invoke it on the command line. Alternatively, you can use the command **g++**, which invokes the **gcc** compiler with the C++ Class library.

C++ source code files have a different extension than regular C files. Several different extensions are recognized for C++: **.C**, **.cc**, or **.cxx**, where *xx* can be any character, as in **.cpp**. Other than this difference, you compile C++ programs just as you would C programs. Instead of **gcc**, it is preferable to use the **g++** command. The following example compiles a C++ program, **myprog.cpp**.

```
$ g++  myprog.cpp  -o myprog
```

The **gcc** compiler also supports Objective-C programs. Objective-C is an object-oriented version of C originally developed for NeXT systems. To compile a program in Objective-C, you use the **gcc** command with the **-lobjc** option. **-lobjc** links to the Objective-C

library, **libobjc.so**. The following example compiles an Objective-C
program **myprog.c**.

```
$ gcc  myprog.c  -o myprog  -lobjc
```

Other Compilers: Pascal, Ada, Lisp, and Fortran

4

A great many programming languages are supported on your
Linux system. Many are available on your OpenLinux CDROM. In
addition to C and C++, you can compile Pascal, Ada, Lisp, Basic,
and Fortran programs. In several cases, the compiling is handled
by the **gcc** compiler, which is designed to recognize source code
files for other programming languages. For example, G77 is the
GNU Fortran compiler. This compiler is integrated with the **gcc**
compiler. The command **g77** will compile a Fortran program by
invoking the **gcc** compiler with options to recognize Fortran code,
using the G77 features of **gcc**.

The ADA 95 compiler is called **gnat**. The **info** file on ADA provides
detailed information on **gnat**. You can compile an ADA program
using the command **gnatmake** with the filename. The following
example compiles the ADA program called **hello.ada**.

```
$ gnatmake hello.ada
```

The compiling operation is invoked by **gcc**, which recognizes the
.ada extension and then calls the **gnat1** compiler. The **gnatbind**
and **gnatlink** commands then link the object code file into an
executable ADA program. The following table lists the commands
for the various compilers available on Linux:

Command	Description
gnat	ADA 95 compiler.
g++	C++ compiler (front end to **gcc**).
gcc	C compiler. Also compiles other languages such as Fortran. Can act as front end to other compilers.
gcc -lobjc	Objective C compiling.

Command	Description
g77	The GNU Fortran 77 compiler
p2c	The Pascal-to-C translator for **gcc**
basic	The Basic interpreter
gcl	The Common Lisp Interpreter, CLISP
modula-2	Modula-2 compiler
smalltalk	Smalltalk interpreter

Creating and Using Libraries: Static, Shared, and Dynamic

There are usually functions in a C program that rarely need to be compiled. There may also be functions that you want to use in different programs. Often such functions perform standardized tasks, such as database input/output operations or screen manipulation. You can precompile such functions and place them together in a special type of object code file called a *library*. The functions in such a library file can be combined with a program by the linker. They save you the trouble of having to recompile these functions for each program you develop.

Different types of applications make use of specialized libraries that are placed in system directories and made available for use in developing programs. For example, there is a library, **libdbm**, that contains **dbm** functions for implementing database access to files. You can use these functions in your own programs by linking to that library. Mathematical applications would use the math library, **libm**, and X-Window applications would use the Xlib library, **libX11**. These libraries are placed within system directories such as **/usr/lib**, where they can be accessed by anyone on the system. You can also create your own library just for use with your own particular program, or make one that you would want accessed by others.

Libraries can be either static, shared, or dynamic. A *static* library is one whose code is incorporated into the program when it is compiled. A *shared* library, however, has its code loaded for access whenever the program is run. When compiled, such a program simply notes the libraries it needs. Then, when it is run, that library is loaded and the program can access its functions. A *dynamic* library is a variation on a shared library. Like a shared library, it can be loaded when the program is run. However, it does not actually load until instructions in the program tell it to. It can also be unloaded as the program runs, and another could be loaded in its place. Shared and dynamic libraries make for much smaller code. Instead of a program including the library as part of its executable file, it only needs a reference to it.

Most libraries currently developed are shared libraries. Shared libraries were made feasible by the implementation of the ELF binary format, though there is an older **a.out** format for shared (tagged) libraries. ELF is currently the standard format used for all binary files in Linux.

The GNU libraries are made available under a Library GNU Public License (LGPL). The conditions of this license differ from the Standard GNU license in that you are free to charge for programs developed using these libraries. However, you do have to make available the source code for those libraries you used.

Library Names

Libraries made available on your system reside in the **/usr/lib** and **/lib** directories. The names of these libraries always begin with the prefix **lib** followed by the library name and a suffix. The suffix differs depending on whether it is a static or shared library. A shared library has the suffix **.so** followed by major and minor version numbers. A static library simply has a **.a** extension. A further distinction is made for shared libraries in the old **a.out** format. These have the extension **.sa**.

```
libname.so.major.minor
libname.a
```

The *name* can be any string, and uniquely identifies a library. It can be a word, a few characters, or even a single letter. The name of the shared math library is **libm.so.5**, where the math library is uniquely identified by the letter **m**, and the major version is 5. **libm.a** is the static math library. The name of the X-Window library is **libX11.so.6**, where the X-Window library is uniquely identified with the letters **X11**, and its major version is 6.

4

Invoking Libraries: -l

You can link libraries to your programs using the **gcc** compiler. For example, the **libc.so.5** library contains the standard I/O functions. This library is automatically searched and linked whenever the linker generates an executable file. The standard I/O library contains numerous functions that include input/output operations, such as **printf**. There are other system libraries that you can access, such as the math library. Though the **libc.so.5** library is automatically linked, most other system libraries need to be explicitly referenced on the command line.

Most shared libraries are found in the **/usr/lib** and **/lib** directories. These will always be searched first. Some shared libraries are located in special directories of their own. A listing of these is placed in the **/etc/ld.conf** configuration file. These directories will be searched also for a given library. By default, Linux will first look for shared libraries, then static ones.

To reference a library file in one of these searchable directories when you invoke the **gcc** compiler, you use the -l option followed by the unique part of a system library's name: -l*name*. To instruct the linker to use the standard math library, you enter **-lm** on the **gcc** command line. -l will look first for a **lib***name***.so** file, in this case, **libm.so**. This is a link to the actual library file. In the next example, the **bookrec** program is created and linked to the math library. Notice the **-lm** option.

```
$ gcc main.c io.c -o bookrec -lm
```

There are many different libraries currently available for your use. One of the more popular is the **libncurses.a** library, which contains simple cursor movement routines. You would reference the **libncurses.so** library on the command line with **-lncurses**. In the next example, the user invokes both the math and cursor libraries.

```
$ gcc main.c io.c -o bookrec -lm -lncurses
```

To reference a library in another directory, you have to specify that directory using the -L*dir* option. This option adds the specified directory to the list of directories that will be searched with the -l option. In the following example, the user links to a library in the **mydir** directory called **myio.so**. For a shared library, you will first have to have the **dl** and **ld** link names set up, such as

libmyio.so and **libmyio.so.1** for a **libmyio.so.1.0** file (see the next section).

```
$ gcc main.c -o bookrec -Lmydir -lmyio
```

Shared Libraries

Shared libraries are designed to be used by many different applications. This way the applications do not have to repeat code. Most libraries used by applications are shared libraries. Shared libraries have a different extension than ordinary libraries. Instead of **.a** extensions, shared libraries have **.so** extensions, followed by major and minor version numbers. The minor version number is optional and can be anything you want. For example, the shared library for X-Window is **libX11.so.6**.

However, the linker (**ld**), which searches for the library at compile time, and the dynamic linker (**dl**), which searches for it whenever the program is run, search for different forms of a shared library's name. The linker searches for a name that ends only with the extension **.so** with no version numbers. The dynamic linker, on the other hand, searches for what is called a *soname,* a name held within the library file itself that identifies it. Both are different from the actual name of the library file. For the linker and the dynamic linker to locate a library file, there have to be links to that library file, with names in forms that the linkers can recognize. In referencing the link, they will reference the library file. For the linker (**ld**), there has to be a link whose name ends with a **.so** extension. For the dynamic linker (**dl**), there has to be a link whose name is the same as that of the soname. Then, there needs to be a link to that soname with the **.so** extension. This is the link that the linker (**ld**) will recognize. For example, the **libc.so.5.4.22** will have a link named **libc.so.5** (the soname) to which there will be another link named **libc.so**.

name.so → soname   → lib*name*.so.*ver*.*min*
libc.so   → libc.so.5 → libc.so.5.4.22

The soname is the name that the dynamic linker uses to identify a shared library. When compiling a program that references a shared library, it is this soname that is placed in the program's executable code and that identifies what library to load at run time. (With a static library, the entire code of the file is incorporated into the program's executable code.) You generate the link to the soname using the **ldconfig** command. **ldconfig** will automatically read the soname from a library file and create a link of that name to the file. At boot time, the **ldconfig** program automatically updates these links for libraries located in the shared library directories, those in **/usr/lib**, **/lib**, and listed in /etc/ld.conf. On the other hand, the links for the linker with **.so** extensions have to be created manually.

You begin creating a shared library by first generating the object code files you want in it. You compile a source code file for use in a shared library using the **-fPIC** option, which generates position-independent code suitable for shared libraries. The following example creates such an object code file called **io.o**. (The **-c** option instructs **gcc** to generate just an object code file.)

```
$ gcc -fPIC -c io.c
```

You can create a shared library using the **gcc** compiler with the **-shared** and **-W1** options. In this case the compiler will place the compiled files into a library file, instead of an executable file. The **-o** option will specify the name of the directory. You can list as many object files as you want. The **-W1** passes options to the linker, in this case, the **soname** option that specifies a soname for the library. This soname will be placed within the library file and later used by **ldconfig** to generate the soname link. The following example creates a library called **libmyio.so.1.0** using the **io.o** file. The soname for this library is **libmyio.so.1**.

```
$ gcc -shared -W1,soname,libmyio.so.1 -o
libmyio.so.1.0 io.o
```

If you are ready to place it in a library directory you can just copy it there. Then run **ldconfig** to generate the **dl** link names. (This will also be done automatically when you boot up.)

```
$ cp libmyio.so.1.0 /usr/lib
$ ldconfig  /usr/lib
```

You then have to create a link that the linker (**ld**) can recognize. **ld** looks for library names that have the form **lib**name.**so** with no version numbers. You need to create a link of that form to the link whose name is the soname. The following example creates a link called **libmyio.so** that references the link **libmyio.so.1** and through that the **libmyio.so.1.0** library file. You use the **ln** command to create a link to a file.

```
$ ln -s /usr/lib/libmyio.so.1  /usr/lib/libmyio.so
```

Once you have both the **ld** and **dl** links in place, you can compile programs using that library. In the next example, the **bookrec** program is compiled using the **libmyio.so.1.0** library. It is referenced as **-lmyio**, which will look for and reference **libmyio.so**. The preceding **"lib"** and the extension are left out. That link, in turn, links to **libmyio.so.1** and from there to the **libmyio.so.1.0** file.

```
$ gcc main.c -o bookrec  -lmyio
```

The **ldd** command will display the shared libraries that a program uses. The following example shows that the **bookrec** program uses the **libmyio.so.1** and **libc.so.5** shared libraries. The first name is the soname, and the next name is the library filename.

```
$ ldd bookrec
    libmyio.so.1 => /usr/lib/libmyio.so.1.0
    libc.so.5 => /lib/libc.so.5.4.22
```

If you want to keep your shared library in a directory of your own, create the **ld** and **dl** links with that library. The **ldconfig** command with the -l option allows you to specify a particular file instead of a directory. You use this option to reference your library file and create a **dl** link for it. Be sure to use full path names. Then make another link to that link using a name ending in the **.so** extension, which will be recognizable to the **ld** command.

```
$ ldconfig -l /home/dylan/libmyio.so.1.0
$ ln -s /home/dylan/libmyio.so.1 /home/dylan/libmyio.so
```

When you compile a program, you will have to use the **-L***dir* option to specify the directory where your library is kept.

```
$ gcc main.c -o bookrec  -L/home/dylan -lmyio
```

Dynamically Linked Libraries

You can also dynamically load shared libraries. This means that they are not loaded and referenced by the program until the program is running and specifically loads the library. With dynamically loaded libraries, a program could load one library, use its functions, unload it, and then load another library. This can drastically cut down on memory needed by a program. It may also mean that updating a library would not require that the program be recompiled. The program is never compiled with the library, it only loads it in at run time.

A dynamically loaded library should be a shared ELF library compiled with the **-fPIC** option. This is different from the **-fpic** option used for regular shared libraries. The **-fPIC** option generates position-independent code suitable for dynamically loaded libraries. The following example creates a **libmyio.so** library prepared for dynamic loading.

```
$ gcc -fPIC -c io.c
$ gcc -shared -Wl,-soname,libmyio.so.1
     -o libmyio.so.1.0 io.o
$ cp libmyio.so /usr/lib
```

The process of dynamically loading a library is handled by the program itself. Special function calls in the program will load a library and reference its functions. These functions are part of the dynamic linker library (**libld.so**). The special function for dynamically loading a library is the **dlopen** function. This function takes as its arguments the name of the library and a permission, usually **RDT_LAZY**. The function returns a pointer, usually called a *handle*, that is used to reference that library. Functions in a loaded library are referenced within a program through function pointers. These pointers obtain the address of a function in the library with the **dlsym** function. **dlsym** takes as its argument the name of the function you want, and returns its address. This address should be assigned to a function pointer. That function pointer can then be used to call the function.

In the **maindym.c** example, the dynamic linker functions are used to load the **libmyio.so** library and access its functions. First, the **dlfcnt.h** header file is included, providing the function declarations for the dynamic linker functions. Then the **dlopen** function loads the **libmyio.so** library and assigns its address to the **handle** variable. The **dlsym** function obtains the address of the **bookinput** function in that library and assigns it to the **bkinput** function pointer. Then the **dlsym** function assigns the address of the **printbook** function to the **prbook** function pointer. These two pointers are then used to call their respective functions. The **dlclose** function then unloads the library.

maindym.c

```
#include <stdio.h>
#include <dlfcnt.h>

void bookinput(char[], float*);
void printbook(char[], float);

void main(void)
```

```
    {
        char title[20];
        float price;
        void *handle;
        void (*bkinput) (char*,float*);
        void (*prbook) (char*,float);

        handle = dlopen ("/usr/lib/libmyio.so",
                            RTLD_LAZY);
        if(!handle) {
            fputs(dlerror(), stderr);
            exit(1);
            }
        bkinput = dlsym(handle, "bookinput");
        prbook = dlsym(handle, "printbook");

        (*bkinput)(title, &price);
        (*prbook)(title, price);

        dlclose(handle);
    }
```

A program that uses dynamic linking is compiled with the **libld.so** library, **-ldl**. The libraries it loads are not linked by the compiler. The following example creates a program called **bookrecd** that can load the **libmyio.so** library and reference its **bookinput** and **printbook** functions. Notice the use of -**ldl** to reference the dynamic loader library, **libld.so**.

```
$ gcc bmain.c -o bookrecd  -ldl
```

The **ldd** command shows that the **bookrecd** program uses the **libdl.so** library, the dynamic loader library. It does not show the **libmyio.so.1.0** library.

```
$ ldd bookrecd
    libdl.so.1 => /lib/libdl.so.1.7.14
    libc.so.5 => /lib/libc.so.5.4.22
```

Static Libraries: ar

Instead of a shared library, you can create a static library using the **ar** command. The name for a library created with **ar** should have a **.a** extension. With **ar** you can easily maintain your library, adding or updating files and removing ones you no longer need.

The action performed by the **ar** command is determined by the **ar** command's option. An **ar** option consists of a single letter placed after the **ar** command. There is no hyphen before the option. Three of the more common options are **r**, **x**, and **t**. The **r** option instructs **ar** to copy a file into the library. The **x** option extracts files, and the **t** option displays a list of files in the library. The syntax for the archive operation is the keyword **ar**, the option, the library filename, and a list of files archived in the library:

```
ar option library-file list-of-object-code-files
```

You create a library using the **ar** command's **r** option. If the library file used in the **ar** command does not exist, it will be created. You also use the **r** option to update the library and to add new files to it. The **r** option stands for replace. If you are archiving a file and a copy of that file is already in the library, it will be replaced (overwritten). If the file being archived is not already in the library, it will be added. Using the **r** option, you can update files already in your library with new versions. As an example of how to create a library, the files **input.o** and **print.o** are used to create the **iolib.a** library.

```
$ ar r iolib.a input.o print.o
```

Once you have created a library file and you want to use it in a program, you need to first prepare it to be used by the linker with the **ranlib** command. **ranlib** organizes a library file so that it can be effectively searched by the linker.

```
$ ranlib iolib.a
```

The library is now ready for use with the compiler.

```
$ gcc main.c iolib.a -o bookrec
```

Should you want to remove functions from a library, you need to remove the files they are in. The **ar** command with the **d** option will delete a file from a library.

```
$ ar d iolib.a input.o
```

Option	Function
r	Create a library file or add and update files in the library.
d	Delete files from the library.
x	Extract files from the library.
t	Produce a listing of all files in the library.

Development Libraries

If you download software from ftp sites in their source code form, and then compile them on your Linux system, there may be specialized libraries that you will need. This is particularly true of X-Window-based software. Many X-Window-based programs use special libraries. Xview programs use their own special libraries. Other software may use specialized graphic libraries such as the QT libraries or **xforms**. Most are included on your OpenLinux CD-ROM, though they are not installed with a standard install. You may have to download others, such as QT, from a Linux ftp or Web site. Standard Linux libraries are usually located in the **/usr/lib** directory, whereas X-Window libaries are usually found in the **/usr/X11R6/lib** directory, and OpenLook libraries are found in the **/usr/opwnwin/lib** directory. The following table lists several of the more commonly used libraries:

Library	Description
libc.so	The standard library for the C programming language.
libg++.so	The classes library for C++, supported by the **gcc** compiler.
libobjc.so	The Objective-C library. Required for compiling Objective-C programs.
libm.so.5	The math library.
libdb.so.2	The BSD database library for C.
libelf.so	The library for manipulating ELF objects.
libgdbm.so	The **gnu** version of the **dbm** library for database access to files.
libgpm.so	The general-purpose mouse support library.
libncurses.so	The **ncurses** terminal control library.
libtiff.so.1	The TIFF library used for managing TIFF image files.
libdl.so	The dynamic loader library.
libforms.so	The forms library.
libtcl.so	The TCL library.
libtk.so	The TK library.
libtix.so	A collection of meta-widgets for TK.
libqt.so	The QT library.
libX11.so.6	The Xlib library (X-Window operations).
libX.so	The X-Window library.

Library	Description
libXaw.so	The Athena widget library.
libXaw3d.so	The 3-D Athena widget library.
libXpm.so	The Pixmap library.
libICE.so	The ICE library.
libXview.so	The library for the Xview (Open Look) interface.

The gdb Symbolic Debugger

gdb is the symbolic debugger available on your Linux system. If you run your program and it crashes for some reason, you can use a symbolic debugger to track down the error. A symbolic debugger allows you to step through your program line by line, displaying the source code for each line as you execute it. You can decide to stop in specific functions and display the contents of active variables. You can even check specific addresses and the contents of the stack.

To be able to use an executable file with a symbolic debugger, you need to compile and link your program using the **-g** option. Once you have a prepared executable file, you can then use it with the symbolic debugger. In the next example, a program is compiled and prepared for the symbolic debugger.

```
$ gcc -g main.c io.c
```

You invoke the **gdb** debugger with the keyword **gdb** and the name of the executable file. In the next example, the name of the executable file is **a.out**.

```
$ gdb a.out
```

The **gdb** command will place you in the debugger, replacing the Linux prompt ($) with the **gdb** prompt (gdb). You run your program in the debugger by typing the command **run** at the prompt.

```
(gdb) run
```

If your program has in it an **fopen** or **open** statement, it means it will be using a data file at some point in the program. If this is so, then **gdb** needs also to know the name of that file. When you type

run in **gdb** to run your program, you must also supply the actual name of such data files.

```
(gdb) run filename
```

When you have finished, leave the debugger with the **quit** (or **q**) command.

```
(gdb) quit
```

Most **gdb** commands have a single-letter equivalent, consisting of the first letter of the command. Commands for running **gdb** programs are listed here:

Command	Single-Letter Equivalent	Function
run	r	Run the program.
quit	q	Quit **gdb**.

Displaying Variables and Arguments

If you have an error in your program, **gdb** will stop at the error. You can then use **gdb** commands to examine what went wrong. Several of the different **gdb** commands that you can use are listed in the following table and described in this section. Many are comparable to those used in **sdb**.

Command	Single-Letter Equivalent	Function
print variable	**p** variable	Display the contents of a variable.
print &variable	**p &**variable	Display the address of a variable.
set variable = value		Assign a value to a variable during the **gdb** session.
where		Display a stack trace showing the sequence of function calls with function names and their arguments.
info locals		Display defined variables and arguments.
list line-number	l line-number	Display lines beginning at the specified line-number.

Command	Single-Letter Equivalent	Function
list *function*	l *function*	Display lines in a *function*.
list *num,num*	l *num,num*	Display a range of line numbers.

You display the contents of a variable using the **print** command. Enter the word **print** followed by the variable name. In the next example, the user displays the contents of the **count** variable.

```
(gdb) print count
10
```

Sometimes you may need to change the value of a variable during the **gdb** session. You can do this with the **set** operation. Enter the **set** keyword followed by the variable, then the equal sign and the value. In the next example, the user sets the **count** variable to 41.

```
(gdb) set count = 41
41
```

With the **where** command you can display the function names and the arguments of the functions that have been called at any point in your program. In the next example, the user is currently in the **calc** function. Entering the **where** command displays the function **main** as well as **calc** and its arguments.

```
(gdb) where
#3   calc(newcost = 2.0) at calc.c:25
#1   main () at main.c:19
#2   0x8000455 in ___crt_dummy__ ()
```

You can obtain a listing of all the variables and arguments defined in a function. The **info locals** command will display variable and argument values currently defined. In the next example, the user displays the defined variables.

```
(gdb) info locals
cost = 2
name = "Richard\000\000"
count = 10
count2 = 10
nameptr = 0x8000570 "petersen"
countptr = (int *) 0xbffffde8
```

You can display source code lines by specifying a line, range of lines, or function. The **list** command by itself displays the next ten lines beginning with your current line. To display the lines in a function, follow the **list** command with the name of the function. To list a specific line, enter the line number after the **list** command. If you want to display a range of lines, enter the **list** command followed by the first and last lines separated by a command.

Command	Function
list 17	Display the next ten lines, beginning with line 17.
list 12,15	Display lines 12 through 15.
list calc	Display the lines for the **calc** function.

In the next example, the user lists lines 14 to 17.

```
(gdb) list 14,17
14  cost   = 2.00;
15  count  =  calc (cost);
16  *countptr  =  count;
17  strcpy (name,"Richard");
```

Pointers

Pointers are used in three ways: as pointers to simple variables, as pointers to structures, and as pointers to arrays. As a pointer to a variable, what the pointer points to is displayed with this command:

```
print *pointer
```

In the next example, the user displays the contents of the variable that **countptr** is pointing to.

```
(gdb) print *countptr
4
```

Many errors occur when a pointer holds the wrong address. If a pointer is supposed to point to a certain variable, you may need to compare the address in the pointer to the address of a variable to see if they are the same. To obtain the address of a variable, you precede it with an ampersand. When placed before a variable, the ampersand becomes the address operator. In the next example, the user displays the address of **count** and the contents of **countptr** to see if they are the same.

```
(gdb) print &count
0x7fffbcd4
(gdb) print countptr
0x7fffbcd4
```

Pointers are also used to reference arrays. In this case, you need only specify the pointer itself. Referencing the pointer itself will display the entire array.

```
print pointer
```

To display elements of a structure using the structure's pointer, two things are needed: the pointer to the structure and the element of the structure you want printed. The following command uses a pointer to a structure to display a particular element in it. Notice the arrow. It is necessary.

```
print pointer->elementname
```

Stopping and Stepping

Though you may not have an error that stops your program, your program may, for some reason, give the wrong answers. This is called a *run-time error*. You then need to be able to stop a run of your program in **gdb** at a place in the program that you want to examine. (You can then check out the values of variables at that point.) You then may want to step through the program line by line to see where the error occurs.

You can set breakpoints in your program using the **break** command. When you reach a breakpoint, your program will stop. You can then step through your program, line by line, using the **next** or the **step** command. When you wish, you can advance to the next breakpoint by using the **cont** command.

Command	Single-Letter Equivalent	Function
next	**n**	Perform single-step execution, line by line, executing the current line and displaying the next line to be executed.

Command	Single-Letter Equivalent	Function
step	s	Perform single-step execution, line by line, executing the current line and displaying the next line to be executed.
cont	c	Continue execution of the program.

The **break** command has several variations (see the following table) depending on how you specify your breakpoint. You can specify a line at which to set the breakpoint, simply by entering the line number after the word **break**. You can also specify a function in which you want to stop. Just enter the **break** command followed by the function name. In the next example, the user sets breakpoints at line 17 and in the function **calc**.

```
(gdb) break 17
Breakpoint 1 at 0x80004cb: file main.c, line 17
(gdb) break calc
Breakpoint 2 at 0x80004f6: file main.c, line 25
```

Command	Single-Letter Equivalent	Function
break	b	Set breakpoint at current line.
break *line*	**b** *line*	Set breakpoint at specified *line*.
break *function*	**b** *function*	Set breakpoint at first line in the specified *function*.

You can display the breakpoints you have set by entering the **info break** command. Before each breakpoint there will be a number that identifies the breakpoint. You can use this number with the **delete** command to delete the breakpoint if you want to. In the next example, the user displays the breakpoints that have been set, and then deletes the first one.

```
(gdb) info break
Num Type          Disp Enb Address    What
1   breakpoint    keep y   0x080004cb in main at main.c:17
2   breakpoint    keep y   0x080004f6 in main at main.c:25
(gdb) delete 1
(gdb) info break
2   breakpoint    keep y   0x080004f6 in main at main.c:25
```

You can clear all your breakpoints by entering the **delete** command alone.

(gdb) **delete**

The commands for listing and deleting breaks are shown here:

Command	Single-Letter Equivalent	Function
info break	(none)	List all breakpoints.
delete	**d**	Delete all breakpoints.
delete *number*	**d** *number*	Delete specific breakpoint. You need to specify the *number* of the breakpoint to be deleted.

Example Run of gdb

In this example run, the **gdb** utility is used to examine the **calc.c** program. First, breakpoints are set using the **break** commands. The **status** command lists the active breakpoints. The **run** command then executes the program, stopping in the **main** function. Then the user steps through the program line by line, displaying the different values of variables. At line 15 the user jumps to the next breakpoint with the **cont** command. At the end, the user displays a list of all active variables and functions using the **info locals** command. Notice that single-letter versions of commands are used in places.

calc.c

```
#include <stdio.h>

 int calc(float);

 void main(void)
{
float cost;
char name[10];
int count, count2;
char *nameptr;
int *countptr = &count2;

cost  = 2.00;
count =  calc (cost);
```

```
*countptr = count;
    strcpy (name,"Richard");
nameptr = "petersen";
}

 int calc (float newcost)
{
int result;

result = newcost * 5;
return (result);
}
```

4

```
$ cc -g calc.c
$ gdb a.out
```
GDB is free software and you are welcome to distribute
copies of it under certain conditions; type "show
copying" to see the conditions. There is absolutely
no warranty for GDB; type "show warranty" for details.
GDB 4.14 (linuxelf), Copyright 1995 Free Software
Foundation, Inc...
```
(gdb) break main
Breakpoint 1 at 0x80004a6: file main.c, line 12.
(gdb) break 17
Breakpoint 2 at 0x80004cb: file main.c, line 17.
(gdb) info b
Num Type           Disp Enb Address    What
1   breakpoint     keep y   0x080004a6 in main at main.c:12
2   breakpoint     keep y   0x080004cb in main at main.c:17
(gdb) run
Starting program: /root/a.out

Breakpoint 1, main () at main.c:12
12   int *countptr = &count2;

(gdb) next
14   cost  = 2.00;

(gdb) n
15 count  = calc (cost);

(gdb) print cost
$1 = 2
(gdb) cont
Continuing.
```

```
Breakpoint 2, main () at main.c:17
17   strcpy (name,"Richard");

(gdb) p count
$2 = 10
(gdb) print *countptr
$3 = 10
(gdb) p countptr
$4 = (int *) 0xbffffde8
(gdb) n
18   nameptr =  "petersen";

(gdb) p name
$5 = "Richard\000\000"
(gdb) n
19   }

(gdb) print *nameptr
$6 = 112 'p'
(gdb) p nameptr
$7 = 0x8000570 "petersen"

(gdb) list 14,17
14   cost  = 2.00;
15   count =  calc (cost);
16   *countptr =  count;
17   strcpy (name,"Richard");

(gdb) info locals
cost = 2
name = "Richard\000\000"
count = 10
count2 = 10
nameptr = 0x8000570 "petersen"
countptr = (int *) 0xbffffde8
(gdb) where
#0   main () at main.c:19
#1   0x8000455 in ___crt_dummy__ ()
(gdb) c
Continuing.

Program exited with code 0360.
(gdb) q
```

xxgdb

xxgdb provides easy-to-use X-Window access to the **gdb** debugger. **xxgdb** is organized into a set of vertically positioned subwindows. Initially, five subwindows are displayed. A top subwindow, called the file window, displays the name of the file currently being displayed. The next subwindow displays the program's source code file and is called the source window. A scroll bar to the left allows you to scroll through the text. Below that is the message window for displaying **gdb** status and error messages. The bottom subwindow, called the *dialog window,* is used for entering **gdb** commands and displaying their results. A scroll bar to the left allows you to view previous commands and their results. Above the dialog window is the command window. This is a subwindow that lists a series of buttons for different **gdb** commands. To execute a command such as **run** or **step**, just click on that button. You can horizontally change the size of any window using the small squares located on the right side of the dividers between subwindows.

With command buttons, you can easily set **gdb** commands, indicating breakpoints or specifying what variables to display. If the command is designed to operate on an object such as a variable or function name, you first need to select that object in the source-code window. For example, to set a breakpoint on a function, you first click on that function name in the source-code window, then click on the break button. You will see a red hand appear in the source-code window pointing to the first line of code in that function. As you step through the code, a blue pointer to the left will show you what line of code was just executed.

To display the contents of variables, you first select them and then click on the display button. This will open up another subwindow, called the display window, at the bottom of the screen that will display the selected variable. As you choose more variables for display, they will be added to the window.

The print button will print the contents of a selected variable or expression in the message window. However, if you right-click on the print button, then a separate pop-up window displays the contents of that variable. Above the display of the object's contents is the pop-up's label with the object's name. To close the pop-up window, click on that label. If you right-click on any address displayed as a pointer value, this will bring up a pop-up to display the contents of the object it points to.

The file button brings up a window that lists all files in the current directory. To load a new source-code file, just click on its name. The search button brings up a window that lets you enter a search pattern. It will display a button labeled << for searching backward in a file, and >> for searching forward in a file. Close the window by clicking on the done button.

Programming Tools

There are several tools available that help you prepare and organize your source code. **f2c** and **p2c** can translate Fortran and Pascal programs into C programs. **cproto** generates a list of function declarations for all your defined functions, for use in header files. The **indent** utility will indent the braces used for blocks in a consistent format, making the code easier to read. **xwpe** is an X-Window programming environment similar to Turbo C.

Conversion Utilities for C: f2c and p2c

f2c and **p2c** perform source-code conversion from Fortran and Pascal into C code. Both generate a C source-code file with the extension .c. The original name is retained. They also have options for handling the conversion of complex programs. The following example will convert the Pascal program **mytitle.pas** to a C source-code file named **mytitle.c**.

```
$ p2c mytitle.pas
```

cproto

With a program made up of several source-code files, functions defined in one file may have to be used in another. To allow such use, the function has to be declared in that file. A function declaration is the function return value, followed by the function name and the list of that function's parameter types. When there are many functions involved, programmers often find themselves creating large lists of function declarations. Errors in typing this list can lead to subtle compiler or run-time bugs. **cproto** helps to avoid this problem by automatically generating a list of function declarations for a given file. You list several files or just one. The function declarations can then be easily placed in header files for inclusion in the source-code files that need them.

indent

The **indent** utility is designed to make C source code more readable for programmers. **indent** will indent opening and closing braces, {}. C functions and control structures make extensive use of braces to enclose the code they affect. As far as the compiler is concerned, the braces can occur with any number of intervening spaces, tabs, or carriage returns. For example, the opening brace for a function is placed right after the function parameters, but it can be placed on the same line, on the next line, or on the next line and indented several spaces, and you can do it differently for each function. This leads to code that can be hard to read. With **indent** you can avoid this problem. **indent** will place such braces in the same position for each function. It has numerous options for specifying how you want the indentation performed.

xwpe

xwpe is an X-Window program that has an interface similar to Borland's TurboC user interface. Program source files are displayed in windows. A window at the bottom shows error messages. Menus across the top provide different operations, such as loading files, running your program, setting up projects, and configuring your interface. The project capabilities of **xwpe** allow you to easily create programs using many different source-code files. Simply list the source-code files in the project file and then use **make** in the Compile menu to create the program.

Copying the Run of a Program: The script Command

There may be times when you want to make a copy of the run of a program. Suppose you want a printout of an interactive session with a program to show others how it works. You can obtain such a printout using the **script** command. The **script** command creates a new shell in which everything that appears in the standard input and output is copied to a file. Since both standard input and output are copied, **script** can be used to keep a record of an interactive run of a program. Everything typed in, as well as output to the screen, will be recorded in a file.

script takes as its argument the name of the file to which the copy of the session is to be written. If no argument is given, then a file with the default name of **typescript** is created. The file will be created and opened, recording all input and output. The file will remain open until the script shell is ended with the end-of-file character, CTRL-D, entered on the command line. Once the CTRL-D is entered, the script file is closed and the script shell is ended. The script file will then contain a copy of the run of your program. This file can be printed out with **lp**, like any other file. **script** will also record the date and time in the file.

In the next example, the user runs the **bookrec** program within a script shell. All input and output is saved in the file **runbook**. After the run of the program, the user ends the script shell with a CTRL-D. You can then examine the run of your program by displaying or printing out your script file, in this example, **runbook**.

```
$ script runbook
$ bookrec
Please enter a book record : Raven 2.50
The book record is : Raven 2.50
$ ^D
Script done, file is runbook
```

Be sure to end the script shell before you examine your script file. If you don't, and you use the **cat** command to display the script file, not only will characters be output to the screen, but they will also be recorded as more added input for the script file. Furthermore, you will not be able to log out while the script shell is active. If you have been using the **script** command and find yourself unable to log out, then a script shell is still active and must first be ended with a CTRL-D.

It is also possible to nest script shells. Executing a second **script** command before ending the first one simply records all input and output in the second script shell to the first script file. When the first script shell is finally ended, its file will contain everything in the first script shell, as well as everything in the second script shell.

| Packaging Your Software: |
| autoconf and rpm |

Once you have finished developing your software, you may then want to distribute it to others. Ordinarily you would pack your program into a **tar** archive file. People would then download the file and unpack it. You would have to have included detailed instructions on how to install it and where to place any supporting documentation and libraries. If you were distributing the source code, users would have to figure out how to adapt the source code to their systems. There are any number of variations that may stop compilation of a program.

The Redhat Package Manager (**rpm**) and **autoconf** are designed to automate these tasks. **autoconf** is used to automatically configure source code to a given system. **rpm** will automatically install software on a system in the designated directories, along with any documentation, libraries, or support programs. Both have very complex and powerful capabilities and are able to handle the most complex programs. Simple examples of their use are provided here.

autoconf

A Unix system can compile any software written in the C programming language. However, different Unix systems have different configurations, some using different compilers or placing programs and libraries in different system directories. Different types of support libraries may be present. In the past, in order to compile software on different systems, the software had to be manually configured for each system. For example, if your system has the **gcc** compiler instead of the **cc** compiler, you would have to set that feature in the software's makefile.

The **autoconf** program is designed to automate the configuration process. It automatically detects the configuration of the current Unix system and generates an appropriate makefile that can then be used to compile that software on this particular system. Much of the current software on the Internet in source form uses **autoconf**. A detailed manual on **autoconf** can be found in the **/usr/info** directory and is called **autoconf.info**. You can use the

info command to view it. (You can also view the text with any text editor.) The general operations are described here.

Software that uses **autoconf** performs the configuration without any need of the actual **autoconf** software. Special shell scripts included with the software will detect the different system features that the software needs. The **./configure** command usually will automatically configure the software for your system. As the configuration is performed, it checks for different features one by one, displaying the result of each check. The operation is entirely automatic, not even requiring the identity of the system it is working on.

To create a configuration script for your own software, you need to use special **autoconf** commands. The **autoconf** applications package is available on your OpenLinux CD-ROM. Generating the configurations involves several stages, using several intermediate configuration files. **autoconf** has many options designed to handle the requirements of a complex program. For a simple program you may only need to follow the basic steps.

The goal is to create a **configure** script. There are two phases in this process, using the **autoscan** and **autoconf** commands. The first phase creates a **configure.scan** file using the **autoscan** command. The **autoscan** command is applied directly to your source-code files. You then check the **configure.scan** file for any errors and make any changes or additions you want, then rename it as the **configure.in** file. This file is used as input for the **autoconf** command, which then generates the **configure** script.

The **autoscan** step is an aid in the creation of the **configure.in** file, but **autoscan** and the **configure.scan** file it generates are optional. You can create your own **configure.in** file, entering various **autoconf** macros. These are described in detail in the **autoconf.info** file, and the steps are described here:

> *source-code-files* → [autoscan] → [configure.scan]
> [configure.scan] → configure.in
> configure.in   → autoconf   → configure

In addition, you need to create a version of the makefile for your program named **makefile.in**. This is essentially your original makefile with reference to special **autoconf** variables. When the software is compiled on another system, the **configure.in** will detect the system's features and then use this information with the **makefile.in** file to generate a makefile for that particular system. It is this new makefile that is used to compile the program.

autoconf is designed to create values for different features that can then be used with the **makefile.in** to create a new makefile containing those features. The feature values are placed in special shell variables called *output* variables. You should place references to these shell variables in the **makefile.in** file wherever you want to use these values. For example, the **CC** variable will hold the name of the C compiler on your system (**cc** or **gcc**). The **AC_PROG_CC** macro in the **configure** script will detect the C compiler in use and place its name in the **CC** variable. A reference to this variable should be placed in the **makefile.in** file wherever you would invoke the C compiler. The variable name is bounded by two @ symbols. For example, @CC@ in the **makefile.in** will reference the **CC** variable, and its value will be substituted in that place.

The following is an example of the **autoscan** process using the source-code files for the **bookrec** program. The files are kept in a directory called **bookrec-1.0**. The **autoscan** command takes as its argument the directory that holds the source-code files. Be sure that it also includes the **makefile.in** file for that program. **autoscan** will create a new file called **configure.scan** in that directory. You then rename the **configure.scan** file to **configure.in**. **autoconf** will only read from a file named **configure.in**.

```
$ autoscan bookrec-1.0
$ ls bookrec-1.0
configure.scan      io.c     main.c        makefile.in
$ cd bookrec-1.0
$ mv configure.scan configure.in
$ ls
configure.in        io.c     main.c        makefile.in
```

An example of a simple **configure.in** file is shown next. The last line, the **AC_OUTPUT** macro, instructs **autoconf** to generate the makefile. There are many such **autoconf** macros that you can include in your **configure.in** file.

```
$ cat configure.in
dnl Process this file with autoconf to produce
    a configure script.
AC_INIT(main.c)
dnl Checks for programs.
AC_PROG_CC
```

```
dnl Checks for libraries.
dnl Checks for header files.
dnl Checks for typedefs, structures, and compiler
    characteristics.
dnl Checks for library functions.
AC_OUTPUT(makefile)
```

The **autoconf** command is then entered to generate the **configure** file. You enter **autoconf** by itself, with no arguments. It will automatically look for and read from the **configure.in** file.

```
$ autoconf
$ ls
configure   main.c   configure.in   io.c   makefile.in
```

If your program uses special system header files, such as those found in special libraries, you will need to perform a parallel process to create a **config.h.in** file. For example, suppose your program uses the Xview library to create Xview windows. Your program will need to know where the Xview header files are located on a particular system. The **config.h.in** file is generated by the **autoheader** command. The **autoconf.info** file goes into detail about creating such a file.

Once you have the **configure** file, you no longer need the **configure.in** file. You only need **configure**, **makefile.in**, and the source-code files along with any header files. The **configure** file is a shell script designed to execute on its own. It does not need **autoconf**.

Once another user has received the software package and unpacked all the source-code files, there are only three steps to take: configuration, compilation, and installation. **./configure** will generate a customized makefile for the user's system, **make** will compile the program using that makefile, and **make install** will install the program on the user's system.

```
./configure
make
make install
```

The **make install** operation is performed by a **make** command to copy the files to certain directories. Be sure to place it in the original **makefile.in** file. An example is shown here.

```
install:
        chmod 644 bookrec
        cp bookrec  /usr/local/bin
```

The following example shows all three operations for the **bookrec**
program. The **configure** script will generate two status files:
config.log and **config.status**. **config.log** lists all the actions that
configure took and **config.status** contains any error messages.

```
$ ls bookrec-1.0
configure   io.c     main.c     makefile.in
$ cd bookrec-1.0
$ ./configure
creating cache ./config.cache
checking for gcc... gcc
checking whether we are using GNU C... yes
checking whether gcc accepts -g... yes
updating cache ./config.cache
creating ./config.status
creating makefile
$ ls
config.cache    config.status    io.c       makefile
config.log      configure        main.c     makefile.in
$ make
cc     -c main.c -o main.o
cc     -c io.c -o io.o
cc main.o io.o -o bookrec
$ ls
bookrec    config.status   io.o      makefile
           config.cache    configure
main.c   makefile.in   config.log      io.c      main.o
$ make install
chmod 644 bookrec
cp bookrec /usr/local/bin
```

autoconf also supports complex programs using many source
code files distributed among several subdirectories. It is of special
help when dealing with specialized libraries that can be located in
different system directories on different systems.

rpm

The Redhat Package Manager (**rpm**) is designed to provide easy
installation of software on a system. It will install programs,
configuration files, and documentation, as well as source-code
files. **rpm** has options to allow you to create your own **rpm**
packages. Users can use such packages to automatically install
your software on their systems. Components such as the program,

man pages, and supporting libraries will be placed in the correct directories on the given system. Such packages can contain executable binaries or source-code files. You can find detailed information on how to use **rpm** to build packages on the www.rpm.org Web site. This site has the **RPM-HOWTO** that describes the process in detail.

The package-creation process is designed to take the program through several stages, starting with unpacking it from an archive, then compiling its source code, and finally generating the **rpm** package. You can skip any of these stages, up to the last one. If your software is already unpacked, you can start with compiling it. If it is compiled, you can start with installation. If already installed, you can go directly to creating the **rpm** package.

rpm makes use of three components to build packages: the build tree, the **/etc/rpmrc** configuration file, and an **rpm** spec script. The build tree is a set of special instructions used to carry out the different stages of the packaging process. The **rpm** spec script contains instructions for creating the package as well as the list of files to be placed in it. The **/etc/rpmrc** file is used to set configuration features for **rpm**. **rpm** has several options you can set in the **/etc/rpmrc** file. To obtain a listing, enter

```
$ rpm -showrc
```

The build tree directories, listed in the following table, are used to hold the different files generated at each stage of the packaging process. The **SOURCES** directory holds the compressed archive. The **BUILD** directory holds the source code unpacked from that archive. The **RPMS** directory is where the **rpm** package containing the executable binary program is placed, and **SRPMS** is where the **rpm** package containing the source code is placed. If you are creating a package from software stored in a compressed archive, such as a **tar.gz** file, you will have to first copy that file to the build tree's **SOURCES** directory.

Directory Name	Description
BUILD	The directory where **rpm** does all its building
SOURCES	The directory where you should put your original source archive files and your patches
SPECS	The directory where all spec files should go

Directory Name	Description
RPMS	The directory where **rpm** will put all binary RPMs when built
SRPMS	The directory where all source RPMs will be put

The following example copies the compressed archive for the **bookrec** software to the **SOURCES** directory:

```
$ cp bookrec-1.0.tar.gz  /usr/src/redhat/SOURCES
```

The **topdir:** entry in the **/etc/rpmrc** file specifies the location of the build tree directories. In that file you will find an entry for **topdir:**. Currently, the OpenLinux system has already set this directory to **/usr/src/redhat**. Here you will find the **SOURCES**, **BUILD**, **RPMS**, and **SRPMS** directories. You can specify a different directory for these subdirectories by changing the entry for **topdir:** in the **/etc/rpmrc** file.

```
topdir: /usr/src/redhat
```

By default, **rpm** is designed to work with source code placed in a directory consisting of its name and a release number, separated by a hyphen. For example, a program with the name *bookrec* and *release 1.0* should have its source-code files in a directory called **bookrec-1.0**. If **rpm** needs to compile the software, it will expect to find the source code in that directory within the **BUILD** directory, **BUILD/bookrec-1.0**. The same name and release number also need to be specified in the spec file. The following example shows how the **bookrec** software was archived using a directory called **bookrec-1.0** that holds the source-code files.

```
$ tar cvf bookrec-1.0.tar bookrec-1.0
bookrec-1.0/
bookrec-1.0/io.c
bookrec-1.0/main.c
bookrec-1.0/makefile
bookrec-1.0/bookrec.1
bookrec-1.0/README
$ gzip bookrec-1.0.tar
```

rpm Spec File

To create a package you have to first create an **rpm** spec file for it. The **rpm** spec file specifies the files to be included, any actions to

build the software, and information about the package. The spec
file is designed to take the program through several stages,
starting with unpacking it from an archive, then compiling its
source code, and finally generating the **rpm** package. In the spec
file, there are segments for the different stages and special **rpm**
macros that perform actions at these stages. These are
listed here:

File Segment or Macro	Description
%description	A detailed description of the software.
%prep	The prep stage for archives and patches.
%setup	The prep macro for unpacking archives. A **-n** *name* option resets the name of the **BUILD** directory.
%patch	The prep macro for updating patches.
%build	The build stage for compiling software.
%install	The install stage for installing software.
%files	The files stage that lists the files to be included in the package. A **-f** *filename* option specifies a file that contains a list of files to be included in the package.
%config *file-list*	A file macro that lists configuration files to be placed in the **/etc** directory.
%doc *file-list*	A file macro that lists documentation files to be placed in the **/usr/doc** directory with the subdirectory of the name-version-release.
%dir *directory-list*	The specification of a directory to be included as being owned by a package. (A directory in a file list refers to all files in it, not just the directory.)
%pre	A macro to do pre-install scripts.
%preun	A macro to do pre-uninstall scripts.
%post	A macro to do post-install scripts.
%postun	A macro to do post-uninstall scripts.

A spec file is divided into five basic segments; the header, prep,
build, install, and files. They are separated in the file by empty
lines. The header segment contains several lines of information,
each preceded by a tag and a semicolon. For example, the
following tag is used for a short description of the software.

```
Summary: bookrec program to manage book records
```

The Name, Version, and Release tags are used to build the name of the **rpm** package. The name, version, and release are separated with hyphens. For example, the name *bookrec* with the *version 1.0* and *release 2* will have the following name:

```
bookrec-1.0-2
```

The Group entry is a list of categories for the software. It is used by the Redhat **glint** utility to place the software in the correct **glint** display folder. The Source entry is the compressed archive where the software is stored on your system. Description is a detailed description of the software.

Following the header are the three stages for creating and installing the software on your system, indicated by the **%prep**, **%build**, and **%install rpm** macros. It is possible to skip any of these stages, say if the software is already installed. You can also leave any of them out of the spec file or comment them out with a preceding **#**. The spec file is capable of taking a compressed archive, unpacking it, compiling the source-code files, and then installing the program on your system. Then the installed files can be used to create the **rpm** package.

The **%prep** macro begins the **prep** segment of the spec file. The **prep** segment's task is to generate the software's source code. This usually means unpacking archives, but it may also have to update the software with patches. The tasks themselves can be performed by shell scripts that you write. There are also special macros that will automatically perform these tasks. The **%setup** macro will decompress and unpack an archive in the **SOURCES** directory, placing the source-code files in the **BUILD** directory. The **%patch** macro will apply any patches.

The **%build** segment contains the instructions for compiling the software. Usually this is a simple **make** command, depending on the complexity of your program. The **%install** segment contains the instructions for installing the program. You can use simple shell commands to copy the files or, as in the **bookspec** example that follows, the **install** command that installs files on systems. This could also be the **make install** command, provided your makefile has the commands to install your program.

The **%files** segment contains the list of files you want placed in the **rpm** package. Following the **%files** macro you list the different files, including their full path names. The macro **%config** can be used to list configuration files. Any files listed here are placed in the **/etc** directory. The **%doc** macro is used for documentation such as README files. These will be placed in the **/usr/doc** directory under a subdirectory consisting of the software's name, version, and release number. In the **bookspec** example, the **README** file will be placed in the **/usr/doc/bookrec-1.0-2** directory.

bookspec

```
Summary: bookrec program to manage book records
Name: bookrec
Version: 1.0
Release: 2
Copyright: GPL
Group: Applications/Database
Source: /root/rpmc/bookrec-1.0.tar.gz
%description
This program manages book records by title, providing
price information

%prep
%setup

%build
make RPM_OPT_FLAGS="$RPM_OPT_FLAGS"

%install
install -s -m 755 -o 0 -g 0 bookrec /usr/bin/bookrec
install -m 644 -o 0 -g 0 bookrec.1 /usr/man/man1

%files
%doc README

/usr/bin/bookrec
/usr/man/man1/bookrec.1
```

rpm Commands for Creating a Package

To create an **rpm** software package you use the **rpm** build options (listed in the following table) with the **rpm** command, followed by the name of a spec file. The -**bl** option checks to see if all the files used for the software are present. The -**bb** option builds just the binary package, whereas -**ba** builds both binary and source packages. They expect to find the compressed archive for the software in the build tree's **SOURCES** directory. -**ba** and -**bb** will execute every stage specified in the **rpm** spec script, starting from the prep stage to unpacking an archive and then compiling the program, followed by installation on the system and then creation of the package. The completed **rpm** package for executable binaries is placed in a subdirectory of the build tree's **RPMS** directory. This subdirectory will have a name representing the current platform. For a PC this will be **i386**, and the package will be placed in the **RPMS/i386** subdirectory. The source-code package is placed directly in the **SRPMS** directory.

The following program generates both a binary and a software package, placing them in the build tree's **RPMS/i386** and **SRPMS** directories. The name of the spec file in this example is **bookspec**.

```
rpm -ba bookspec
```

An executable binary package will have a name consisting of the software name, the version number, the release number, the platform name (**i386**), and the term **rpm**. The name, version, and release are separated by hyphens, whereas the release, platform name, and the **rpm** term are separated by periods. The name of the binary package generated by the previous example, using the **bookspec** spec script, will generate the following name:

```
bookrec-1.0-2.i386.rpm
```

The source-code package will have the same name, but with the term **src** in place of the platform name:

```
bookrec-1.0-2.src.rpm
```

The following example shows the complete run of the **rpm** packaging operation, beginning with the unpacking of the **bookrec** archive, **bookrec-1.0.tar.gz**, that has been placed in the **SOURCES** directory.

```
$ rpm -ba bookspec
* Package: bookrec
+ umask 022
+ echo Executing: %prep
Executing: %prep
+ cd /usr/src/redhat/BUILD
+ cd /usr/src/redhat/BUILD
+ rm -rf bookrec-1.0
+ gzip -dc /usr/src/redhat/SOURCES/bookrec-1.0.tar.gz
+ tar -xvvf -
drwxr-xr-x root/root         0 1997-08-10 15:09
```

```
 bookrec-1.0/
-rwxr-xr-x root/root    256 1997-08-10 15:02
 bookrec-1.0/io.c
-rwxr-xr-x root/root    174 1997-08-10 15:02
 bookrec-1.0/main.c
-rw-r--r-- root/root     49 1997-08-10 15:06
 bookrec-1.0/makefile
-rw-r--r-- root/root   1161 1997-08-10 15:09
 bookrec-1.0/bookrec.1
-rw-r--r-- root/root  19538 1997-08-10 15:09
 bookrec-1.0/README
+ [ 0 -ne 0 ]
+ cd bookrec-1.0
+ cd /usr/src/redhat/BUILD/bookrec-1.0
+ chown -R root.root .
+ chmod -R a+rX,g-w,o-w .
+ exit 0
+ umask 022
+ echo Executing: %build
Executing: %build
+ cd /usr/src/redhat/BUILD
+ cd bookrec-1.0
+ make RPM_OPT_FLAGS=-O2 -m486 -fno-strength-reduce
cc    -c main.c -o main.o
cc    -c io.c -o io.o
cc main.o io.o -o bookrec
+ exit 0
+ umask 022
+ echo Executing: %install
Executing: %install
+ cd /usr/src/redhat/BUILD
+ cd bookrec-1.0
+ install -s -m 755 -o 0 -g 0 bookrec /usr/bin/bookrec
+ install -m 644 -o 0 -g 0 bookrec.1 /usr/man/man1
+ exit 0
+ umask 022
+ echo Executing: special doc
Executing: special doc
+ cd /usr/src/redhat/BUILD
+ cd bookrec-1.0
+ DOCDIR=//usr/doc/bookrec-1.0-2
+ rm -rf //usr/doc/bookrec-1.0-2
+ mkdir -p //usr/doc/bookrec-1.0-2
+ cp -ar README //usr/doc/bookrec-1.0-2
```

```
+ exit 0
Binary Packaging: bookrec-1.0-2
Finding dependencies...
Requires (1): libc.so.5
usr/bin/bookrec
usr/doc/bookrec-1.0-2
usr/doc/bookrec-1.0-2/README
usr/man/man1/bookrec.1
48 blocks
Generating signature: 0
Wrote: /usr/src/redhat/RPMS/
i386/bookrec-1.0-2.i386.rpm
+ umask 022
+ echo Executing: %clean
Executing: %clean
+ cd /usr/src/redhat/BUILD
+ cd bookrec-1.0
+ exit 0
Source Packaging: bookrec-1.0-2
bookspec
bookrec-1.0.tar.gz
18 blocks
Generating signature: 0
Wrote: /usr/src/redhat/SRPMS/bookrec-1.0-2.src.rpm
#
```

There are several other options that execute different stages in
the packaging process, without generating an **rpm** package.
These build commands have the following format.

```
rpm -bx [build-options] spec-file
```

The **-bp** option executes just the prep stage, unpacking source
files held in an archive and then applying any update patches to
it. The **-bc** option executes both the prep stage and the build
stage, unpacking files to the **BUILD** directory and compiling the
source-code files into an executable program. The **-bi** option
executes the prep, build, and install stages. It unpacks, compiles,
and then installs the software files on your system. It does not,
however, create the **rpm** package. These options are designed to
let you perform different tasks in the process, depending on what
stage you may be working at. If you just want to unpack the
archive and then make modifications to the software, you can use
the **-bp** option. The **-bl** option checks to see if all the files used for
the software are present.

If you already have an **rpm** package for the source-code files, you can use the **--rebuild** option to create a package for the binaries. This option will install the source-code files, compile the program, install it, and then incorporate the program into an **rpm** binary package. With the **--recompile** option, it will only compile and install the program without creating the binary package.

Option	Function
-ba	Create both the executable binary and source-code packages. Perform all stages in the spec file: prep, build, install, and create the packages.
-bb	Create just the executable binary package. Perform all stages in the spec file: prep, build, install, and create the package.
-bp	Run just the prep stage from the spec file (**%prep**).
-bl	Do a "list check". The **%files** section from the spec file is macro-expanded, and checks are made to ensure the files exist.
-bc	Do both the prep and build stages, unpacking and compiling the software (**%prep** and **%build**).
-bi	Do the prep, build, and install stages, unpacking, compiling, and installing the software (**%prep**, **%build**, and **%install**).
--short-circuit	Skip to specified stage, not executing any previous stages. Only valid with **-bc** and **-bi**.
--clean	Remove the build tree after the packages are made.
--test	Do not execute any build stages. Used to test out spec files.
--recompile *source_package_file*	**rpm** installs the source-code package and performs a prep, compile, and install.
--rebuild *source_package_file*	**rpm** first installs the named source package, and does a prep, compile, and install, and then rebuilds a new binary package.
--showrc	List the configuration variables for the **/etc/rpmrc** file.

Installing the Package

Once you have created the package you can then distribute it. You could post it on an ftp site for downloading or just place it on a floppy and give it to someone. When a person has placed it on their system, they can then use the **rpm** command with the **-i** option to install it. The program will be installed, along with any documentation, **man** files, or configuration files. The following example installs the **bookrec** package on a system. The different directories are checked to see that the installation was made.

```
$ rpm -i bookrec-1.0-2.i386.rpm
$ ls /usr/bin/book*
/usr/bin/bookrec
$ ls /usr/doc/book*
/usr/doc/bookrec-1.0-2:
README
$ ls /usr/man/man1/book*
/usr/man/man1/bookrec.1
```

4

Chapter 5
Development Tools

An application is an executable program created by a programmer using one of several programming languages. Linux provides several utilities with which a programmer can control development of an application. Foremost among these is the **make** utility. The **make** utility interfaces with the Linux operating system to provide an easy way to maintain and compile programs. The **rcs** utility allows you to better control program changes. It organizes changes into different versions that can be stored and later accessed. You can even use the **man** utility to create your own online documentation for your applications. All of these utilities are complex and powerful tools.

The make Utility

You will often be working with a program that has many source-code files. As you develop the program and make modifications, you will need to compile the program over and over again. However, you need only compile those source-code files in which you made changes. The linker then links the newly generated object-code files with previously compiled object-code files creating a new executable file. The fact that only a few of your source files are actually compiled each time drastically cuts down on the work of the compiler. Each time you need a new executable program, you do not need to recompile each source-code file.

It can be very difficult in large programs, with many source-code files, to keep track of which files have been changed and need to be compiled and which files need only to be linked. The **make** utility will do this for you. **make** was designed for a development environment in which different source-code files in a program are constantly being modified. **make** keeps track of which source files have been changed and which have not. It then recompiles only those that have been changed, linking them with the rest of the object-code files to create a new executable file. In the next example, the user enters the command **make** on the command

207

line to invoke the **make** utility. **make** then compiles those files that have recently been modified and creates a new executable file. **make** displays each Linux command it executes.

```
$ make
gcc -c main.c
gcc -c io.c
gcc main.o io.o
```

If all the files in your program are up to date, then the **make** utility only returns a message telling you so.

```
$ make
'a.out' is up to date.
```

To understand how the **make** utility works, you need to realize that it uses a source-code file's time stamp to determine whether or not it should be compiled. When a file is created, re-created, or modified in any way, a new time stamp is placed on it by the Linux operating system. If you create a file at 1:00, that file is stamped with the time 1:00. If you then change the file at 6:00, the file is restamped with the time 6:00. When compiling a program, only those source-code files that have been changed need to be recompiled, and the time stamp can be used to determine which files those are. In this way, **make** selects the files to be compiled for the programmer.

In the next example, the user manages a program consisting of two source-code files: **main.c** and **io.c**. Both files have corresponding object-code files: **main.o** and **io.o**. These are used to create an executable file called **a.out**. If either **main.c** or **io.c** have been modified since **a.out** was last created, then **make** will again compile the modified source-code file, generating a new object-code file, and then create a new executable file. Below, the **ls -l** command lists all files using a long format that includes the time the file was last modified. Notice that all files, except for **main.c**, have times earlier than the executable file **a.out**.

```
$ ls -l
-rwxr-xr-x  1 rich     48728 Nov  3 04:31 a.out
-rw-r--r--  1 rich       256    Nov  3 04:30 io.c
-rw-r--r--  1 rich      2080    Nov  3 04:30 io.o
-rw-r--r--  1 rich       136    Nov  3 05:05 main.c
-rw-r--r--  1 rich       604    Nov  3 04:30 main.o
-rw-r--r--  1 rich        66    Nov  3 03:00 types.h
```

The user then executes the **make** command. **make** finds that **main.c** was changed more recently than **a.out**, so **main.c** is compiled creating a new **main.o** file. Both the new **main.o** and the old **io.o** file are then used to create a new **a.out** file. The following **ls -l** command shows that the times for **main.o** and **a.out** are now more recent than **main.c**.

```
$ make
gcc -c main.c
gcc main.o io.o
$ ls -l
total 56
-rwxr-xr-x  1 rich    48728 Nov  3 05:06 a.out
-rw-r--r--  1 rich      256 Nov  3 04:30 io.c
-rw-r--r--  1 rich     2080 Nov  3 04:30 io.o
-rw-r--r--  1 rich      136 Nov  3 05:00 main.c
-rw-r--r--  1 rich      604 Nov  3 05:05 main.o
-rw-r--r--  1 rich       66 Nov  3 03:00 types.h
```

make does not automatically compile any source-code file that has been changed. You need to first provide the **make** utility with a coded set of instructions that tell **make** how to determine what files are to be compiled. These instructions are often referred to as dependency lines and are placed in a file called **makefile**. **make** will automatically read and execute the dependency lines that it finds in the **makefile**.

By default, **make** will look for a file called **makefile** in your current working directory. Each directory can have its own file called **makefile**. Suppose, however, that you needed to have more than one makefile in your current directory. Using the **-f** option, **make** can read a file that contains dependency lines, but has a name other than "makefile". In the next example, the user reads dependency lines from a file called **prog.mak**. By convention, such files often have the extension **.mak**. However, this extension is not required.

```
$ make -f prog.mak
gcc -c io.c
gcc main.o io.o
```

Another **make** option that you may find helpful as you learn **make** is the **-n** option. With this option, **make** does not execute any actual Linux commands. Instead it only displays those commands that would be executed by **make**. In this way you can see how your **make** instructions are operating and if they are performing as you want them to.

Dependency Lines

A *dependency line* specifies a dependency relationship between files. **make** operates in terms of dependencies. A source-code file is used to create an object-code file, which in turn is used to create a runable program. The program can be said to be dependent on the object-code file, which in turn is dependent on the source-code file. You need to specify the dependency relationship between a source-code file and an object-code file in a dependency line. In another dependency line you need to specify the dependency relationship between an executable file and all its object-code files.

A dependency line can be thought of as a kind of conditional statement. The dependency relationship is its test condition. If an object-code file depends on a source-code file and the source-code file has been recently modified, then the test condition is true and the file is then recompiled. However, the syntax for a dependency line is a bit more complex than a standard conditional statement. A dependency line consists of three components: a target file, a list of dependency files, and a Linux command. If any of the dependency files has been modified more recently than the target file, then the Linux command is executed. The target file and the dependent files are written on the same line, separated by a colon. You can either place the Linux command on the same line, separated from the dependent files by a semicolon, or you can place the Linux command on the next line, preceded by a tab. You can list more than one Linux command if you wish. When entered on the same line, you separate Linux commands with semicolons. On separate lines, each Linux command has to be preceded by a tab. The dependency line ends with a following empty line. In these examples, the Linux command is an invocation of the **cc** compiler, compiling a source-code file or linking object-code files. The syntax for a dependency line is as follows:

```
target file : dependent files ; Linux command
empty line

target file : dependent files
tab    Linux command
empty line
```

In the following makefile we construct the dependency lines for a C program consisting of two source-code files: **main.c** and **io.c**. In such a two-file program there are really five files to manage. For each **.c** file there is a corresponding **.o** file, and there is the executable file, **a.out**. You need to set up your makefile with dependency lines to manage all of these files, specifying dependencies for each. An object-code file (**.o**) is dependent on a source-code (**.c**) file. An executable file, **a.out**, is dependent on several object-code files (**.o**). In the following example, **a.out** is dependent on (made up of) the two object-code files **main.o** and **io.o**. Each object-code file is, in turn, dependent on their respective source-code files; **main.o** on **main.c**, and **io.o** on **io.c**.

In the makefile, three dependency lines are needed for the **a.out**, **main.o**, and **io.o** files, respectively. Notice that the linking and compilation of the program are split up among the different dependency lines. The Linux command for the **a.out** target only links the two object-code files, creating a new executable file. It invokes **gcc** with only object-code files (**.o**), causing only the linker to be invoked. The Linux commands for the **main.o** and **io.o** targets only compile, creating **.o** object files. The -c option used with **gcc** means that no linking is done, only compilation, generating the object-code file for this source-code file.

makefile

```
a.out : main.o io.o
gcc main.o io.o

main.o : main.c
gcc -c main.c

io.o : io.c
cc -c io.c
```

The flow of control for a dependency line operates somewhat like a series of function or procedure calls. Control is transferred from one dependency line to another, each time checking the time stamps of files in the list of dependent files. The flow of control operates according to three basic rules applied to each dependency line.

1. Start checking the list of dependent files. Take the first dependent file and check to see if it is itself a target file in another dependency line. If it is, then suspend operation on the current dependency line and transfer control to that other dependency line. This operation is similar to a function call, where control is transferred from one part of the program to

another. Notice that the target files form a left-hand column on the left edge of the file.

2. When control has returned to the dependency line after another dependency line has finished, or if the dependent file is not itself a target file, then continue on to the next dependent file in the list of dependent files. Check, in turn, to see if this next dependent file is itself a target file in another dependency line. If so transfer control.

3. After all the dependent files have been processed, **make** then checks if any of the time stamps for the dependent files is more recent than that of the target file. If so, the dependency line executes the Linux command. If not, the Linux command is not executed.

Header Files

Dependency relationships can be set up between files of any type, not just source-code and object-code files. For example, you can set up a dependency relationship between an object-code file and what is known in C programs as a header file. A header file is a text file that contains segments of source code that are inserted into your main source-code files by your compiler. They become an actual part of the program. In this respect, an object-code file may not only be dependent on a source-code file, but also a particular header file. By convention, header files all have the extension **.h** attached to their names. In the next makefile example, both the **types.h** header file and the **main.c** source-code file are used to create the **main.o** file. An **include** instruction in **main.c** instructs the compiler to include the function declaration in **types.h** as part of the **main.c** source code. Both **main.c** and **types.h** are now used to create the **main.o** file. Should you make changes to the **types.h** file, you would want to have **make** generate a new **main.o** file. To do this, you need to place **types.h** as a dependent file in the **main.o** dependency line. If there are any changes to either **main.c** or to the **types.h** header file, then **main.c** will be recompiled.

makefile

```
a.out : main.o io.o
gcc main.o io.o

main.o : main.c types.h
gcc -c main.c

io.o : io.c
gcc -c io.c
```

Implied make Dependencies

The **make** utility has a set of implied dependency relationships
that it automatically applies to source-code and object-code files.
In Linux, the source-code file for any given programming language
must contain a specific suffix. C source-code files require **.c**
suffixes. Fortran files require a **.f** suffix. **.s** is used for assembler
source-code files. **make** will examine the source-code file suffix
of a corresponding object-code file in a dependency list and
automatically invoke the appropriate compiler for that source-code
file. This means that by using implied dependencies, you can
dispense with the dependency lines for compiling source-code
files. You can then reduce your makefile to one Linux command:
the command to link files.

Exactly how **make** implements implied dependencies is discussed
later, during the examination of suffix rules. Using such rules you
will learn how to create your own implied dependencies. For now
it is enough to know that you can drastically reduce the number of
dependency lines in your makefile if you wish to do so.

In the next example, by relying on implied dependencies, the
makefile for the **bookrec** program is reduced to two dependency
lines. When examining the dependency list for the **bookrec**
dependency line, **make** will look for corresponding source-code
files in the current directory. It will find **main.c** and **io.c**. Since
these files have a **.c** extension, the dependency line would
recognize these as C source codes and would invoke the **gcc**
compiler if necessary. Suppose the user recently modified **io.c**.
Then **make** would know to compile **io.c** with the C compiler, **gcc -c**.

makefile

```
bookrec : main.o io.o
    gcc main.o io.o -o bookrec

$ ls *.c
main.c io.c
$ make
gcc -c io.c
gcc main.o io.o -o bookrec
```

To denote the dependency of header files on an object-code file,
you need to add a dependency line, but one without a following
Linux command. **make** will locate the source-code file and compile
it to create the object-code file. In the next makefile example,
another dependency line is added for the **main.o** and **types.h**
dependency.

makefile

```
bookrec : main.o io.o
   cc main.o io.o -o bookrec

main.o: types.h
```

Specifying Dependency Lines Using Target Arguments

Suppose that you want to use **make** to execute a specific Linux command for you. For example, suppose you would like to use **make** to execute the Linux command to print out all your source-code files. Instead of entering the names of all the files on the command line each time you want to print them out, you can have **make** do it for you. Remember that the Linux command in a dependency line can be any Linux command, not just a **gcc** compiler command. You could enter a dependency line whose Linux command is an **lpr** command to print files.

You would then be using your makefile for two very different purposes: to compile a program and to print files. You will have dependency lines that compile your program, as well as another dependency line to print your files. However, whereas the dependency lines for compiling are all interdependent, the one for printing would be independent of any other dependency lines. You do not want to print each time you compile and vice versa. You could have a dependency line whose target is not listed as a dependent file in any other dependency line. Such a dependency line would be disconnected from all others. The target itself does not have to be an actual file. It can be what is known as a *zero-length file*—one that **make** creates for its own purposes. In the next example, the user creates such a dependency line whose target is the word **print**. **print** is a zero-length file created by **make**. It is not one that you have created.

makefile

```
bookrec: main.o io.o
   gcc main.o io.o -o bookrec

main.o :types.h

print :
lpr main.c io.c &
```

Since the target in such a dependency line is not in any way related to any other dependency line, how then could it ever be executed? By default, **make** begins processing with the first dependency line in the makefile. However, you can direct **make** to begin processing with a specific dependency line by using its target as an argument on the command line. If you list the target of a dependency line, then **make** will execute that dependency line, ignoring the others. In the previous makefile, the last dependency line only prints files. Its target is the word **print**. There is no dependency list, so if this dependency line is ever processed, it will always execute its Linux command.

```
$ make print
lpr main.c io.c
$
```

5

You can actually specify any target on the command line. For example, you could explicitly specify **main.o** as a target on the command line. Then **make** would only execute the **main.o** dependency line, checking to see if the **main.c** file should be compiled. Notice that for this makefile, the **make** command by itself and **make** with the **bookrec** argument have the same effect. **bookrec** is the target of the first dependency line in the file and thus also the default.

A **make** argument commonly used with software that you may download is the **install** argument. Usually the makefile is used to both compile a program and then to install it into system directories on your system. To compile, you usually just enter the **make** command by itself. To install, you would enter **make** with the **install** target.

```
$ make install
```

Updating a File's Time Stamp: touch and -t

Using the previous makefile as an example, suppose you have added some new options to your **cc** command and want to recompile your program to include those new options, such as the -O optimizing option. Since you have not actually modified any of your source code or header files, **make** will consider the program to be up to date and will not recompile. You need to be able to change the time stamp of the source-code files for the program. For this task you can use the **touch** command to directly change the time stamp of your files. The **touch** command is designed to go hand in hand with **make**. It allows you to force execution of dependency lines, even though you may not have actually changed any files. **make** looks only at the time stamp of files, not whether they have actually been modified or not. In the next example, the **touch** command updates the time stamps of the **main.c** and **io.c** files. Then, when the user executes the **make** command, the program is recompiled.

```
$ touch main.c io.c
```

Should you not want a target file recompiled, even though you may have changed one of its dependent files, you can update the target file using **make**'s -t option. Enter the option -t and the target as an argument on the command line.

make Variables

You may often need to use a list of filenames in more than one place in a makefile. Instead of retyping the list in several dependency lines, you could assign the list to a variable and use the variable in its place. In your makefile you can define variables and assign values to them. You can then evaluate the variables in different dependency lines throughout the makefile. To evaluate a **make** variable, you first encase the variable name within parentheses and then precede the parentheses with a dollar sign (**$**). For example, if you assign a variable a list of filenames, the list of filenames that it holds will be substituted for the variable name when you evaluate the variable.

In the next makefile example, a list of object-code files is assigned to a variable called **OBJECTS**. In previous makefile examples, the **bookrec** dependency line required that you enter the list of object-code files, both in the list of dependent files and also in the **cc** command to link those files. In this makefile, you simply enter an evaluation of the **OBJECTS** variable in both places with **$(OBJECTS)**. Also in the makefile, the **CFILES** variable is defined and assigned the list of all C source-code files. This variable is then used in the print dependency line to provide the **lp** command with a list of all C source-code files. Notice that **make** variables operate somewhat like shell variables. You use the assignment operator to assign a string to a variable. Then the dollar sign is used to evaluate the variable. However, unlike shell variables, when evaluating a variable you must place the variable name within parentheses.

A **make** variable has as its value a string. The string can be any set of characters. For example, in the next makefile example, the string "Printing out the source-code files" is assigned to the variable **PRINTNOTICE**. This variable is then evaluated in the print dependency line as the argument to an **echo** command. The string is displayed on the screen, notifying the user that the source-code files are being printed. The **echo** command itself is preceded by an @ operator, which suppresses display of the actual **echo** command. **make** will display each command that it executes, unless instructed not to with the @ operator.

The list of filenames assigned to a variable is really just a string. Just as you can assign filenames to a variable, you can also assign compiler options. The options are really just strings as far as the variable is concerned. Options are represented with a hyphen followed by a letter code and sometimes an argument. In the following example, the variable **LINKFLAGS** holds the linker option **-o** followed by a filename. This option allows the user to specify another name for the executable file, in this case **bookrec**.

makefile

```
CFILES = main.c io.c
OBJECTS = main.o io.o
LINKFLAGS = -g -o bookrec
PRINTNOTICE = Printing out the source-code files

bookrec : $(OBJECTS)
    cc $(LINKFLAGS) $(OBJECTS)

print :
    @echo $(PRINTNOTICE)
    lp $(CFILES) &

$ make print
Printing out the source-code files
lp main.c io.c &
```

make Predefined Variables

When executing the **make** command, **make** defines all exported variables from the shell, as well as several standard variables for its own use. The predefined variables hold compiler command names and compiler options. For example, **CC** holds the command name of the system's C compiler, usually **cc.**, and **FC** holds the command name of the system's Fortran compiler. Compiler options are held in variables whose names end with **FLAGS**. For example, **CFLAGS** holds the standard C compiler options such as -O, which invokes the optimizer. **FFLAGS** holds the Fortran compiler's standard options.

The predefined variables, listed in the following table, are useful if you have several different compilers for the same computer language, or if the system compiler changes frequently. Suppose that you have several different C compilers on your system to choose from. One of them will be considered the default and have its name assigned to the **CC** variable. However, in your makefile, you can change the value of any of the predefined variables. To use one C compiler or the other, just assign that compiler's command name to the **CC** variable. The same is true for the option variables. To add the **-g** option to the **CFLAGS** variable, just assign **-g -O** to it in your makefile. The advantage of using the predefined variable is that the command names held in them are also used in implied **make** operations, ones that you do not explicitly enter in a dependency line.

Predefined Variable	Default Value	Description
CC	gcc	C compiler
CFLAGS	-O	Options for the C compiler
AS	as	Assembler
ASFLAGS		Options for Assembler
FC	f77	Fortran compiler
FFLAGS		Options for the Fortran compiler
LD	ld	Loader to link object-code files
LDFLAGS		Options for loader
LEX	lex	Lexical Analyzer: creates .c files from .l files
LFLAGS		Lexical options
MAKE	make	The make utility
MAKEFLAGS	b	Options for make

make Special Variables

make has a set of specially defined variables that hold information about the current dependency line. Their values change from one dependency line to another. There are three special variables that you can use in any ordinary dependency line: **$@**, **$$@**, and **$?**. The **$@** and **$$@** variables hold the name of the current target. The **$?** variable holds a list of those dependent files whose time stamps are more recent than those of the target file. Some of the special variables apply only to special kinds of dependency lines. For example, the **$*** and **$<** are used only with suffix rules, and the **$%** is used only with library dependency lines. They are discussed in later sections. The **make** special variables are listed in the following table.

Variable	Description
$@	The name of the target file in a dependency line.
$$@	The name of the target file. This variable can only be used in the list of dependent files.
$?	The dependent files that are more recent than the target. This variable can only be used in the Linux command of a dependency line.
$%	Member files of a library file that are more recent than the library file. If **iolib.a** is composed of **input.o**, and **input.o** is more recent than **iolib.a**, then **$%** evaluates to **input.o**.
$<	In suffix rules, this variable evaluates to the dependent files that are more recent than the target (like **$?**).
$*	In suffix rules, this variable evaluates to the name of the target file without its suffix (like **$@**).

In the previous makefile example, the print dependency line printed out all the source-code files. Suppose, however, you want to print only those files in the dependency list that were most recently changed. The **$?** variable will hold the names of the most recently changed source-code files in the dependency list. You can use that variable with the **lpr** command to print out only the recently changed files. The following dependency line for **print** shows how to do this. The **main.c** file has been changed since the print dependency line was last executed. Notice that there is a **touch** command after the **lpr** command in the print dependency line. The **touch** command updates the time stamp for print. The @ before **touch** is a special **make** instruction to suppress display of the command.

```
print : main.c io.c
lp $?
@touch print
```

The **$@** variable holds the name of the target. It becomes helpful when you need to reference the target name in a dependency line's Linux command. In the previous makefile example, instead of repeating the term **bookrec** in the **gcc** command, the **$@** variable is used. This would ensure that if you ever change the name of the target, the same name would be used in the **gcc** command as the name of the executable file.

```
bookrec : main.o io.o
        gcc main.o io.o -o $@
```

make Special Targets

In addition to the special variables, **make** has a set of special targets used to provide different features. A special target is preceded by a period and entered in uppercase. For example, the special target **.SILENT** will suppress the usual display of Linux commands as they are executed in dependency lines. The special target **.IGNORE** will allow your makefile to continue execution even if a Linux command fails. By default, **make** will stop if it executes a Linux command that returns an error code. The **.IGNORE** special target ignores all error codes.

The **.PRECIOUS** special target specifies those targets you do not want removed should **make** be interrupted. In some cases you need to retain the target file in order to preserve its time stamp. For example, the time stamp of the print target file is used to print out those files that have recently been changed. If, for some reason, the **lp** command in the print dependency line is interrupted during its execution, then **make** will by default remove the target, the print file. However, you can override this default action by listing **print** with the **.PRECIOUS** special target. The print file will not be removed.

The **.DEFAULT** special target is executed if there is no dependency line or builtin rule to handle a target. For example, if the user enters a target that does not exist as an argument to **make**, then the **.DEFAULT** target is executed. (Note that a target does not have to be explicit; it can be builtin.)

In the next makefile example, the user suppresses the display of commands with the **.SILENT** target; ignores command errors with the **.IGNORE** target; preserves the print target in case of interruptions; and outputs an error message if there is not a dependency line, explicit or implied, for the target.

makefile

```
.SILENT:
.IGNORE:
.PRECIOUS: print

bookrec : main.o io.o
    cc main.o io.o -o $@

print : main.c io.c
    lp $?
    touch print

.DEFAULT:
    echo The target $@ does not exist.
```

```
$ make myindex
The target myindex does not exist.
```

There are other special targets, such as **.SUFFIXES**, that are described later. The **make** special targets are listed in the following table.

Target	Function
.DEFAULT: *Linux commands*	Execute if there is no dependency line for a specified target.
.IGNORE:	Ignore error values returned by Linux commands. Continue on with makefile execution.
.PRECIOUS: *targets*	Should **make** be interrupted, do not remove *targets* listed with **.PRECIOUS**.

Target	Function
.SILENT:	Do not display commands when executed.
.SUFFIXES: *suffixes*	Add *suffixes* to the list of valid suffixes referenced by suffix rules. If no suffixes are listed, erase the list of valid suffixes.

Suffix Rules

A suffix rule is a special dependency that specifies how files with different suffixes depend on each other. For example, the **main.c** file and the **main.o** file have the same name but different suffixes: .c and .o. A suffix rule for files ending in .c and .o would show how a **main.o** file depends on a **main.c** file. In other words, how you would use a **main.c** file to create a **main.o** file.

Suffix rules provide generality to the dependency line. Instead of applying to one specific set of files, a suffix rule applies to whole categories of files. The categories are determined by the suffixes. For example, you can write a suffix rule that applies to all files ending in .o and those ending in .c. Because of this generality, suffix rules can drastically reduce the number of dependency lines you may need in your makefile. This is particularly true of dependency lines that perform the same actions and differ only according to the name of the files specified. In previous makefile examples, the **main.o** and io.o dependency lines are identical in every respect except for the names of their files. Both perform the same action, specifying how a .o file depends on a .c file and how the **gcc** command creates the .o file. You can replace both of these dependency lines with one suffix rule that specifies the dependency of .o and .c files. Moreover, this suffix rule would apply to all files you may later add that end in .c and .o. You would not have to add any new dependency lines for them.

The target of a suffix rule consists of a sequence of two suffixes, each beginning with a period. The second suffix depends on the first suffix. The target for a suffix rule for .c and .o files would consist of the suffix .c followed by .o: .c.o. A .o file depends on a .c file. The syntax for a suffix rule follows.

```
.suf1.suf2:
    Linux command
```

Notice that the suffix rule has no list of dependent files following the colon. In a sense, the dependent files are those specified by the first suffix in the target, and the target file is the one specified by the second suffix. In the case of a **.c** and **.o** dependency, if you change a **.c** file and then execute **make**, the **.c.o** suffix rule would be activated and its Linux command executed. The **.c.o** suffix rule will be activated for each **.c** file that has been recently changed. However, each time you activate the rule, you need to be able to reference, in the Linux command, the particular **.c** file you are dealing with at the time. When the **.c.o** suffix rule is invoked for, say, the **main.c** file, you need to be able to reference the **main.c** file in the Linux command. The **$<** special variable evaluates to the name of the current dependent file that is causing the suffix rule to activate. For example, if you change your **main.c** file, then, in the **.c.o** suffix rule, **$<** will be set to **main.c**. If you change several **.c** files, then **$<** will be set in turn to each one as the suffix rule is invoked for them.

We can now construct a suffix rule for the source-code files and their object-code files. The target consists of the suffixes **.c** and **.o** and the Linux command consists of **the gcc -c** command with the **$<** special variable:

```
.c.o:
    gcc -c $<
```

In the next makefile example, the dependency lines for the **main.o** and **io.o** files are now replaced by the **.c.o** suffix rule. Notice that should you have a program consisting of many source-code files, you now need only one suffix rule to cover them all, instead of a dependency line for each one.

makefile

```
bookrec : main.o io.o
    cc main.o io.o -o bookrec

.c.o:
    cc -c $<

$ make
gcc -c main.c
gcc -c io.c
gcc main.o io.o -o bookrec
```

Another special variable used in suffix rules is **$***. This variable holds the name of the current target without its suffix. If the current target was **main.o** then the value of **$*** would be just "main". The variable is helpful when you need to specify the name of the target in the Linux command, without its extension. For example, if you want to make a backup copy of the object file, but give it the extension **.bak**, you could specify the target with **$*.o** and the backup name with **$*.bak**. Notice that the **$@** variable holds the full name of the target, whereas the **$*** variable only holds the target name without its suffix. In the next example, the backup command is added to the suffix rule. Using the following suffix rule in your makefile, an object-code file is copied after the source-code file is compiled.

```
.c.o:
    gcc -c $<
    cp  $*.o  $*.bak
```

Implied make Dependencies and the Standard Suffix Rules

The **make** utility has a standard set of suffix rules that automatically provide **make** with built-in dependencies. **make** automatically applies these rules to any files for which there are not explicit dependency lines. Using just the suffixes of files and the appropriate suffix rule, **make** can execute the appropriate Linux command. For example, if you do not specify a dependency line for the **main.o** file, then **make** will use the standard suffix rule for **.c** and **.o** files to determine that **main.o** depends on **main.c** and, if **main.c** is more recent, **make** will recompile **main.c**.

Creating Suffix Rules for Your Own Suffixes

Suppose that you want **make** to manage files that have a suffix that you made up. The suffix for a file can be any set of characters. For example, say you want to automatically back up your updated C source-code files. Your C files have the suffix **.c**, but you want to give the copies a suffix that you have made up yourself, **.bk** for backup. You now want to create a suffix rule that will copy updated C files automatically, giving the copies the suffix **.bk**. You can easily create such a suffix rule using the target **.c.bk**. However, before you can use the new suffix rules, you need to inform **make** that the new suffix is a valid suffix that can be applied to suffix rules. **make** maintains a list of valid suffixes, including the standard suffixes such as **.c** and **.o**. You can add to this list as many suffixes of your own as you want. You add a

suffix using a dependency line whose target is the special target
.SUFFIXES. You then list your new suffixes after the colon. Before
you create a suffix rule for the **.c** and **.bk** suffixes, you need to add
.bk to the suffix list using the **.SUFFIXES** target.

```
.SUFFIXES: .bk
```

You can now create a suffix rule for **.bk** files using the target **.c.bk**.
Notice the use of the special variables **$<** and **$@** to specify the
dependent file and the target file. **$<** holds the filename with the **.c**
extension; **$*** holds the filename without the **.bk** extension.

```
.c.bk:
    cp $< $@
```

In the next makefile example, the user adds the **.bk** suffix to the
list of valid suffixes and then adds the suffix rule for **.c.bk** files.
The actual backup file, in this case **main.bk**, is placed in the list of
dependent files in the **bookrec** dependency line.

makefile

```
.SUFFIXES: .bk

bookrec! : main.o io.o main.bk
        gcc main.o io.o -o bookrec

.c.o:
        cc -c $<

.c.bk:
      cp $< $@

$ touch main.c
$ make
gcc -c main.c
cp main.c main.bk
gcc main.o io.o -o bookrec
```

Library Dependencies and Standard Suffix Rule

There is also a special implied dependency for libraries and their
member files. **make** is able to compile and replace a member file
in an archive automatically for you. You only need to specify the
member with its library name on the dependency line. Specifying
a library member takes the form *library(member)*. The member file
is enclosed in parentheses and preceded by the library name. To

specify the **input.o** member of the **iolib.a** library, you enter
iolib.a(input.o). **make** will then use a special library suffix rule to
determine if the library member needs updating. If so, **make** will
recompile the source-code file for the library member and then,
using the **ar** command with the **r** option, will write the resulting
object-code file to the library file. For example, the **iolib.a** library
consists of the **input.o** and **print.o** files. In the next makefile
example, the user specifies both files as members of the **iolib.a**
library on the **bookrec** dependency line: **iolib.a(input.o)**
iolib.a(print.o). If you should change **input.c**, then, when you
execute **make**, **input.c** will be recompiled and the resulting
input.o file will be written to the **iolib.a** library.

makefile

```
bookrec : main.o iolib.a(input.o) iolib.a(print.o)
   ranlib iolib.a
   cc main.o iolib.a -o bookrec

$ touch input.c
$ make
gcc -c -O input.c
ar rv iolib.a input.o
a - input.o
rm -f input.o
ranlib iolib.a
gcc main.o iolib.a -o bookrec
```

Notice that the standard library suffix rule also removes the
object-code file after it has been copied to the library file. At this
point, the object-code file is no longer needed, since it has already
been added to the library.

The standard library suffix rule uses the special suffix **.a** to denote
library files. A library file does not actually have to have a **.a**
extension, though. The **.a** extension used in the target of the
library suffix rule applies to all library files, no matter what their
extension or whether they have one. In the library suffix target,
the **.a** is preceded by a **.c** indicating that the library file depends
on C source-code files, files with a **.c** extension. An example of a
standard library suffix rule follows.

```
.c.a:
   gcc -c $<
   ar rv $@ $%
   rm -f $%
```

The library suffix rule has three Linux commands. The first compiles the source-code file, creating an object-code file. In the **gcc** command, the **$<** variable references the current .c file that needs to be updated. For example, if the **print.c** file had been changed, then the value of **$<** would be **print.c**. The second command is an archive command that adds the object-code file to the library file. In the **ar** command, the **$@** variable holds the name of the target file, in this case the library file. If the target library is **iolib.a**, then the value of **$@** would be **iolib.a**. The **$%** variable holds the name of the library member that is being updated. If the **print.o** member file needed to be updated, then **$%** would hold that member name, **print.o**. In the last command, the **rm** command removes the object-code file. Again the **$%** variable holds the name of the member file. The **$%** variable is a special variable used only with library dependencies. You can use it either in dependency lines that have library members, or in the library suffix rule.

You can, if you wish, create your own library suffix rule using the .c.a target. Suppose, for example, you do not want the object-code file deleted after it is added to the library. In the next makefile example, the user creates a library suffix rule that does not delete the object-code file. It also suppresses the messages that each of the Linux commands would output by preceding them with an @ operator. Instead of the command outputs, the suffix rule prints a message saying which member file is being updated to which library.

makefile

```
bookrec : main.o iolib.a(input.o) iolib.a(print.o)
    ranlib iolib.a
    cc main.o iolib.a -o bookrec

.c.o:
    cc -c $<

.c.a:
@cc -c $<
@ar r $@ $%
@echo Member $% updated in library $@
```

Libraries and Directories

As you develop larger programs, you may end up using several libraries, each with its own set of source-code files. One way of keeping your libraries organized is to place them in their own directories. You could then create a separate makefile for each directory that updates that library. The makefile and source-code files for your main program would reside in their own directory. Though you could explicitly run each makefile in the library directories, you can also instruct your main makefile to change to those directories and execute the makefiles in them. For the next example, the user has created a directory called **iodir** in which is placed the files for the **iolib.a** library: **input.c** and **print.c**, as well as the **iolib.a** file. Within the **iodir** directory, the user creates a makefile consisting of one dependency line that is used to update members of the **iolob.a** library. In **iodir**'s parent directory resides the program source-code files, such as **main.c** and the executable file **bookrec**. The makefile in the parent directory, shown below, specifies two Linux commands for special targets that the user named **ilib**. The **ilib** target will always be out of date. Its dependency line holds the **cd** command that changes to the **iodir** directory, and a **make** command to execute the makefile in the **iodir** directory. Since **ilib** is always out of date, the library will always have its makefile run to check for any out-of-date members.

makefile

```
bookrec : main.o ilib
    cc main.o iodir/iolib.a -o bookrec

ilib:
    cd iodir ; make
```

makefile in iodir Library Directory

```
iolib.a:iolib.a(input.o)  iolib.a(print.o)
    ranlib iolib.a

$ touch iodir/input.c
$ make
cd iodir; make
gcc -c -O input.c
ar rv iolib.a input.o
r - input.o
rm -f input.o
ranlib iolib.a
gcc main.o iodir/iolib.a -o bookrec
```

Sometimes targets for programs and libraries in a makefile are separated so that you could independently update a library. In this case you would use a zero-length target consisting of a name you made up for use in the makefile. In the next makefile example, the target **ilib** is a name made up by the user to serve as a target for the dependency line that manages the **iolib.a** library. The user can now either update the library or compile the program by invoking **make** with either an **ilib** or **bookrec** argument. Notice, however, that the **bookrec** dependency line is no longer connected to the **ilib** dependency line. If you change a library member file, such as **print.c**, and then invoke **make** with the **bookrec** target to compile the program, the library is not going to update the changed member. To restore the connection, you need to create a new dependency line using **ilib** and **bookrec** as dependent files. The target can be any name you make up, such as the term **all**. Notice that in the makefile example, the **all** dependency line is the first one listed. When you enter **make** with no arguments, this will be the default. **make** will first update the library using the **ilib** dependency line, and then update the program using the **bookrec** dependency line. **ilib**, in turn, will change to the **iodir** directory and execute the makefile that updates the **iolib.a** library file.

makefile

```
all: ilib bookrec

bookrec : main.o iodir/iolib.a
    cc main.o iodir/iolib.a -o bookrec

ilib:
    cd iodir ; make iolib.a
```

makefile in iodir Library Directory

```
iolib.a:iolib.a(input.o) iolib.a(print.o)
    ranlib iolib.a
```

makefile Example

Bringing together all these features, we can now create a powerful makefile. In the next makefile example, the user first defines variables to hold different lists of filenames and compiler options. The different variables are then used throughout the dependency lines.

Two suffix rules follow, one for creating object-code files from C source-code files, and the other for updating libraries. The target for the object-code files is **.c.o**. The **$<** variable holds the name of the C source-code file that needs to be compiled. The target for the suffix rule for making libraries is **.c.a**. The out-of-date member's C source-code file is compiled, creating a new object-code file. The **$<** holds the name of the member's C source-code file, such as **print.c**. This object-code file is then written to the library using the **ar** command. The **$@** variable holds the name of the library, in this case **iolib.a**. The **$%** variable holds the name of the member to be written to the library, such as **print.o**. The @ operator preceding these commands suppresses their display as they are executed. Instead, a message is output telling which member is being updated in which library. You can, of course, do away with the suffix rules listed here, and rely on the standard suffix rules to determine how to update object-code files and libraries.

The dependency lines follow, beginning with the **bookrec** dependency line. In this line, both object-code files and libraries form the list of dependent files. Its Linux command uses the **cc** compiler to create an executable program called **bookrec**. The **$@** holds the name of the target, in this case **bookrec**. The **CC** variable is a builtin variable that holds the name of the compiler command, **gcc**.

The next two dependency lines lack any Linux commands. They will rely on suffix rules to update their targets. If **types.h** is out of date, then its target, **main.o**, needs to be updated and will make use of the suffix rule for updating **.o** files. The next dependency line makes the library **iolib.a** dependent on its members. Should the source code for any of its members be changed, then **iolib.a** will need to be updated. Since there is no Linux command, the suffix rule for updating libraries will be used.

The next dependency line is used to print source-code files that have been recently modified. Its target is the zero-length file called **print**. The C source-code files form the list of dependent files. The **$?** special variable in the **lp** command holds only the names of those files that were modified since the last printing. **$?** literally holds the filenames in the list of dependent files on a dependency line whose time stamp is more recent than that of the targets. Following the **lp** command, the **touch** command updates the print file. The @ operator preceding the **touch** command suppresses its display when it is executed.

Finally, the .**DEFAULT:** special target displays an error message
should the user specify a target that does not exist.

makefile

```
CFILES = main.c input.c print.c
OBJECTS = main.o
LIBS = iolib.a
IOLIBMEMS = iolib.a(input.o) iolib.a(print.o)
SYSLIBS = -lm
CFLAGS = -g -O
.c.o:
    $(CC) $(CFLAGS) -c $<

.c.a:
    @$(CC) $(CFLAGS) -c $<
    @ar r $@ $%
    @echo Member $% updated in library $@

bookrec : $(OBJECTS) $(LIBS)
$(CC) $(CFLAGS) $(OBJECTS) $(LIBS) $(SYSLIBS) -o $@

main.o: types.h

iolib.a: $(IOLIBMEMS)
    @ranlib iolib.a

print : $(CFILES)
lp $?
@touch print

.DEFAULT:
    @echo Unknown target $@
```

The Revision Control System: RCS

5

When you work on a major project, you are continually changing
source code. You may detect bugs or you may add other features.
Sometimes changes may unintentionally result in new bugs. A
record of all the changes to your program may help you track
down bugs and any possible design errors. The Revision Control
System (RCS) is a Linux utility that keeps track of all changes that

you have made to a program. In effect, RCS provides you with a set of prior versions of your program. You can view each version and examine the changes made in each.

RCS is very helpful in a situation in which a team of programmers is working on the same program. Each programmer may make changes to the program at different times. RCS can record each change a programmer makes and when it was made. It can even include notes about a change.

RCS stores an original version of a file and then records all changes to the file. Using this information it can generate any one of several possible versions of a file. RCS does not actually store separate full versions of a file. Instead it uses the change information and the original file to create a full version of the file.

A set of recorded changes to a file is called a *version*. Each version is assigned a version number that has several components, the first two of which are the release and level numbers. By default, the first version is assigned a release number of 1 and a level number of 1. A version is often referred to by its release and level numbers. The first version is called version 1.1 or delta 1.1. Subsequent versions will have the same release number with an incremented level number. The next version will be 1.2, then 1.3, etc. You can also change the release number manually.

Versions are usually generated sequentially. Each version holds all changes made in previous versions. However, you can create a branch version that is a modification of one of the particular versions. Changes made to a branch would not be included in later versions. A branch version has four elements: release, level, branch, and sequence. The release and level numbers reference a particular version. Then the branch specifies a branch of that version. The sequence number is the number of the version in that branch. Each branch can itself have several versions. In a sense, a branch can be thought of as starting a whole new sequence of versions. The branch number 1.1.1.1 references the first branch of the first version. 1.1.1.2 references that same branch but the second version in the branch. 1.1.2.1 references a second branch of the first version.

You can easily create extremely complex RCS files that have a multitude of releases, versions, and branches, each with their own versions and other branches. You should be careful to generate versions only as they are needed and maintain as simple a structure as possible.

Creating an RCS File

To create an RCS file, you first create an RCS directory. Within this directory are placed the RCS files for your programs. You can then create an RCS file with the **ci** command.

ci

```
ci -options filename
```

The **ci** command takes one argument, the name of the original file. The RCS file will be created in the RCS directory with the extension **,v**. A **main.c** file will have an RCS file called **main.c,v** in the RCS directory.

You can use the **-r** option to specify the release and version number you want to begin with when creating a new version, as shown here:

```
$ ci -r5.2 main.c
```

If your program is initially made up of several source-code files, you need to create an RCS file for each one, including its source code suffix. In the next example, the user creates an RCS file for the **main.c** program.

```
$ ci main.c
RCS/main.c,v <-- main.c
enter description, terminated with single '.' or end
of file:
NOTE: This is NOT the log message!
>> bookrec main program
>> .
initial revision: 1.1
done
```

Ordinarily, a project is worked on by several different programmers at once. Each would have access to, and make changes to, the source code.

rcs

```
rcs -options filename
```

You can use the **rcs** command with the **-a** option to restrict access to an RCS file. Attached to the **-a** option, type the login name of the user permitted to access this file. Use a **-a** option for each user permitted access. In the next example, access is restricted to larisa and mark.

```
$ rcs -amark -alarisa main.c
```

Should someone decide to drop out of the project, you can deny them access to the source code. The **rcs** command with the **-e** option removes a user from the list of users that have permission to access the file. In the next example, the user larisa no longer has access to the **main.c** code.

```
$ rcs -elarisa main.c
```

At times, you may decide that no further changes are to be made to a release. You can then lock the release with the **-l** and **-L** options. The **-l** option locks all other programmers from accessing the program, whereas the **-L** option locks all programmers and the creator of the file from the program. You can later unlock a version with the **-u** or **-U** option and the version number. The next example locks release 2. Any attempt to modify versions in release 2 will be denied. The version is then unlocked with the **-u** option.

```
$ rcs -l2 main.c
$ rcs -u2 main.c
```

Option	Description
-ausername	Add usernames to the list of users that can access a specified RCS file.
-eusername	Remove usernames from the list of users that can access a specified RCS file.
-lrelease	Lock a specific release for everyone but the creator of the file.
-urelease	Unlock a specific release.
-Lrelease	Lock a specific release for everyone including the creator of the file.
-Urelease	Unlock a specific release for everyone including the creator of the file.
-orelease	Delete a version from an RCS file.

Retrieving and Recording RCS Files

To edit your source-code file using RCS, you must first have RCS generate a copy of the source-code file. This copy will have the same name as the RCS file, but without the **,v** suffix. For the

main.c,v file, RCS will generate a file called **main.c**. To save the copy once you have made changes, you simply register any changes you make to the RCS file.

co

co *option filename*

The RCS **co** command generates a copy of the source-code file. The **co** command has several options. The **co** command with no options simply generates a read-only copy of the source-code file. The -l option generates a copy of the source-code file that you can edit. -l stands for lock, and when you use this option, the **main.c** program in the RCS **main.c,v** file is locked. No other programmers can access it, even if they would normally have access. This means that only one programmer at a time can change a given file. When finished, you check in the program, registering your changes and unlocking it for use by others.

In the next example, the **co** command generates an editable copy of the source-code file **main.c,v**.

```
$ co -l main.c
RCS/main.c,v  -->  main.c
revision 1.1 (locked)
done
```

ci

ci *filename*

Once you have finished editing your source-code file, you then register your changes in the RCS file with the **ci** command. You enter the keyword **ci** followed by the name of the RCS file. You are then prompted to enter comments. In effect, editing a copy of the file generated with **co** creates a new version of the source-code file, a new set of changes constituting a new version. The new version number (1.2) is displayed. In the next example, the user saves the changes to **main.c** by generating a new version, 1.2.

```
$ ci main.c
RCS/main.c,v <-- main.c
new revision: 1.2; previous revision: 1.1
enter log message, terminated with single '.' or end
of file:
>> Added prompts
>> .
done
```

You can use the **-r** option with the **ci** command to specify your own number for a new version, as described in the section "Retrieving and Removing Specific RCS Versions," later in this chapter.

rlog

rlog *option filename*

As you add more versions, it may help to have a list describing each one. The **rlog** command will print out the summaries of all the versions in the RCS file, giving you an idea of what each version is. Each summary has a header with the date and time; the user who created it; the version's sequence number; and the number of lines inserted, deleted, or unchanged. The comments for the version are then printed. Such information will give you a clear idea of how your program has progressed and changed from one version to the next.

```
$ rlog main.c
RCS file: RCS/main.c,v
Working file: main.c
head: 1.2
branch:
locks: strict
access list:
symbolic names:
keyword substitution: kv
total revisions: 2;   selected revisions: 2
description:
Calculation program
----------------------------
revision 1.2
date: 1999/11/07 22:52:41;  author: root;  state:
Exp;  lines: +1 -0
Added prompt
----------------------------
revision 1.1
date: 1999/11/07 22:50:20;  author: root;  state:
Exp;
Initial revision
==================================================
```

Option	Description
-r*version*	Output information about a specific version.
-d*date*	Output information about versions created on a specified date. (The format for the date is *yy/mm/dd* and *hh:mm:ss*. All except the year are optional.)

Option	Description
-d<*date*	Output information that is earlier than a specified date.
->d*date*	Output information that is later than a specified date.

Retrieving and Removing Specific RCS Versions

You can use the -r option with the **ci** command to specify your own number for a new version. You enter the version number attached to the -r option. In the next example, the user has specified a new version number with the -r option.

```
$ ci -r3 main.c
RCS/main.c,v <-- main.c
new revision: 3.1; previous revision: 1.2
enter log message, terminated with single '.'
or end of file:
>> A new version Number
>> .
done
```

You use the **co** command with the -l option to retrieve a specific version of a file. However, checking in that edited version with **ci** creates a branch version. The changes you make are saved in a branch of the version you retrieved. The original version remains unchanged. In the next example, the -r option retrieves version 1.1 and then **ci** creates a new branch of that version, 1.1.1.

```
$ co -l -r1.1 main.c
RCS/main.c,v  -->  main.c
revision 1.1 (locked)
done
```

```
$ ci main.c
RCS/main.c,v <-- main.c
new revision: 1.1.1.1; previous revision: 1.1
enter log message, terminated with single '.'
or end of file:
>> A new branch
>> .
done
```

You can then use **rlog** to see a list of all the versions and branches for a given file.

```
$ rlog main.c
RCS file: RCS/main.c,v
Working file: main.c
head: 3.1
branch:
locks: strict
access list:
symbolic names:
keyword substitution: kv
total revisions: 4;    selected revisions: 4
description:
Calculation program
----------------------------
revision 3.1
date: 1999/11/07 23:15:23;  author: root;
state: Exp;  lines: +1 -1
A new version Number
----------------------------
revision 1.2
date: 1999/11/07 22:52:41;  author: root;
state: Exp;  lines: +1 -0
added prompt
----------------------------
revision 1.1
date: 1999/11/07 22:50:20;  author: root;
state: Exp;
branches:  1.1.1;
Initial revision
----------------------------
revision 1.1.1.1
date: 1999/11/07 23:01:57;  author: root;
state: Exp;  lines: +1 -1
A new branch
================================
```

You can remove a version from the RCS file with the **rcs** command using the -**o** option. In the next example, version 3.1 is removed.

```
$ rcs -o3.1 main.c
```

make Suffix Rules for RCS Files

The **make** utility, described previously in this chapter, has several standard suffix rules for managing RCS files. **make** assumes that an RCS file corresponds to a source-code file and includes a source-code suffix, such as **.c**. For example, the RCS file for **main.c** is **main.c,v**, the **,v** being the suffix for RCS files. **make** will then use a standard suffix rule for the RCS file suffix to extract the source-code file using the RCS **co** command; then **make** will compile that source-code file to create an object-code file. In the case of files with a **.c,v** suffix, **make** will use the C compiler to create the object-code file. If the RCS file had a **.f,v** suffix, **make** would use the Fortran compiler.

In the next example, the user has only two RCS files in the directory, one for each source-code file in the program. The makefile consists of one dependency line for making the **bookrec** program. Since there are no dependency lines for making the object-code files, and there are no source-code files in the directory, **make** will use a standard RCS suffix rule to create the object-code files.

makefile

```
bookrec : main.o io.o
    cc main.o io.o -o bookrec OK
```

```
$ make
co main.c
gcc -O -c main.c
rm -f main.c
co  io.c
gcc -O -c io.c
rm -f io.c
gcc main.o io.o -o bookrec
```

Notice that the source-code file is immediately deleted by an RCS suffix rule. If a source-code file were to remain, then the next time you used **make**, that source-code file would be used instead of the RCS file.

An example of a standard RCS suffix rule for **.c** files follows. The **$<** variable holds the name of the RCS file, such as **main.c,v**. The

$* variable holds the name of the target without its suffix, such as **main** derived from the target **main.o**. Here the **$*** variable is used to construct the name of the C source-code file that ends with a **.c**. When the RCS suffix rule operates on the file **main.c**, the variable **$<** holds the name **main.c,v**, **$*** holds the name **main**, and **$*.c** constructs the name **main.c**.

```
.c,v.o:
   co $<
   gcc -O -c $*.c
   rm -f $*.c
```

The target for an RCS suffix rule consists of an RCS suffix followed by the suffix for the dependent file. The RCS suffix consists of a source-code suffix followed by a **,v**. The target for the suffix for the rule that compiles a **.c** file into a **.o** file using an RCS file is **.c,v.o**. For Fortran it is **.f,v.o**. For a library member the target is **.c,v.a**.

You can create your own suffix rule for your RCS files. If you are using C source-code files, you can use the target **.c,v.o**, and then specify your own commands. In the next makefile example, the suffix rule allows the user to extract a specific version from all the RCS files. The version number is held in the variable **SVER**.

```
.c,v.o:
   co   -r$(SVER) $<
   gcc -O -c $*.c
   rm -f $*.c
```

An RCS suffix is used in the next example to the **bookrec** program.

makefile

```
SVER = 1.2

bookrec : main.o io.o
   cc main.o io.o -o bookrec

.c,v.o:
   co -p -r$(SVER) $<
   cc -O -c $*.c
rm -f $*.c[
```

```
$ make
co  -r1.2 main.c
gcc -O -c main.c
rm -f main.c
gcc main.o io.o -o bookrec
```

RCS Suffix Rules for Header Files

make also has a standard suffix rule for header files, files with a **.h** suffix. You can maintain your header files in an RCS file that has a **.h** suffix, for example **types.h,v**. **make** will always extract the header file before it compiles the source-code files that depend on that header file. In the next example, **main.o** depends on **types.h**. The **types.h** file is extracted from the **types.h,v** RCS file before **main.o** is created.

5

makefile

```
bookrec : main.o io.o
    cc main.o io.o -o bookrec
    main.o: types.h
```

```
$ make
co  types.h,v
co  main.c
gcc -O -c main.c
rm -f main.c
gcc main.o io.o -o bookrec
```

Notice that the header file was not removed after it had been extracted and used. The reason for this is that several files may depend on **types.h**. Suppose both **main.o** and **io.o** depended on **types.h** as specified in a dependency line: **main.o io.o: types.h**. Should you need to update **main.o**, then the RCS suffix rule for header files would extract a copy of **types.h**. However, in doing so, the suffix rule has created a file, **types.h**, that is also more recent than **io.o**. It is as if you not only changed **main.c**, but also changed **types.h**. Since **io.o** also depends on **types.h**, it also will be recompiled—an unnecessary compilation since you never changed **io.c**. The current solution is to simply leave the most recently extracted **types.h** file in your directory. If you need to update **types.h** using the RCS file **types.h,v**, you can first remove the **types.h** file.

Online Manuals for Applications: man

As you develop a program for use on Linux, you may need to document it. If it is a large application worked on by several programmers at once, documentation may become essential. Documentation often takes the form of a manual describing different commands and features of a program. Many times an application is broken down into separate programs. It is very helpful to both users and program developers to be able to retrieve and display appropriate sections of an application's manual. Such an online manual provides instant access to documentation by all users and developers. The **man** command provides access to an online manual for Linux commands, and you can also use the **man** command to manage your own online manual for your own applications. You can create **man** documents using special **man** text-processing macros. You can then instruct the **man** command to read these documents.

One of the more common uses today of **gnroff** is the creation of online manual documents. The online manual that you find on your Linux system is actually a **gnroff** document. You use a set of macros called the **man** macros to create your own online manual entries. If you create a new command and want to document it, you can create a manual document for it and read this document with the **man** command.

When you call the **man** command with the name of a document, the **man** command uses **gnroff** to format the document and then display it. The actual document that you create is an unformatted text file with the appropriate **man** macros. The **man** macros are very similar to the **ms** macros. You can actually format and display a manual document directly by using the **gnroff** command with the -**man** option. In the next example, both commands display the manual document for the **ls** command.

```
$ man ls
$ gnroff -man /usr/man/man1/ls | more
```

man Document Files

You can create a **man** document file using any standard text editor. The name that you give to the text file is the name of the command or topic it is about, with a section number as an extension. The name of a document about the **who** command would be called **who.1**. In the example described here, the document is about the **bookrec** command and has a section number **1**. Its name is **bookrec.1**. Section numbers are discussed in the next section, "man Document Directories."

A **man** document is organized into sections with a running title at the top. The sections may be named anything you wish. By convention, a **man** document for Linux commands is organized into several predetermined sections, such as NAME, SYNOPSIS, and DESCRIPTION. You are, however, free to have as many sections as you want and to give them names of your own choosing. The actual document that you create is an unformatted text file with the appropriate **man** macros. A manual document requires at least two different **man** macros: .TH and **.SH**. .TH provides a running title that will be displayed at the top of each page of the document as well as the document's section number. You use the **.SH** macro for each section heading. You can add other macros as you need them, such as a **.PP** macro for paragraph formatting, or an **.IP** macro for indented paragraphs.

You enter a macro in your document at the beginning of a line, preceded by a period. Any text that you enter in the lines after the macro will be formatted by it. A macro stays in effect until another macro is reached. Some macros, like **.SH** and **.TH**, take arguments. You enter in arguments after the macro on the same line. The **.SH** macro takes as its argument the name of a section. You enter the section name on the same line as the **.SH** macro. The body of the section then follows. The body of the section text is entered in as a series of short lines. These lines will later be formatted by **man** into a justified paragraph. In the next example, the user enters a **.SH** macro and follows it with the section name DESCRIPTION. In the following lines, the user enters the text of the section.

```
.SH DESCRIPTION
myulistopt provides alternative ways
of displaying your grocery list.
You can display it with numbers, dates, or save
the list in a file.
```

Your **man** document is organized into a series of section-heading macros with their names and text. The template below gives you an idea of how to organize your **man** document. It is the organization usually followed by the online manual for Linux commands.

```
.TH COMMAND    Section -number
.SH NAME
 Command and brief description of function.
.SH SYNOPSIS
 Command and options.  Each option is encased in
brackets.  This section is sometimes called
the SYNTAX.
.SH DESCRIPTION
 Detailed description of command and options.  Use
paragraph macros for new paragraphs: PP, LP, and IP.
.SH OPTIONS
 Options used for the command.
.SH EXAMPLES
 Examples of how a command is used.
.SH FILE
 Files used by the command.
.SH "SEE ALSO"
 References to other documentation or manual documents.
.SH DIAGNOSTICS
 Description of any unusual output.
.SH WARNINGS
 Warnings about possible dangerous uses of the command.
.SH BUGS
 Surprising features and bugs.
```

Within the text of a section, you can add other macros to perform specific text-processing operations. You enter these macros on lines by themselves. Some will also take arguments. The **.PP** macro starts a new paragraph. The **.IP** macro starts an indented paragraph and is usually used to display options. You enter in the option as an argument to the **.IP** macro and then the following text is indented from it. The **.I** macro underlines text. The **.B** macro will boldface text. Both the **.B** macro and **.I** macro take as their argument the word you want to boldface or underline. By convention, the command name and options in the **NAME** section are set in boldface with the **.B** macro. Any other use of command names is usually underlined with the **.I** macro. One final note, if you use any hyphens, you need to quote them with a backslash. The macros for the **man** utility are listed here:

Macro	Function
.TH *title* *section-number*	Enter running title of the online document.
.SH *section-name*	Enter section headings.
.B *word*	Boldface words such as command names.
.I *word*	Underline text.
.IP *option*	Format indented paragraph; enter options in the OPTIONS section.
.PP	Format paragraph; start new paragraph.

In the next example, the user creates an online document for the **bookrec** program described earlier. Notice how the text is formatted into justified paragraphs. The options are displayed using indented paragraphs specified by the **.IP** macro.

bookrec.1: man Document File

```
.TH    BOOKREC    1
.SH NAME
bookrec  \-Input and display a book record
.SH SYNOPSIS
.B bookrec
[ \-t ] [ \-p] [ \-f]
.SH DESCRIPTION
.I  bookrec
 allows the user to input a title and price
for a book.  Then both elements
of the record are displayed.
.SH  OPTIONS
.IP t
Display only the title.
.IP p
Display only the price.
.IP f
Save the record to a file.
.SH FILES
  The command uses no special files.
.SH "SEE ALSO"
    printbook (1)
.SH DIAGNOSTICS
 Date output has the form of m/d/y.
```

```
.SH BUGS
 The program can only read and display one record.
.br
 It does not as yet allow you to read records
from a file.
```

Output of bookrec1

```
BOOKREC (1)                                    BOOKREC (1)

 NAME
bookrec  -  Input and display a book record

 SYNOPSIS
. bookrec  [ -t ]  [ -p ]  [ -f ]

 DESCRIPTION
bookrec allows the user to input a title and
price for a book.  Then both elements of the
record are displayed.

 OPTIONS
-t    Display only the title.

-p    Display only the price.

-f    Save the record to a file.

 FILES
The command uses no special files.
 SEE ALSO
 printbook (1)
 DIAGNOSTICS
 Date output has the form of m/d/y.
 BUGS
The program can only read and display one record.
 It does not as yet allow you to read records from
 a file.
```

man Document Directories

The **man** utility looks for a particular manual document in a
system directory set aside for manual documents, such as

/usr/man. The **/usr/man** directory itself does not contain manual documents. Rather, it contains subdirectories called *section directories*, which in turn contain the documents. The name of a section directory begins with the word **man** and ends with the section number. **man1** is the name of the first section directory in a manual. There are usually about seven section directories, beginning with **man1** and ending with **man7**. In your own manual directory you can have as many or as few section directories as you want, though you always have to have a **man1** directory.

Section directories allow you to create several documents of varying complexity and subject matter for the same command or topic. For example, the document in section 1 for the **man** command gives only a general description, whereas the document in section 7 for the **man** command lists all the **man** macros. These documents are identified by section numbers and reside in the appropriate section directory. The section number of a document, as noted previously, is entered in as an argument to the **.TH** macro. To retrieve an online document from a particular section, enter in the section number before the command name. The next example displays the document on the **bookrec** command that is in the third section directory. If you enter no section number, the first section is assumed.

```
$ man 3 bookrec
```

When creating your own manual directory, you need to add in section directories. Within the section directories you can then place the **man** documents that you have created. At a minimum, you need to have a **man1** section directory. The **man** command will always look for a section directory, and if none is specified, will choose **man1**. In the next example, the user creates a directory called **man** in the user's home directory, in this case **/home/chris/man**. Within the **man** directory the user creates a section directory called **man1** and then copies in the document **bookrec.1** to it.

```
$ mkdir man
$ cd man
$ mkdir man1
$ cp ../bookrec.1 man1
$ cd man1
$ pwd
/home/chris/man/man1
$ ls
bookrec.1
```

To have the **man** utility retrieve a manual document from your
own manual directory, you can use the -**M** option with that
directory path name. The -**M** option instructs **man** to search a
local directory for a **man** directory. You enter the local directory's
path name on the command line after the -**M** option. In the next
example, the user looks for a manual document in the user's own
directory: **/home/chris/man**.

```
$ man -M $HOME/man bookrec
```

Instead of having to explicitly specify your own **man** directory,
you can have **man** automatically search it by adding the path
name to your **MANPATH** special variable. You follow the same
rules for assigning new values as for any shell special variable.
You may want to place this assignment in your initialization file
so that your own **man** directory will be automatically added to
MANPATH each time you log in. The assignment syntax differs
in the BASH and TCSH shells. In the BASH shell, as illustrated
below, any new added directories are separated by a colon:

```
$ MANPATH=$MANPATH:/$HOME/man
```

In the TCSH shell, as illustrated below, any new directories are
added as elements in a TCSH shell array. Such an assignment
should be placed in your **.cshrc** initialization file.

```
% setenv MANPATH ($MANPATH  /$HOME/man)
```

Using **MANPATH**, the **man** command will search all system
manual directories, as well as your own. Should you want to
restrict **man** to search only your own **man** directories when
looking for your own online documents, you can do so by simply
creating your own variation of the Linux **man** command. In the
next example, the user creates a shell script **myman** consisting of
the **man** command and the -**M** option with a specified local **man**
directory. The script will only search for manual documents in
that directory.

myman
```
man -M $HOME/man $1
```

```
$ myman bookrec
```

Chapter 6
Gnome Programming

Gnome programming involves a very extensive set of functions and structures contained in many libraries, making up the different components that go into creating a Gnome application. This chapter can only provide a general overview of these libraries and how you use them to create Gnome programs. Gnome applications make use of Gnome, Gnome Toolkit, Gnome Drawing Kit, and GNU libraries. For detailed descriptions of the functions, definitions, and structures contained in these libraries, it is strongly recommended that you use the extensive documentation available on the Gnome developer's Web site at **developer.gnome.org**. The Documentation section includes detailed tutorials, manuals, and reference works, including the complete reference for the Gnome, GTK, and GDK APIs.

Gnome applications are created using functions provided by the Gnome libraries. Many of these make use of functions in the GTK+ libraries as well as the Glib libraries. The Gnome libraries provide the highest-level function used in Gnome applications. Below them are the GTK+ libraries. GTK+ is the toolkit developer for the GNU Image Manipulation Program (GIMP). GTK+ is made up of the Gimp Toolkit (GTK) and Gimp Drawing Kit (GDK) libraries. GTK contains the functions and structures to manage widgets and user interface tasks. These can be accessed directly in any Gnome program. In fact, a Gnome application is a GTK program with Gnome library functions. GTK functions and structures are C++ program objects, designed to be used in a C++ style program. GDK, in turn, contains lower-level functions that are used to connect GTK to the Xlib libraries. The Xlib libraries hold functions that perform the actual X Window System operations. Both GTK and Gnome also make use of the standard C functions provided by the Glib library. Table 6-1 lists the different Gnome components.

Though developed in ANSI C, there are wrappers available in other languages for the Gnome and Gtk+ libraries. There are wrappers for most languages including Ada, Scheme, Python, Perl, Dylan, Objective C, and, of course, C++.

In addition, Gnome applications also make use of ORBit and Imlib. ORBit is a version of the Common Object Request Broker Architecture (CORBA). With it, programs can locate and request

Gnome libs	High-level gnome functions
GTK	Widgets and GUI functions
GDK	Low-level wrapper for Xlib
Xlib	X Window operations
Glib	GNU C library of standard functions

Table 6-1. Gnome Components

services from an object, even one located across a network. For example, an editor could request the use of a spreadsheet. Imlib (Image Library) contains functions for managing images in various formats, letting you display, scale, save, and load images into your program.

Gnome Libraries

With the Gnome libraries, applications can have the same kind of GUI interface with the same look and feel. Though a Gnome application is a GTK program with Gnome library functions, the Gnome library provides several complex higher-level widgets as well as many simple operations not in the GTK+ libraries. Table 6-2 lists the Gnome libraries.

Libgnome and libgnomeui are the two main libraries needed for any Gnome applications. Libgnome is a set of functions designed to be independent of any particular toolset. These functions could be used in any kind of program, whether it be one with just a command line interface or even no interface. These functions are independent of any particular GUI toolkit. The libgnomeui library contains functions that provide GUI interface operations. These are tied to a particular GUI toolset, such as the GTK toolset. It is possible to create a libgnomeui library that is tied to a different GUI toolset.

The libgnome library provides many utility routines related to the Gnome desktop environment. Among the capabilities provided are config file support for applications to store persistent data, support for metadata (data attached to file objects, like the icon to display for a particular file type), and support for loading help documents into the GNOME help browser. An interface is also provided so GNOME applications can talk to the GNOME session manager. Finally, routines exist to configure how different MIME types are handled by GNOME and the GNOME file manager.

GNOME applications use the libgnomeui library extensively. This library contains toolkit extensions to the GTK+ widget set. Users can easily create dialog boxes and message boxes, as well as menu bars, toolbars, and status lines. An extensive array of stock icons is provided for the programmer's use in dialog boxes, menu entries, and buttons. Because all GNOME applications will use libgnomeui to create these common GUI elements, visual consistency is guaranteed. Another important capability provided is the GNOME canvas, which allows painless creation of complex interfaces. Similar in many ways to the Tk canvas, the GNOME canvas provides a framework to create address books, calendar applications, and spreadsheets.

The libaudiofile library can read a wide variety of audio file formats (AIFF, AIFC, WAV, and NeXT/Sun au). Once samples have been loaded using libaudiofile, libesd routines are available to play these samples via the Esound sound daemon. The Esound sound daemon allows several processes to access the sound hardware simultaneously.

GUI applications require extensive use of images to create a friendly and comfortable user interface. Traditionally, it has been difficult to load all the common graphic file formats into X11 applications. The libbgdk_imlib library addresses this issue by providing convenient and powerful functions to load multiple file formats (JPEG, GIF, TIFF, PNG, XPM, PPM, PGM, PBM, and BMP). These files are converted to an internal 24-bit RGB representation, and utility functions exist to scale as well as render from 24-bit RGB to a variety of other color depths (with dithering if desired). Input image files are cached internally by libbgdk_imlib to improve performance in applications that repeatedly use images.

The libgtk library is the GIMP Toolkit library. It is a professional-quality widget set that in many ways is superior to other widget sets. GNOME applications are written entirely using libgtk for all GUI elements (buttons, menus, scroll bars, etc.). Libgnorba provides support or CORBA operations such as obtaining references to objects and requesting new instances of an object. Libzvt is a simple library containing a terminal widget. Libar_lgpl holds graphic functions that can be used with the GnomeCanvas widget.

libaudiofile	Read a wide variety of audio file formats (AIFF, AIFC, WAV, and NeXT/Sun au). Libesd routines are available to play these samples via the Esound sound daemon.
libgdk_imlib	Functions to load multiple file formats (JPEG, GIF, TIFF, PNG, XPM, PPM, PGM, PBM, and BMP).
libgtk	GIMP Toolkit library. GNOME applications are written entirely using libgtk for all GUI elements (buttons, menus, scroll bars, etc.).
libgnome	Utility routines for the GNOME desktop environment such as configuration, help, MIME types, session management, toolkit independent.
libgnomeui	Toolkit extensions to the GTK+ widget set for creating dialog boxes and message boxes, menu bars, toolbars, status lines, etc. Includes icons for use in dialog boxes, menu entries, and buttons. Also provides the GNOME canvas for the easy creation of complex interfaces such as address books, calendar applications, and spreadsheets. This is a toolkit-dependent library currently using the Gimp Toolkit.
libgnorba	Library for using ORBit CORBA implementation with Gnome.
libzvt	Library containing terminal widget.
Libart_lgpl	Graphic functions used for GnomeCanvas.

Table 6-2.   Gnome Libraries

Compiling Gnome Programs

Given the extensive number of libraries involved in creating Gnome applications, the compiler command with all its listed libraries and flags can be a very complex operation to construct. For this reason, Gnome provides the gnome-config script. You place a call to this script as an argument to the compiler operation instead of manually listing Gnome libraries and flags. gnome-config takes two options, –cflags and –libs. The –cflags option will generate all the flags you need and the –libs options generates the list of needed Gnome libraries. You do need to specify the libraries you want to use, such as gnomeui and gnome, as shown here:

```
gnome-config --cflags --libs gnome gnomeui
```

For the compiler operation, you would place the gnome-config operation in back quotes to execute it:

```
gcc myprog.c -o myprog `gnome-config --cflags --libs
gnome gnomeui`
```

To simplify matters, you can place this operation in a **Makefile**. Recall that in a **Makefile** the compiling is performed separately from the linking. For compiling, you would use gnome-config with the –cflags option and for linking use the –libs option. In the following example, CFLAGS and LDFLAGS macros are used to hold the compiling and linking results, respectively. Notice the use of back quotes in the code below:

```
CFLAGS=`gnome-config --cflags gnome gnomeui`
LDFLAGS=`gnome-config --libs gnome gnomeui`

all: bookrec

bookrec: file.o calc.o
        cc $(LDFLAGS) main.o -o bookrec
main.o: main.c
        cc $(CFLAGS) main.c
file.o: file.c file.h
        cc $(CFLAGS) file.c
```

Gnome Program Example

The following is a simple Gnome application for the Hello World program. Gnome functions begin with the term "gnome," whereas GTK functions begin with "gtk." Notice that the initialization function is a Gnome function, gnome_init. Gnome programs are event-driven. You first define your objects, such as windows, then set their attributes and the bind signals from events like mouse clicks to given objects like windows and to functions that process these events. Such functions are often referred to as callback functions.

To compile a Gnome program, you start up Gnome, open a terminal window, and execute the **compile** command at the shell

6

prompt. Then, you execute the program from within the terminal window and it will show up on your Gnome interface. The following **hello1.c** program creates a simple window with a button that displays a message on the standard output of your terminal window. When the user clicks the Close box (delete_event), the window closes. The first gtk_signal_connect connects the application with a delete_event signal, which occurs when the user clicks the Close box. This executes the closeprog function, which uses gtk_main_quit to end the program. The second gtk_signal_connect connects the button to the mouse click event (clicked) and then executes the hello function. Whenever the user clicks the button, "Hello World" is displayed on the standard output. See the section on GTK for a more detailed analysis of gtk_signal_connect and other GTK functions.

Gtk_widget_show_all shows all the displays the widgets that have been defined and set up. Then, gtk_main starts an infinite loop that constantly checks for any of the bound signals (like mouse clicks) and executes their associated functions, for example closeprog for a closebox click.

```c
#include <gnome.h>

    void hellomessage( GtkWidget *widget, gpointer
data )
    {
        g_print ("Hello World\n");
    }

    gint closeprog ( GtkWidget *widget, GdkEvent
                    *event, gpointer   data )
    {
        gtk_main_quit();
    }

    int main( int   argc, char *argv[] )
    {
        GtkWidget *app;
        GtkWidget *mybutton;

        gnome_init ("", "0.1", argc, argv);

        mybutton = gtk_button_new_with_label
                        ("Click Me");
        app = gnome_app_new ("Hello-World",
                            "Hello App");
```

```
gnome_app_set_contents (GNOME_APP (app),
                        mybutton);
gtk_signal_connect (GTK_OBJECT (app),
            "delete_event", GTK_SIG NAL_FUNC
            (closeprog),NULL);
gtk_signal_connect (GTK_OBJECT (mybutton),
              "clicked", GTK_SIGNAL_FUNC
              (hellomessage), NULL);
gtk_widget_show_all(app);
gtk_main ();

return(0);
}
```

To compile this program you would use the following compiling
command in a Gnome terminal window. Then, just enter
hello to run it. The –o option specifies the name of the program,
in this case hello. Be sure to use back quotes for the gnome-
config segment.

```
gcc hello.c -o hello `gnome-config --cflags --libs
gnome gnomeui`
```

You will usually be integrating GTK functions into Gnome
programs. In the following program, the Hello program is modified
to use a window to display the hello message. The GTK functions
used here are explained in more detail in the section on GTK.

```
#include <gnome.h>

gint closeprog( GtkWidget *widget, GdkEvent   *event,
                               gpointer   data )
    {
        gtk_main_quit();
    }

void hellowin( GtkWidget *widget,GdkEvent *event,
                               gpointer   data )
    {
        GtkWidget *mywindow;
        GtkWidget *label;

        mywindow = gtk_window_new
                        (GTK_WINDOW_TOPLEVEL);
        gtk_container_set_border_width (GTK_CONTAINER
                        (mywindow), 10);
        label = gtk_label_new("Hello World\n");
        gtk_container_add (GTK_CONTAINER (mywindow),
```

6

```
label);
        gtk_widget_show (label);
        gtk_widget_show (mywindow);
    }

    int main( int    argc, char *argv[] )
    {
        GtkWidget *mybutton;
        GtkWidget *app;

        gnome_init ("Hellowin", "0.1", argc, argv);
        app = gnome_app_new ("Hellowin", "Hello
                             World Window");
        gtk_signal_connect (GTK_OBJECT (app),
                    "delete_event", GTK_SIGNAL_FUNC
                    (closeprog), NULL);
        mybutton = gtk_button_new_with_label
                    ("Click Me");
      gtk_signal_connect (GTK_OBJECT(mybutton),
     "clicked", GTK_SIGNAL_FUNC (hellowin), NULL);
        gnome_app_set_contents (GNOME_APP (app),
                            mybutton);
        gtk_container_set_border_width (GTK_CONTAINER
        (app), 10);
         gtk_widget_show_all(app);
        gtk_main ();
        return(0);
    }
```

libgnome Libraries

The libgnome library provides nontoolkit-specific functions for
operations such as reading configuration files, handling the gnome
.desktop files, managing mime types, sound operations, etc. All of
these are GUI-independent operations. You can use them in
applications that use a different GUI interface, like KDE, to let them
work more easily with other Gnome applications. The various kinds
of functions you can find in this library are listed in Table 6-3.

Configuration

The gnome-config functions let you store configuration information
to files for easy access. Each function begins with the term
"gnome-config." There are functions for accessing information,
saving information, and managing information. The functions all
take as their argument a relative path name for a file. The file,

gnome-config	Simple access to configuration values
gnome-defs	GNOME definitions for C++ linking
gnome-dentry	Manipulation of **.desktop** files
gnome-exec	Execution of programs from GNOME applications
gnome-fileconvert	File format conversion functions
gnome-help	Routines for displaying help
gnome-history	Keeping track of recently used documents
gnome-i18n	Support for localization and internationalization
gnome-metadata	File metadata information storage
gnome-mime-info	Routines to get information bound to a MIME type
gnome-mime	Routines to find out the MIME type of a file
gnome-paper	Paper dimensions, printing unit conversions
gnome-popt	Command line argument parser
gnome-regex	Regular expression cache implementation
gnome-remote	User preference routines for executing commands on a remote host
gnome-score	Tracking score for games
gnome-sound	Sound-playing routines for GNOME applications
gnome-triggers	Hierarchical signal mechanism for application events
gnome-url	Launch viewers for documents based on their URL
gnome-util	Miscellaneous utility functions for GNOME and C programs
libgnome	Non-GUI part of the GNOME library

Table 6-3.   Gnome Library

along with its specified directory, is assumed to be located in the user's **.gnome** directory, ~/**.gnome**.

You read configuration data using the gnome_config_get functions. There is a particular function for each type of data you want to retrieve. Each function begins with the term gnome_config_get and ends with the type of data to be accessed. For example, gnome_config_get_int retrieves integer data and gnome_config_get_vector retrieves string data. You can specify a default to be returned by entering it after an = sign following the path name. The default is returned if the data is not found.

```
char *text;
text = gnome_config_get_string("/example/sec-
tion/text=TEXT");
```

You write configuration information using the gnome_config_set functions. Like the gnome_cponfig_get functions, there are particular functions for each type of data you want to store. Any specified directories that do not exist will be automatically created. To actually write to the files, you use the gnome_config_sync command.

```
char *text;
gnome_config_set_string("/example/sec-
tion/text",text);
gnome_config_sync();
```

To delete a configuration file you use the gnome_config_clean_file function. When you run gnome_config_sync again, the file will be deleted. If you want to cancel changes (quit without saving), use the gnome_config_drop_file.

To provide some security from other users, you can store information in the ~/.**gnome_private** directory instead of the ~/.**gnome** directory. To do this, you use functions with the term "private" in them such as gnome_config_private_set_string. There are corresponding private functions for the gnome_config_get and gnome_config_set functions. However, for some tasks you use the same functions, such as gnome_config_sync.

You can modify the default path using the gnome_config_push_prefix function. This functions adds a pathname to the ~/.**gnome** path and lets you use this extended path name as the default. This is helpful if you are performing several read and write operations from the same file. To remove the path name, use the gnome_config_pop_prefix function.

.desktop

The .**desktop** directory contains files that provide configuration information about applications on your desktop and Applications menu. The configuration files are in the gnome-config format, and these functions are used to read and write to them. To manage these files, you use the gnome_desktop_entry functions. These make use of a GnomeDesktopEntry structure into which the data in a configuration file can be loaded. The gnome_desktop_entry_load function loads data from a file into a GnomeDesktopEntry structure, and the gnome_desktop_entry_launch function will start an application specified in the GnomeDesktopEntry structure given as its argument.

Files

There are also several functions for managing files. A group of functions is designed to extract the full path name of files used in the Gnome installation. For example, gnome_libdir_file returns the full path name of a file in the library directory and gnome_datadir_file returns the full path of a file in the data directory. In addition, there are several Glib-like functions for performing simple file operations such as g_file_exits which detect if a file exists. g_concat_dir_and_file attaches a file name to a directory path with an intervening /. To check for a MIME type of a file, you use the gnome_mime_type function. It tries to detect the MIME type from the file name. You can select a default MIME type using the gnome_mime_type_or_default function.

With the gnome-metadata functions, you can save data that you want associated with a particular file name. The gnome_metadata_set function stores data associated with a file name and gnome_metadata_get retrieves it. Other functions record actions that have been taken on a file such as gnome_metadata_copy for file copy operations, gnome_metadata_delete for deletions, and gnome_metadata_rename for a rename file.

Gnome User Interface Library: libgnomeui

The libgnomeui library contains the functions and structures you need to create Gnome user interfaces for your applications. It contains many functions for performing standard user interface tasks, including session management and utilities. The library also contains the GnomeCanvas widget designed to make GUI operations easy to do, rather than resorting to lower-level GTK+ functions. The various kinds of functions you can find in this library are listed in Table 6-4.

gnome-app-helper	Simplified menu and toolbar creation
gnome-app-util	Utility functions for manipulating GnomeApp container widgets
gnome-canvas-util	Auxiliary canvas functions
gnome-dialog-util	Convenience functions for making dialog boxes
gnome-dns	Nonblocking name resolver interface
gnome-geometry	Window geometry utility functions
gnome-ice	Integrates the ICE library with the GTK+ event loop
gnome-icon-text	Text-wrapping functions for icon captions
gnome-init	Initialize GNOME libraries
gnome-mdi-session	Routines providing GnomeMDI state saving and restoration
gnome-popup-help	A pop-up help system for GtkWidgets
gnome-popup-menu	Routines for attaching pop-up menus to widgets
gnome-preferences	Fetching and setting GNOME preferences
gnome-properties	Deprecated/experimental/unfinished
gnome-property-entries	Deprecated/experimental/unfinished
gnome-startup	Internal routines for session management
gnome-types	Some global types used by the GNOME libraries
gnome-uidefs	Useful GNOME macros
gnome-winhints	Manipulate GNOME-specific window manager hints
gtkcauldron	Produce gtk/Gnome dialog boxes from format strings

Table 6-4.   Gnome User Interface Library

Gnome App, Toolbar, and Menu Widgets

The GnomeApp widget is the basic widget for Gnome applications. This widget is the main window holding menus, toolbars, and data. You use the gnome_app_new function to create a new GnomeApp widget. It takes as its argument the name of the application. To add elements like toolbars, menus, and status bars, you just use the appropriate function. For example, to add a menu you use gnome_app_set_menus, and to add a status bar you use gnome_app_set_statusbar. To add just a single toolbar, you use gnome_app_set_toolbar, and to add multiple toolbars you use gnome_app_add_toolbar. A listing of Gnome widgets is provided later in Table 6-8.

With the gnome-app-helper functions, you can generate menus and toolbars automatically using GnomeUIInfo structures. For toolbars and menus, you can create structures with the appropriate values and then use gnome_app_create_menus to create menus and gnome_app_create_tool-bars to create toolbars.

For simple menu entries you can use one of many macros. Table 6-5 lists the Gnome menu macros. With the GNOMEUIINFO_ITEM macro, you can add an item to a menu. The GNOMEUIINFO_SEPARATOR adds a separator line and the GNOMEUIINFO_END specifies the end of a menu. In the following example label is the text of the label, tooltip is the tooltip when the pointer moves over that item, and callback is the function that is executed when the user presses that item. You can add another argument for an icon image if you want an icon displayed in the menu item. This is usually a **.xpm** image.

To specify an accelerator key for a particular item, you just place an underscore before the letter in the label for the key you want to use. An accelerator key is an alternative key you can use to access the menu item. This is usually an ALT key. In the following example, the menu item will have an Exit label with the "x" underlined, indicating that you can use an ALT-X key combination to access this item.

```
    GNOMEUIINFO_ITEM("E_xit", "Exit the pro-
gram", exitfunc),
```

The macro generates the values to be used in a GnomeUIInfo structure. You can assign these values to such a structure. In the following example, a menu is created consisting of an array of

GnomeUIInfo structures. GnomeUIInfo macros are used to assign values to each GnomeUIInfo structure in this array. In this example, a simple File menu is created with two entries, one for Open and one for Exit. A line separator will be displayed between them.

```
GnomeUIInfo file_menu[] = {
        GNOMEUIINFO_ITEM("_Open", "Open a document",
                         openfunc),
        GNOMEUIINFO_SEPARATOR,
        GNOMEUIINFO_ITEM("E_xit", "Exit the
                         program", exitfunc),
        GNOMEUIINFO_END
        };
```

A number of macros are provided for standard menu items like the Save and Open entries in a File menu. These take as their arguments the function to be executed when the item is selected (cb) and any icon image you want displayed for the entry (data).

```
GNOMEUIINFO_MENU_OPEN_ITEM(cb, data)
```

The following example creates the same simple File menu as in the previous example, but uses specialized macros to create each item. Here, the GNOMEUIINFO _MENU_EXIT_ITEM macro creates the Exit entry for the menu:

```
GnomeUIInfo file_menu[] = {
        GNOMEUIINFO_MENU_OPEN_ITEM(openfunc),
        GNOMEUIINFO_SEPARATOR,
        GNOMEUIINFO_MENU_EXIT_ITEM(exitfunc),
        GNOMEUIINFO_END
        };
```

For submenus and for menus added to your menu bar, you use the GNOMEUIINFO_SUBTREE(label, tree) macro, where tree is the array of GnomeUIInfo structures to be used for that submenu. The following example assigns the File menu defined earlier and an Edit menu to a menu bar. Again, these are GnomeUIInfo structures for which the macros generate values. Notice the use of underscores in the labels to designate ALT keys to use to access the menus.

```
GnomeUIInfo menubar[] = {
        GNOMEUIINFO_SUBTREE("_FILE", file_menu),
        GNOMEUIINFO_SUBTREE("_EDIT", edit_menu),
        GNOMEUIINFO_END
    };
```

For particular menus on a menu bar you use the menu TREE macros as shown in Table 6-5. The tree argument is the array of GnomeUIInfo structures for the menu. For example, the File menu

File Menu	Description
GNOMEUIINFO_MENU_NEW_ITEM(label, hint, cb, data)	"New" menu item (you need to provide label and hint yourself here)
GNOMEUIINFO_MENU_OPEN_ITEM(cb, data)	"Open" menu item
GNOMEUIINFO_MENU_SAVE_ITEM(cb, data)	"Save" menu item
GNOMEUIINFO_MENU_SAVE_AS_ITEM(cb, data)	"Save as..." menu item
GNOMEUIINFO_MENU_REVERT_ITEM(cb, data)	"Revert" menu item
GNOMEUIINFO_MENU_PRINT_ITEM(cb, data)	"Print" menu item
GNOMEUIINFO_MENU_PRINT_SETUP_ITEM(cb, data)	"Print Setup" menu item
GNOMEUIINFO_MENU_CLOSE_ITEM(cb, data)	"Close" menu item
GNOMEUIINFO_MENU_EXIT_ITEM(cb, data)	"Exit" menu item

6

Edit Menu	
GNOMEUIINFO_MENU_CUT_ITEM(cb, data)	"Cut" menu item
GNOMEUIINFO_MENU_COPY_ITEM(cb, data)	"Copy" menu item
GNOMEUIINFO_MENU_PASTE_ITEM(cb, data)	"Paste" menu item
GNOMEUIINFO_MENU_SELECT_ALL_ITEM(cb, data)	"Select" menu item
GNOMEUIINFO_MENU_CLEAR_ITEM(cb, data)	"Clear" menu item
GNOMEUIINFO_MENU_UNDO_ITEM(cb, data)	"Undo" menu item
GNOMEUIINFO_MENU_REDO_ITEM(cb, data)	"Redo" menu item
GNOMEUIINFO_MENU_FIND_ITEM(cb, data)	"Find" menu item
GNOMEUIINFO_MENU_FIND_AGAIN_ITEM(cb, data)	"Find Again" menu item
GNOMEUIINFO_MENU_REPLACE_ITEM(cb, data)	"Replace" menu item
GNOMEUIINFO_MENU_PROPERTIES_ITEM(cb, data)	"Properties" menu item

Settings Menu	
GNOMEUIINFO_MENU_PREFERENCES_ITEM(cb, data)	"Preferences" menu item

Windows Menu	
GNOMEUIINFO_MENU_NEW_WINDOW_ITEM(cb, data)	"New window" menu item
GNOMEUIINFO_MENU_CLOSE_WINDOW_ITEM(cb, data)	"Close window" menu item

Help Menu	
GNOMEUIINFO_MENU_ABOUT_ITEM(cb, data)	"About" menu item

Table 6-5.   Gnome Menu Macros

Game Menu

GNOMEUIINFO_MENU_NEW_GAME_ITEM(cb, data)	"New game" menu item
GNOMEUIINFO_MENU_PAUSE_GAME_ITEM(cb, data)	"Pause game" menu item
GNOMEUIINFO_MENU_RESTART_GAME_ITEM(cb, data)	"Restart game" menu item
GNOMEUIINFO_MENU_UNDO_MOVE_ITEM(cb, data)	"Undo move" menu item
GNOMEUIINFO_MENU_REDO_MOVE_ITEM(cb, data)	"Redo move" menu item
GNOMEUIINFO_MENU_HINT_ITEM(cb, data)	"Hint" menu item
GNOMEUIINFO_MENU_SCORES_ITEM(cb, data)	"Scores" menu item
GNOMEUIINFO_MENU_END_GAME_ITEM(cb, data)	"End game" menu item

Menu Tree Macros

GNOMEUIINFO_MENU_FILE_TREE (tree)	"File" menu
GNOMEUIINFO_MENU_EDIT_TREE (tree)	"Edit" menu
GNOMEUIINFO_MENU_VIEW_TREE (tree)	"View" menu
GNOMEUIINFO_MENU_SETTINGS_TREE (tree)	"Settings" menu
GNOMEUIINFO_MENU_FILES_TREE (tree)	"Files" menu
GNOMEUIINFO_MENU_WINDOWS_TREE (tree)	"Windows" menu
GNOMEUIINFO_MENU_HELP_TREE (tree)	"Help" menu
GNOMEUIINFO_MENU_GAME_TREE (tree)	"Game" menu

Table 6-5   Gnome Menu Macros *(continued)*

can be added to the menu bar with the following, where tree is the array of GnomeUIInfo structures for the File menu.

```
GNOMEUIINFO_MENU_FILE_TREE (tree)
```

The following example is a rewritten version of the menu bar assignment using specialized macros for the File and Edit menus:

```
GnomeUIInfo menubar[] = {
        GNOMEUIINFO_MENU_FILE_TREE(file_menu, NULL),
        GNOMEUIINFO_MENU_EDIT_TREE(edit_menu, NULL),
        GNOMEUIINFO_END
 };
```

Once you have defined your menus, you can create them using the gnome_app_create_menus function. This takes as its arguments the Gnome application structure and the pointer to the GnomeUIInfo structures you are using for your menu bar. In this previous example, this pointer is the array name "menubar." Each of the elements making up the menubar array, in turn, references a GnomeUIInfo array for their menu.

```
gnome_app_create_menus (GNOME_APP (app),
                        menubar);
```

The following program implements a Gnome application with two
menus and a toolbar. File and Edit menus are implemented, along
with a toolbar featuring an Exit button.

```
#include <gnome.h>
static void copy_func (GtkWidget *button, gpointer
                       data)
        {
        g_print("Copy operation\n");
        }
static void open_func (GtkWidget *button, gpointer
                       data)
         {
        g_print("Open operation\n");
        }

 GnomeUIInfo file_menu[] = {
        GNOMEUIINFO_MENU_OPEN_ITEM(open_func,NULL),
        GNOMEUIINFO_MENU_EXIT_ITEM(gtk_main_quit,NULL),
        GNOMEUIINFO_END
        };

 GnomeUIInfo edit_menu[] = {
         GNOMEUIINFO_MENU_COPY_ITEM(copy_func, NULL),
         GNOMEUIINFO_END
 };

 GnomeUIInfo menubar[] = {
         GNOMEUIINFO_MENU_FILE_TREE(file_menu),
         GNOMEUIINFO_MENU_EDIT_TREE(edit_menu),
         GNOMEUIINFO_END
 };

 GnomeUIInfo toolbar[] = {
         GNOMEUIINFO_ITEM_STOCK("Exit","Exit the
                     application", gtk_main_quit,
GNOME_STOCK_PIXMAP_EXIT),
         GNOMEUIINFO_END
 };

 int
main(int argc, char *argv[])
 {
         GtkWidget *app;
         GtkWidget *button;
         GtkWidget *label;
```

6

```
            gnome_init ("menu-sample",
                       "0.1", argc, argv);
            /* Create a Gnome app widget */
            app = gnome_app_new ("Menu-App",
                                 "My Gnome Menu");
            gtk_signal_connect (GTK_OBJECT (app),
"delete_event", GTK_SIGNAL_FUNC (gtk_main_quit), NULL);

            label = gtk_label_new("Menu Example");
            gnome_app_set_contents (GNOME_APP (app),
                                    label);

            /*create the menus and toolbar */
            gnome_app_create_menus (GNOME_APP (app),
                  menubar);
            gnome_app_create_toolbar (GNOME_APP (app),
                  toolbar);

            gtk_widget_show_all(app);
            gtk_main ();
            return 0;
    }
```

The libgnomeui library also provides an extensive set of stock
icons for use with menu items and toolbars. Table 6-6 lists many
of the common stock icons. Stock buttons are also provided for
such standard items as OK and Cancel buttons. In the previous
program, a stock icon was used for the Exit button on the icon bar.
The name of the stock Exit icon is GNOME_STOCK_PIXMAP_
EXIT. For an entry in an icon bar, the GNOMEUINFO_ITEM_
STOCK macro is used.

```
GNOMEUIINFO_ITEM_STOCK("Exit","Exit the App",
              gtk_main_quit, GNOME_STOCK_PIXMAP_EXIT)
```

If you want to use a stock icon for something other than a
GnomeUIInfo object, you need to generate a widget for it. For this,
you use the gnome_stock_pixmap_widget function.

For a menu, you use smaller icon stock items. These have the term
MENU in them. You use them for the icon data argument in the
menu and icon macros. For example, for the copy entry in the Edit
menu in the previous program, you could use the following where
GNOME_STOCK_MENU_COPY is a smaller copy icon for use
in menus.

Stock Toolbar Icons

```
#define GNOME_STOCK_PIXMAP_NEW "New"
#define GNOME_STOCK_PIXMAP_OPEN "Open"
#define GNOME_STOCK_PIXMAP_CLOSE "Close"
#define GNOME_STOCK_PIXMAP_REVERT "Revert"
#define GNOME_STOCK_PIXMAP_SAVE "Save"
#define GNOME_STOCK_PIXMAP_SAVE_AS "Save As"
#define GNOME_STOCK_PIXMAP_CUT "Cut"
#define GNOME_STOCK_PIXMAP_COPY "Copy"
#define GNOME_STOCK_PIXMAP_PASTE "Paste"
#define GNOME_STOCK_PIXMAP_PROPERTIES "Properties"
#define GNOME_STOCK_PIXMAP_PREFERENCES "Preferences"
#define GNOME_STOCK_PIXMAP_HELP "Help"
#define GNOME_STOCK_PIXMAP_SCORES "Scores"
#define GNOME_STOCK_PIXMAP_PRINT "Print"
#define GNOME_STOCK_PIXMAP_SEARCH "Search"
#define GNOME_STOCK_PIXMAP_SRCHRPL "Search/Replace"
#define GNOME_STOCK_PIXMAP_BACK "Back"
#define GNOME_STOCK_PIXMAP_FORWARD "Forward"
#define GNOME_STOCK_PIXMAP_FIRST "First"
#define GNOME_STOCK_PIXMAP_LAST "Last"
#define GNOME_STOCK_PIXMAP_HOME "Home"
#define GNOME_STOCK_PIXMAP_STOP "Stop"
#define GNOME_STOCK_PIXMAP_REFRESH "Refresh"
#define GNOME_STOCK_PIXMAP_UNDO "Undo"
#define GNOME_STOCK_PIXMAP_REDO "Redo"
#define GNOME_STOCK_PIXMAP_TIMER "Timer"
#define GNOME_STOCK_PIXMAP_TIMER_STOP "Timer Stopped"
#define GNOME_STOCK_PIXMAP_MAIL "Mail"
#define GNOME_STOCK_PIXMAP_MAIL_RCV "Receive Mail"
#define GNOME_STOCK_PIXMAP_MAIL_SND "Send Mail"
#define GNOME_STOCK_PIXMAP_MAIL_RPL "Reply to Mail"
#define GNOME_STOCK_PIXMAP_MAIL_FWD "Forward Mail"
#define GNOME_STOCK_PIXMAP_MAIL_NEW "New Mail"
#define GNOME_STOCK_PIXMAP_TRASH "Trash"
```

6

Table 6-6.   Stock Toolbar Icons, Menu Icons, and Buttons

Stock Toolbar Icons

#define GNOME_STOCK_PIXMAP_TRASH_FULL "Trash Full"
#define GNOME_STOCK_PIXMAP_UNDELETE "Undelete"
#define GNOME_STOCK_PIXMAP_SPELLCHECK "Spellchecker"
#define GNOME_STOCK_PIXMAP_MIC "Microphone"
#define GNOME_STOCK_PIXMAP_LINE_IN "Line In"
#define GNOME_STOCK_PIXMAP_CDROM "Cdrom"
#define GNOME_STOCK_PIXMAP_VOLUME "Volume"
#define GNOME_STOCK_PIXMAP_BOOK_RED "Book Red"
#define GNOME_STOCK_PIXMAP_BOOK_GREEN "Book Green"
#define GNOME_STOCK_PIXMAP_BOOK_BLUE "Book Blue"
#define GNOME_STOCK_PIXMAP_BOOK_YELLOW "Book Yellow"
#define GNOME_STOCK_PIXMAP_BOOK_OPEN "Book Open"
#define GNOME_STOCK_PIXMAP_ABOUT "About"
#define GNOME_STOCK_PIXMAP_QUIT "Quit"
#define GNOME_STOCK_PIXMAP_MULTIPLE "Multiple"
#define GNOME_STOCK_PIXMAP_NOT "Not"
#define GNOME_STOCK_PIXMAP_CONVERT "Convert"
#define GNOME_STOCK_PIXMAP_JUMP_TO "Jump To"
#define GNOME_STOCK_PIXMAP_UP "Up"
#define GNOME_STOCK_PIXMAP_DOWN "Down"
#define GNOME_STOCK_PIXMAP_TOP "Top"
#define GNOME_STOCK_PIXMAP_BOTTOM "Bottom"
#define GNOME_STOCK_PIXMAP_ATTACH "Attach"
#define GNOME_STOCK_PIXMAP_INDEX "Index"
#define GNOME_STOCK_PIXMAP_FONT "Font"
#define GNOME_STOCK_PIXMAP_EXEC "Exec"
#define GNOME_STOCK_PIXMAP_ALIGN_LEFT "Left"
#define GNOME_STOCK_PIXMAP_ALIGN_RIGHT "Right"
#define GNOME_STOCK_PIXMAP_ALIGN_CENTER "Center"
#define GNOME_STOCK_PIXMAP_ALIGN_JUSTIFY "Justify"
#define GNOME_STOCK_PIXMAP_TEXT_BOLD "Bold"
#define GNOME_STOCK_PIXMAP_TEXT_ITALIC "Italic"
#define GNOME_STOCK_PIXMAP_TEXT_UNDERLINE "Underline"
#define GNOME_STOCK_PIXMAP_TEXT_STRIKEOUT "Strikeout"

Table 6-6.   Stock Toolbar Icons, Menu Icons, and Buttons
(continued)

Stock Toolbar Icons

#define GNOME_STOCK_PIXMAP_EXIT
GNOME_STOCK_PIXMAP_QUIT

Stock Menu Icons

#define GNOME_STOCK_MENU_BLANK "Menu_"

#define GNOME_STOCK_MENU_NEW "Menu_New"

#define GNOME_STOCK_MENU_SAVE "Menu_Save"

#define GNOME_STOCK_MENU_SAVE_AS "Menu_Save As"

#define GNOME_STOCK_MENU_REVERT "Menu_Revert"

#define GNOME_STOCK_MENU_OPEN "Menu_Open"

#define GNOME_STOCK_MENU_CLOSE "Menu_Close"

#define GNOME_STOCK_MENU_QUIT "Menu_Quit"

#define GNOME_STOCK_MENU_CUT "Menu_Cut"

#define GNOME_STOCK_MENU_COPY "Menu_Copy"

#define GNOME_STOCK_MENU_PASTE "Menu_Paste"

#define GNOME_STOCK_MENU_PROP "Menu_Properties"

#define GNOME_STOCK_MENU_PREF "Menu_Preferences"

#define GNOME_STOCK_MENU_ABOUT "Menu_About"

#define GNOME_STOCK_MENU_SCORES "Menu_Scores"

#define GNOME_STOCK_MENU_UNDO "Menu_Undo"

#define GNOME_STOCK_MENU_REDO "Menu_Redo"

#define GNOME_STOCK_MENU_PRINT "Menu_Print"

#define GNOME_STOCK_MENU_SEARCH "Menu_Search"

#define GNOME_STOCK_MENU_SRCHRPL "Menu_Search/Replace"

#define GNOME_STOCK_MENU_BACK "Menu_Back"

#define GNOME_STOCK_MENU_FORWARD "Menu_Forward"

#define GNOME_STOCK_MENU_FIRST "Menu_First"

#define GNOME_STOCK_MENU_LAST "Menu_Last"

#define GNOME_STOCK_MENU_HOME "Menu_Home"

#define GNOME_STOCK_MENU_STOP "Menu_Stop"

#define GNOME_STOCK_MENU_REFRESH "Menu_Refresh"

#define GNOME_STOCK_MENU_MAIL "Menu_Mail"

#define GNOME_STOCK_MENU_MAIL_RCV "Menu_Receive Mail"

#define GNOME_STOCK_MENU_MAIL_SND "Menu_Send Mail"

#define GNOME_STOCK_MENU_MAIL_RPL "Menu_Reply to Mail"

#define GNOME_STOCK_MENU_MAIL_FWD "Menu_Forward Mail"

6

Table 6-6.   Stock Toolbar Icons, Menu Icons, and Buttons
(continued)

Stock Toolbar Icons

#define GNOME_STOCK_MENU_MAIL_NEW "Menu_New Mail"

#define GNOME_STOCK_MENU_TRASH "Menu_Trash"

#define GNOME_STOCK_MENU_TRASH_FULL "Menu_Trash Full"

#define GNOME_STOCK_MENU_UNDELETE "Menu_Undelete"

#define GNOME_STOCK_MENU_TIMER "Menu_Timer"

#define GNOME_STOCK_MENU_TIMER_STOP
"Menu_Timer Stopped"

#define GNOME_STOCK_MENU_SPELLCHECK
"Menu_Spellchecker"

#define GNOME_STOCK_MENU_MIC "Menu_Microphone"

#define GNOME_STOCK_MENU_LINE_IN "Menu_Line In"

#define GNOME_STOCK_MENU_CDROM "Menu_Cdrom"

#define GNOME_STOCK_MENU_VOLUME "Menu_Volume"

#define GNOME_STOCK_MENU_BOOK_RED "Menu_Book Red"

#define GNOME_STOCK_MENU_BOOK_GREEN
"Menu_Book Green"

#define GNOME_STOCK_MENU_BOOK_BLUE "Menu_Book Blue"

#define GNOME_STOCK_MENU_BOOK_YELLOW
"Menu_Book Yellow"

#define GNOME_STOCK_MENU_BOOK_OPEN "Menu_Book Open"

#define GNOME_STOCK_MENU_CONVERT "Menu_Convert"

#define GNOME_STOCK_MENU_JUMP_TO "Menu_Jump To"

#define GNOME_STOCK_MENU_UP "Menu_Up"

#define GNOME_STOCK_MENU_DOWN "Menu_Down"

#define GNOME_STOCK_MENU_TOP "Menu_Top"

#define GNOME_STOCK_MENU_BOTTOM "Menu_Bottom"

#define GNOME_STOCK_MENU_ATTACH "Menu_Attach"

#define GNOME_STOCK_MENU_INDEX "Menu_Index"

#define GNOME_STOCK_MENU_FONT "Menu_Font"

#define GNOME_STOCK_MENU_EXEC "Menu_Exec"

#define GNOME_STOCK_MENU_ALIGN_LEFT "Menu_Left"

#define GNOME_STOCK_MENU_ALIGN_RIGHT "Menu_Right"

#define GNOME_STOCK_MENU_ALIGN_CENTER "Menu_Center"

#define GNOME_STOCK_MENU_ALIGN_JUSTIFY "Menu_Justify"

#define GNOME_STOCK_MENU_TEXT_BOLD "Menu_Bold"

Table 6-6. Stock Toolbar Icons, Menu Icons, and Buttons
(continued)

Stock Toolbar Icons

#define GNOME_STOCK_MENU_TEXT_ITALIC "Menu_Italic"

#define GNOME_STOCK_MENU_TEXT_UNDERLINE
"Menu_Underline"

#define GNOME_STOCK_MENU_TEXT_STRIKEOUT
"Menu_Strikeout"

#define GNOME_STOCK_MENU_EXIT
GNOME_STOCK_MENU_QUIT

Stock Button Icons

#define GNOME_STOCK_BUTTON_OK "Button_Ok"

#define GNOME_STOCK_BUTTON_CANCEL "Button_Cancel"

#define GNOME_STOCK_BUTTON_YES "Button_Yes"

#define GNOME_STOCK_BUTTON_NO "Button_No"

#define GNOME_STOCK_BUTTON_CLOSE "Button_Close"

#define GNOME_STOCK_BUTTON_APPLY "Button_Apply"

#define GNOME_STOCK_BUTTON_HELP "Button_Help"

#define GNOME_STOCK_BUTTON_NEXT "Button_Next"

#define GNOME_STOCK_BUTTON_PREV "Button_Prev"

#define GNOME_STOCK_BUTTON_UP "Button_Up"

#define GNOME_STOCK_BUTTON_DOWN "Button_Down"

#define GNOME_STOCK_BUTTON_FONT "Button_Font"

Table 6-6.   Stock Toolbar Icons, Menu Icons, and Buttons
(continued)

```
GNOMEUIINFO_MENU_COPY_ITEM(copy_func,
                          GNOME_STOCK_MENU_COPY)
```

If you are manually creating menu items, you can use the
gnome_stock_menu_item to create a menu item with a specified
icon. For stock buttons, you can use gnome_stock_buttons.

Dialogs

With the gnome-dialog functions, you can easily create both modal
and nonmodal dialogs. Though nonmodal dialogs tend to be more
user friendly, modal dialogs are easier to program. To create a
dialog, you need to define a GnomeDialog widget using the
gnome_dialog_new function. This function takes as its arguments

the title of the dialog and of any buttons you want displayed on it. To use stock buttons, you can use any of the GNOME_STOCK_BUTTON definitions as arguments.

```
GtkWidget *mydialog;
mydialog = gnome_dialog_new("My Dialog",
            GNOME_STOCK_BUTTON_OK,
            GNOME_STOCK_BUTTON_APPLY,
            GNOME_STOCK_BUTTON_CLOSE, NULL);
```

For a simple modal dialog, you use gnome_dialog_run_and_close functions to execute the dialog. A modal dialog waits for a user to press a button or the window Close box. It will return the number of the button selected (or −1 for a Close box). If you have a dialog where the user needs to press several buttons, then you can use the gnome_dialog_run function. This function does not automatically close the dialog at the first button press. Instead, it returns the number of button pressed and remains displayed. You can use the returned value to execute any operations you have associated with that button and then call gnome_dialog_run again to get the next button press. An effective way to handle this is to place gnome_dialog_run in a loop and to exit the loop when the user presses a Quit button or Close box. Then, use the gnome_dialog_close function to close the dialog.

```
{
GtkWidget *mydialog;
 int drex;
 int dclose;
/*Create a new dialog, Be sure to include the NULL on
the end*/
 mydialog = gnome_dialog_new("My Dialog",
                    GNOME_STOCK_BUTTON_OK,
                    GNOME_STOCK_BUTTON_APPLY,
                    GNOME_STOCK_BUTTON_CLOSE,
                    NULL);
/*add some content to the dialog here*/
dclose = 0;
  while (dclose != 1) {
        dres = gnome_dialog_run(GNOME_DIA-
LOG(mydialog));
          switch(dres){
              case 0:              /* OK button */
              case 2:              /* Close button */
              case -1:             /* close box */
                    dclose = 1;
```

```
                break;
        case 1:                /* Apply button */
            g_print ("User pressed Apply");
            break
        }
    }
    /* close dialog */
    gnome_dialog_close(GNOME_DIALOG(dlg));
}
```

For a nonmodal dialog, you need to bind the click signal to the dialog and provide it with a function to manage the returned value for a clicked button. You use the gtk_signal_connect function to connect the clicking operation (clicked) with dialog buttons on your dialog and have the result passed to a function you defined to manage the results.

```
gtk_signal_connect(GTK_OBJECT(mydialog),"
"clicked",GTK_SIGNAL_FUNC(dialogres), NULL);
```

In the following example, the mydialog dialog is connected to the dialogres function that will handle returned values of clicked buttons.

```
static void dialogres(GnomeDialog *dialog, int but-
ton, gpointer data)
        {
        switch(button) {
        case 1:     /* Apply button */
            g_print ("User pressed Apply");
            break;
            case 0:        /* OK button */
            case 2:        /* Close button */
            gnome_dialog_close(dialog);
            break;
        }
        return;
    }

GtkWidget *mydialog;
mydialog = gnome_dialog_new("My Dialog",
                    GNOME_STOCK_BUTTON_OK,
                    GNOME_STOCK_BUTTON_APPLY,
                    GNOME_STOCK_BUTTON_CLOSE,
                    NULL);
/* Connect the dialog and */
```

```
gtk_signal_connect(GTK_OBJECT(mydialog),"clicked",
                    GTK_SIGNAL_FUNC(dialogres), NULL);
gtk_widget_show(mydialog);
```

The following program example creates an application that
displays a button. When clicked, a dialog is displayed that has
three buttons: OK, Apply, and Close. When the user clicks OK or
Close, the dialog ends. If the user clicks Apply, the text "User
clicked apply" is displayed on the standard output of the
terminal window.

```
#include <gnome.h>

    void do_mydialog( GtkWidget *widget, GdkEvent
*event, gpointer   data )
    {
        GtkWidget *mydialog;
        int dres;
        int dclose;

        mydialog = gnome_dialog_new("My Dialog",
                    GNOME_STOCK_BUTTON_OK,
                    GNOME_STOCK_BUTTON_APPLY,
                    GNOME_STOCK_BUTTON_CLOSE,
                    NULL);
        dclose = 0;
        while (dclose != 1) {
         dres = gnome_dialog_run(GNOME_DIA-
LOG(mydialog));
            switch(dres)
                {
                case 0:
                case 2:
                case -1:
                    dclose = 1;
                    break;
                case 1:
                    g_print ("User pressed Apply");
                    break;
                }
        }
    gnome_dialog_close(GNOME_DIALOG(mydialog));
    }

    gint closeprog ( GtkWidget *widget, GdkEvent
                    *event, gpointer   data )
    {
```

```
        gtk_main_quit();
    }

int main( int    argc, char *argv[] )
{
    GtkWidget *app;
    GtkWidget *mybutton;

    gnome_init ("", "0.1", argc, argv);

    /* Create a Gnome app widget which sets up a
       window
       for your application */
    app = gnome_app_new ("Gnome-dialog", "My
                         Dialog App");

    mybutton = gtk_button_new_with_label
                       ("Click Me");
    gtk_signal_connect (GTK_OBJECT (mybutton),
"clicked", GTK_SIGNAL_FUNC (do_mydialog), NULL);
    gnome_app_set_contents (GNOME_APP (app),
mybutton);
    gtk_signal_connect (GTK_OBJECT (app),
"delete_event",  GTK_SIGNAL_FUNC
 (closeprog),       NULL);

    gtk_widget_show_all(app);
    gtk_main ();

    return(0);
}
```

There are also several specialized dialogs such as message boxes,
property dialogs, and file dialogs. A GnomeMessageBox dialog
works the same way as a GnomeDialog. A message box is initially
set up with a label and an icon determined by the message type.
Table 6-7 lists the different message box types. You create a
message box using the gnome_message_box_new function. It
takes as its first arguments the message text, then the type of
message box, and then the buttons you want displayed on the
dialog, with the last argument being the NULL.

With the GnomePropertyBox dialog, you can set notebook dialog
for different properties, options, or settings for an application. The

```
#define GNOME_MESSAGE_BOX_INFO "info"
#define GNOME_MESSAGE_BOX_WARNING "warning"
#define GNOME_MESSAGE_BOX_ERROR "error"
#define GNOME_MESSAGE_BOX_QUESTION "question"
#define GNOME_MESSAGE_BOX_GENERIC "generic"
```

Table 6-7.   Message Boxes

notebook has pages with tabs you can click on to display different kinds of properties. You create a property dialog with the gnome_property_box_new function. This sets up a notebook and four buttons: OK, Apply, Close, and Help. OK and Apply will call the function you set up to manage the responses selected by the user, also known as the apply handler. OK will further close the dialog. Close will simply close the dialog, and Help will call the help function you set up for this dialog. You can add pages to your property dialog using the gnome_property_box_append_page function. This takes as its arguments the page number and the label. Each time the user makes a change on one of the dialog's widgets, you use the gnome_property_box_changed function to mark the dialog as changed. This enables the Apply and OK buttons to invoke the apply handler to enact the changes.

Entries

You use the gnome-entry widgets for entering text, file names, images, icons, or numeric data. The GnomeEntry widget is used to hold text. First you create the GnomeEntry widget with the gnome_entry_new function. This takes as its argument an identifying string for this object. A GnomeEntry object holds a GtkEntry object that holds the actual text. To modify the text, you have to use a pointer directly to the GtkEntry text object. You can obtain this pointer using gnome_entry_gtk_entry functions.

```
GtkWidget *gnome_text;
GtkWidget *gtk_text;
  gnome_text = gnome_entry_new("text1");
  gtk_text = gnome_entry_gtk_entry(GNOME
            _ENTRY(gnome_text));
```

The GnomeFileEntry not only sets up a text box entry but also adds a Browse button and will accept file drops from the file manager. You create the entry with the gnome_file_entry_new function. You use gnome_file_entry_gtk_entry to obtain a pointer to access the text used for the file name. To obtain the text of the file name, you can use gnome_file_entry_get_full_path.

GnomePixmapEntry is a text entry based on GnomeFileEntry. It displays a preview box for a selected image. You use gnome_pixmap_entry_new to create a new entry and gnome_pixmap_entry_gtk_entry to access its GtkEntry object. You can use gnome_pixmap_entery_get_filename to obtain the pixmap file name.

With GnomeIconEntry you can select and display icons. To the file name text entry is added a button that displays the icon. Clicking on the button displays a listing of images from that icon's directory. Use gnome_icon_entry_new to create a new icon entry and gnome_icon_entry_gtk_entry to access its GtkEntry object. With gnome_icon_entry_get_filename, you can obtain the full name of the icon.

With the GnomeNumberEntry widget, you can enter double precision numbers. It consists of a GnomeEntry widget and a button that invokes a dialog with a calculator. The user can use the calculator and the result will be used to update the number entry. You use gnome_number_entry_new to create a number entry dialog and gnome_number_entry_gtk_entry to access its GtkEntrty. Use gnome_number_entry_get_number to obtain the value. For simple number entries, you would use the GtkSpinButton widget.

Images, Sessions, and MDI

With the GnomePixmap widget, you can easily manage images. Gnome makes use of the imlib image library. There are numerous gnome_pixmap functions available. These operate as higher-level functions allowing you to easily manage images without having to resort directly to the complexities of imlib functions. With the gnome_pixmap_new_from_file function, you can load an image and create a pixmap widget. The gnome_pixmap_new_from_file_at_size will perform the same operation, but will scale the image. The gnome_pixmap_load functions will perform operations on an existing pixmap widget.

With session management, you can have your application save its current settings when it closes and restore them when it starts up again. You can also set up particular sessions that have specified settings.

For applications designed to let you open and work on several documents at once, Gnome provides the Multiple Document Interface (MDI). There are three styles for implementing MDI. In the notebook style, documents can be docked in a notebook and dragged to a separate window. The top-level style displays each document in its own window. The modal style shows only one window and uses a menu to switch between documents. To enable the MDI features, you use a different corresponding set of functions to define your application. Instead of the gnome_app_new functions, you use gnome_mdi_new. For menus and toolbars, you use gnome_mdi_set_menubar_template and gnome_mdi_set_toolbar_template.

Gnome Canvas

A canvas is a simple to use and very powerful graphic drawing widget. It contains support for Xlib graphics and anti-aliasing. You create a canvas widget with the gnome_canvas_new function. You need to make sure that the appropriate visual and color mapping is used. For this, you can use gtk_widget_push_visual and gtk_widget_push_colormap. If you want to enable anti-aliasing, you use the gnome_canvas_new_aa function to create the canvas widget. Anti-aliasing provides more display capabilities than the standard operations. The following example shows how to create a canvas object for imlib graphics:

```
GtkWidget *canvas;

gtk_widget_push_visual(gdk_imlib_get_visual());
  gtk_widget_push_colormap(gdk_imlib_get_colormap());
  canvas = gnome_canvas_new();
  gtk_widget_pop_visual();
  gtk_widget_pop_colormap();
```

Use the gnome_canvas_set_pixels_per_unit function to set the scale of the canvas, gtk_widget_set_usize to set the size of the widget, and gnome_canvas_set_scroll_region to set the region in to scroll in.

To place objects on the canvas, you define GnomeCanvasItem objects and place them in groups. The default group is the root group, which you can access with the gnome_canvas_root function. You create a canvas item with the gnome_canvas_item function. This function takes as its arguments the parent group for the object and the object type, followed by several attributes such as location and color, with the last argument being a NULL. Different types of objects will have different sets of attributes. For example, the rectangle shown in the next example has two sets of x,y dimensions, shades, and color attributes. Canvas item types are shown in Table 6-8.

```
GnomeCanvas *mycanvas;
GnomeCanvasItem *citem1;
citem1 = gnome_canvas_item_new(gnome
        _canvas_root(mycanvas),
        GNOME_TYPE_CANVAS_RECT,
        "x1", 1.0, "y1", 1.0, "x2", 23.0,
        "y2", 20.0,
        "fill_color", "blue", NULL);
```

6

To change any of these attributes, you use the gnome_canvas_item_set function. This function takes as its first argument the pointer to the canvas item, with the remaining arguments being the attributes just as they would be listed for gnome_canvas_item_new. Numerous functions are available for performing operations on objects, such as the gnome_canvas_item_move function that moves an object and the gnome_convas_item_hide function to hide it.

GTK+

GTK+ consists of an extensive set of functions covering widgets of various types. Table 6-9 lists the different kinds of objects that make up GTK+. Check the online documentation for the GTK API at the **www.gtk.org** and **developer.gnome.org** Web sites. The documentation includes a comprehensive listing of all GTK functions as well as a detailed tutorial on GTK programming. It is highly recommended that you make use of this documentation. Due to size constraints, this book can only present brief introductions and list several of the common GTK functions. Also check the header files for a detailed declaration of different functions and structures, including their arguments and return values. Table 6-14 at the end of this section lists the GTK header files.

Widgets and Objects	Description
GnomeAbout	About box for an application
GnomeAnimator	Simple animations for GNOME applications
GnomeApp	The top-level GNOME container
GnomeAppBar	Statusbar/Progress/Minibuffer widget
GnomeCalculator	Calculator widget
GnomeCanvas	Generic engine for structured graphics
GnomeCanvasItem	Create and manage a canvas item
GnomeCanvasGroup	Functions and structures to bind a canvas item to a group
GnomeCanvasLine	A canvas line
GnomeCanvasPolygon	Canvas polygon
GnomeCanvasRE	Canvas Rectangle and Ellipse base class
GnomeCanvasRect	Canvas rectangle
GnomeCanvasEllipse	Canvas ellipse
GnomeCanvasText	Canvas text object
GnomeCanvasImage	Canvas image
GnomeCanvasWidget	Canvas widget
GnomeClient	Routines to provide session management support in your application
GnomeColorPicker	Widget for selecting colors
GnomeDateEdit	Date and time entry widget
GnomeDEntryEdit	Editing object for dentries (**.desktop** files)
GnomeDialog	Transient ("pop-up") dialogs
GnomeDockBand	Widget implementing dock bands
GnomeDockItem	Dockable widget
GnomeDock	Widget supporting movable and detachable widgets
GnomeDruid	The main widget of the GNOME druid system
GnomeDruidPage	Virtual widget defining the druid page
GnomeDruidPageStart	A GnomeDruidPage for the beginning of a DRUID

Table 6-8. GNOME Widgets and Objects

Widgets and Objects	Description
GnomeDruidPageStandard	Standard GnomeDruidPage
GnomeDruidPageFinish	A GnomeDruidPage for the end of a DRUID
GnomeEntry	Entry widget with history tracking
GnomeFileEntry	Entry widget for file names
GnomeFontPicker	Button that displays current font; click to select new font
GnomeFontSelector	Deprecated, use GtkFontSelection in a GnomeDialog or GnomeFontPicker
GnomeGuru	Obsolete, use GnomeDruid instead
GnomeHRef	A link button
GnomeIconEntry	Select an icon
GnomeIconTextItem	Canvas item for editable text captions in icon lists
GnomeIconList	List of icons with captions, with optional caption editing
GnomeIconSelection	Icon listing/chooser display
GnomeLess	Simple file content browser widget
GnomeMDIChild	Abstract MDI child class
GnomeMDIGenericChild	Generic GnomeMDI child
GnomeMDI	GNOME Multiple Document Interface
GnomeMessageBox	Message box display routines
GnomeNumberEntry	Entry line for number input
GnomePaperSelector	Paper selector
GnomePixmapEntry	Selection of large images
GnomePixmap	Display and load images (pixmaps)
GnomePropertyBox	Standardized dialog box for handling configuration
GnomeScores	Dialog box that displays high scores
GnomeStock	Default icons for toolbars, menus, and buttons
GtkClock	Text clock widget, capable of real-time, count-up and count-down modes
GtkTed	Deprecated
GtkDial	Analog dial widget for number selection

6

Table 6-8.   GNOME Widgets and Objects *(continued)*

Widgets and Objects	Description
GtkPixmapMenuItem	Special widget for GNOME menus
GnomeSpell	Deprecated
GnomeDockLayout	Widget for saving and retrieving the layout of a GnomeDock widget
GnomeProcBar	Gnome process bar

Table 6-8. GNOME Widgets and Objects *(continued)*

Several basic functions and components are needed in any GTK program. You first need to include at least the **gtk.h** header file. Other GTK header files may be required, depending on the widgets and functions you are using. You then have to define pointers to the widgets you intend to define and use. Using different GTK functions, you will be defining widgets and assigning their addresses to these pointers. Before you create your widgets, you have to initialize the GTK library with the gtk_init function. You then define your widgets using GTK functions. Then, use GTK functions to specify actions and attributes for the widgets such as displaying them. A close box event (delete event) is connected to the window and the gtk_main_quit function so that when a user clicks the Close box of the window, the program ends. Finally, use the gtk_main function to run the widgets. The following example defines a simple GTK program to display a simple window:

base.c

```
#include <gtk/gtk.h>

int main( int   argc, char *argv[] )
    {
        GtkWidget *window1;

        gtk_init (&argc, &argv);

        window1 = gtk_window_new (GTK
                    _WINDOW_TOPLEVEL);

        gtk_signal_connect (GTK_OBJECT (window1),
     "delete_event", GTK_SIGNAL_FUNC (gtk_main_quit),
```

```
                    NULL);

   gtk_widget_show   (window1);

   gtk_main ();

   return(0);
}
```

The **gtk.h** header file includes GTK variable, macro, and function definitions. Window is defined as a pointer to a structure named GtkWidget. The actual structure pointed to will later be determined by the function used to create a given structure. The gtk_init function creates initial settings, such as the default visual and color map, and then calls the gdk_init function to initialize the GTK library and will check for GTK arguments —gtk-debug for debugging. The gtk_window_new function creates a new window structure, returning its address—which is then assigned to the window pointer. Window is now pointing to GTK window structure. The TOP_LEVEL argument will place the window under the control of the window managers, using its defaults for displaying a window. The gtk_widget_show function then displays the window. Notice that the window pointer is used as the argument to this function. Finally, the gtk_main function starts the interactive process, waiting for events to occur such as button selections and mouse clicks.

You compile a GTK program using the gcc compiler and the GTK libraries. To specify the GTK libraries on the command line, you use the gtk-config command. This command determines the compiler options you need to compile a GTK program.

```
`gtk-config --cflags --libs`.
```

gtk-config is a program that needs to be executed on the command line. To do this, you surround it and its arguments with back quotes. Back quotes are shell operators that are used to execute an enclosed command on the command line and place its returned values on the same place on that line. You can think of this operation as functioning somewhat like a macro, substituting values for the command executed. In this case, the gtk-config command with the cflags and libs arguments will place the compiler GTK flags and libraries you need on the command line with the gcc command. Then, the gcc command is executed with those flags and libraries.

```
gcc hello.c -o hello `gtk-config -cflags -libs`
```

Component	Description
General	General Gtk functions to initialize, start, and quit Gtk programs
Feature test macros	Check Gtk version
Graphics contexts	Return graphic context object
Styles	Functions to manage Gtk styles
Themes	Structures and functions for Gtk theme engine
Resource files	Routines for handling resource files
Keyboard accelerators	Keyboard functions
Selections	Functions for handling interprocess communication via selections
Drag and drop	Functions for controlling drag-and-drop handling
Menu factory	Functions for controlling menus
Signals	Functions and structures to manage signals
Signal marshalers	Functions to marshal signals
Object properties	Functions to determine object properties
Types	Gtk types
Bindings	Binding functions
Standard enumerations	Widget types and flags defined using enum settings
Debugging	Debugging flags
Private information	Functions and flags for managing private data

Table 6-9.   GTK+ Components

The libraries usually used are listed here:

GTK (-lgtk)	GTK widget library.
GDK (-lgdk)	Xlib wrapper.
gmodule (-lgmodule)	Runtime extensions.
GLib (-lglib)	GTK is built on top of glib and always requires it.

Xlib (-lX11)	Used by GDK.
Xext (-lXext)	For shared memory pixmaps and other X extensions.
math (-lm)	Math library.

The types used in GTK+ programming can be categorized into fundamental, built-in, and object types. The fundamental types are basic types such as standard C program types and the base class types for Gtk+ like GTK_TYPE_OBJECT (see Table 6-10). The fundamental types are automatically defined by gtk_init. The built-in types include some basic enumerations, flags, and

GtkType Constant	Corresponding C Type
GTK_TYPE_INVALID	None
GTK_TYPE_NONE	void
GTK_TYPE_CHAR	gchar
GTK_TYPE_UCHAR	guchar
GTK_TYPE_BOOL	gboolean
GTK_TYPE_INT	gint
GTK_TYPE_UINT	guint
GTK_TYPE_LONG	glong
GTK_TYPE_ULONG	gulong
GTK_TYPE_FLOAT	gfloat
GTK_TYPE_DOUBLE	gdouble
GTK_TYPE_STRING	gchar*
GTK_TYPE_ENUM	Any enumeration
GTK_TYPE_FLAGS	guint
GTK_TYPE_BOXED	gpointer
GTK_TYPE_POINTER	gpointer
GTK_TYPE_SIGNAL	GtkSignalFunc, gpointer
GTK_TYPE_ARGS	gint, GtkArg*
GTK_TYPE_CALLBACK	GtkCallbackMarshal, gpointer,GtkDestroyNotify
GTK_TYPE_C_CALLBACK	GtkFunction, gpointer
GTK_TYPE_FOREIGN	gpointer, GtkDestroyNotify
GTK_TYPE_OBJECT	GtkObject*

Table 6-10. GTK+ Fundamental Types

structures like GdkWindow. These are types that Gtk+ need not understand to use. Object types consist of registered GtkObject types.

Signal and Events

Gnome programming works like other GUI programming. It is event oriented. In event-driven programs, you first define the objects that the user can operate on. Then, you start the interaction function that continually checks for certain events such as mouse clicks and menu selections. When one is detected, the event is passed to its appropriate function for handling. For example, if a user clicks on an OK button, the mouse click is detected and control is passed to a function you set up to handle a click on an OK button. When the function is finished, it returns control back to the interaction program. GTK adds a further level of sophistication. When events occur on a certain widget, the widget will emit a signal that is then used to execute a function associated both with that signal and that object. For example, when you click on a Close button, the Close button widget detects the mouse click event and emits a "clicked" signal. The signal is detected and its associated function is executed. You can also, if you wish, associate an event directly with a function. For this to work, the programmer has to connect a signal on a given object with a particular function. Functions associated with a particular signal are commonly referred to as "handlers" or "callbacks." When a signal is emitted, its handlers or callbacks are invoked. This process is referred to as "emission." Callback functions are connected to particular objects by means of a particular signal. When a clicked signal occurs on the OK button in a particular window, the callback function connected to that OK button with the clicked signal is invoked. Note that signals referred to here are in no way like the signal used in Unix systems.

To associate a particular event with the function you want executed for a given signal, you use either the gtk_signal_connect or gtk_signal_connect_object functions. When the signal is detected, its associated function is automatically executed. The syntax for these functions is shown here. The gtk_signal_connect function is used for functions to which you may be passing arguments and gtk_signal_connect or gtk_signal_connect_object is used for functions that require no arguments. The object is the Gtk object you defined, such as an OK button. Then, name is the name of the signal such as mouse click, func is the function you want executed whenever an event for this object occurs, and func_data are any arguments being passed to that function.

```
gint gtk_signal_connect( GtkObject  *object,
        gchar *name,  GtkSignalFunc  func, gpointer
                         func_data );
```

When a signal is detected for that object, its associated function is called and executed. This function is commonly referred to as a "callback function" and for signals has the following syntax:

```
void callback_func( GtkWidget *widget, gpointer
callback_data );
```

For example, to associate a click on a button with the hello function, you use the following example. The object is mybutton, clicked is the click signal, and hello is a function the programmer wrote with code to be executed when this signal is detected. When a user clicks on mybutton, the hello function is called. GTK_OBJECT and GTK_SIGNAL_FUNC are macros that perform type checking and casting to make sure the objects are passed with the appropriate types.

6

```
gtk_signal_connect (GTK_OBJECT (mybutton), "clicked",
                GTK_SIGNAL_FUNC (hello), NULL);
```

You can associate as many callback functions with a particular object and a specific signal as you wish. They will be executed sequentially when the signal occurs. The return value of the gtk_signal_connect function is an identifying tag for that function. If you want to later disassociate that function from the particular object and signal, use the gtk_signal_disconnect function with the identifying tag and object as arguments.

```
void gtk_signal_disconnect( GtkObject *object,
                      gint id );
```

In the following example, the myfunc function is associated with a mouse click on the button1 object. Its identifying tag is saved in the myfuncid variable. Then, this is used in the gtk_signal_connect function to disassociate myfunc from the mouse click operation.

```
Gint myfuncid;

myfuncid = gtk_signal_connect (GTK_OBJECT (button1),
"clicked", GTK_SIGNAL_FUNC (myfunc), NULL);
```

```
gtk_signal_disconnect (GTK_OBJECT (button1),
                       myfuncid);
```

The function gtk_signal_handlers_destroy will disassociate all such associated functions and signals from a particular object.

You can also use the signal connection functions to connect events directly to an object and function. Events are messages transmitted by the X11 server to indicate occurrences like mouse clicks and menu selections. In the gtk_signal_connect function, you use the name of the event instead of the signal. Callback functions for events include an added argument for the event. The type for this parameter can be GdkEvent or any of several event types, should you know the particular type to be used. These are listed in Table 6-11.

```
void callback_func( GtkWidget *widget, GdkEvent
                    *event, gpointer   callback_data );
```

For example, to associate a button_press_event with an OK button you would use "button_press_event" as the signal name. This example associates a button_press_event event on a button with the button_press_callback function:

```
gtk_signal_connect( GTK_OBJECT(button),
            "button_press_event", GTK_SIGNAL_FUNC
            (button_press_callback), NULL);
```

The callback function called button_press_callback has the event type GdkEventButton.

```
    static gint button_press_callback( GtkWidget
*widget, GdkEventButton *event, gpointer data );
```

For example, to associate a click on a window Close box with the close-win function, you use the following example. The object is mywindow, delete_event is the close box event, and close-win is a function the programmer wrote with code to be executed when this event occurs. When a user clicks on the window's Close box, the close-win function is called.

```
gtk_signal_connect (GTK_OBJECT (mywindow),
"delete_event", GTK_SIGNAL_FUNC (close-win), NULL);
```

Signals are stored in a global table. You can create your own signals with the gtk_signal_new function, and then use gtk_signal_emit to have an object emit a signal. Gtk_signal_new will return an identifier for the new signal. You can use this with gtk_signal_emit to have your object emit that signal.

Event Type	GtkWidget Signal
GDK_DELETE	"delete_event"
GDK_DESTROY	"destroy_event"
GDK_EXPOSE	"expose_event"
GDK_MOTION_NOTIFY	"motion_notify_event"
GDK_BUTTON_PRESS	"button_press_event"
GDK_2BUTTON_PRESS	"button_press_event"
GDK_3BUTTON_PRESS	"button_press_event"
GDK_BUTTON_RELEASE	"button_release_event"
GDK_KEY_PRESS	"key_press_event"
GDK_KEY_RELEASE	"key_release_event"
GDK_ENTER_NOTIFY	"enter_notify_event"
GDK_LEAVE_NOTIFY	"leave_notify_event"
GDK_FOCUS_CHANGE	"focus_in_event", "focus_out_event"
GDK_CONFIGURE	"configure_event"
GDK_MAP	"map_event"
GDK_UNMAP	"unmap_event"
GDK_PROPERTY_NOTIFY	"property_notify_event"
GDK_SELECTION_CLEAR	"selection_clear_event"
GDK_SELECTION_REQUEST	"selection_request_event"
GDK_SELECTION_NOTIFY	"selection_notify_event"
GDK_PROXIMITY_IN	"proximity_in_event"
GDK_PROXIMITY_OUT	"proximity_out_event"
GDK_CLIENT_EVENT	"client_event"
GDK_VISIBILITY_NOTIFY	"visibility_notify_event"
GDK_NO_EXPOSE	"no_expose_event"

Table 6-11. GTK Events

The following program shows how to set up a simple object with its event and callback functions. Here, the object button is created using the gtk_button_new_with_label function. Then this button is associated with the function hello message using the gtk_signal_connect function. The hellomessage has been defined at the beginning of the program. It simply prints out "Hello World\n".

```
button = gtk_button_new_with_label ("Click Me");
gtk_signal_connect (GTK_OBJECT (button), "clicked",
GTK_SIGNAL_FUNC (hellomessage), NULL);
```

The program also creates a window object that is also associated
with a callback function—in this case, the delete_win function
that will erase the window object. The delete_win function simply
executes the gtk_main_quit function that stops the gtk_main
function, and, in this case, will end the program. The function is
called when a delete_event is detected. This will occur when the
window manager detects a delete_event event, such as clicking
on the Close box.

```
#include <gtk/gtk.h>

    void hellomessage( GtkWidget *widget,
                       gpointer    data )
    {
        g_print ("Hello World\n");
    }

    gint delete_event( GtkWidget *widget, GdkEvent
                       *event, gpointer    data )
    {
        gtk_main_quit();
    }

    int main( int    argc, char *argv[] )
    {
        GtkWidget *mywindow;
        GtkWidget *mybutton;

        gtk_init(&argc, &argv);

        mywindow = gtk_window_new
                            (GTK_WINDOW_TOPLEVEL);
        gtk_signal_connect (GTK_OBJECT (mywindow),
    "delete_event", GTK_SIGNAL_FUNC (delete_event),
    NULL);
        gtk_container_set_border_width
                        (GTK_CONTAINER (mywindow), 10);

        mybutton = gtk_button_new_with_label
                        ("Click Me");
        gtk_signal_connect (GTK_OBJECT (mybutton),
    "clicked", GTK_SIGNAL_FUNC (hellomessage), NULL);
```

```
gtk_container_add (GTK_CONTAINER (mywindow),
                   mybutton);
gtk_widget_show (mybutton);
gtk_widget_show (mywindow);
gtk_main ();

return(0);
}
```

Widgets

To create a widget, you have to first create it, associate it with events, specify its attributes, pack it into a container, and then display it. The steps can be described as follows:

1. Create the widget with a gtk_*_new function.

2. Associate signals and events for the widget with a specified function using gtk_signal_connect.

3. Specify the widget's attributes.

4. Pack the widget into a container using packing functions like gtk_container_add().

5. Indicate that the widget is ready for display. Use functions like gtk_widget_show().

Table 6-12 lists the kinds of GTK widgets available for use.

Widgets and Objects	Description
GtkAccelLabel	
GtkAdjustment	GtkObject representing an adjustable bounded value
GtkAlignment	Widget which controls the alignment and size of its child
GtkArrow	Produces an arrow pointing in one of the four cardinal directions
GtkAspectFrame	A frame that constrains its child to a particular aspect ratio

Table 6-12. GTK+ Widgets and Objects

Widgets and Objects	Description
GtkButtonBox	Button box
GtkBin	Container with just one child
GtkBox	Base class for box containers
GtkButton	Button
GtkCalendar	Display a calendar and/or allow the user to select a date
GtkCheckButton	Discrete toggle button
GtkCheckMenuItem	Menu item with a check box
GtkCList	Functions to create and manage multicolumn lists
GtkColorSelection	Color selection
GtkColorSelectionDialog	Color selection dialog
GtkCombo	Combo
GtkContainer	Container
GtkCTree	Display a hierarchical tree
GtkCurve	Curves
GtkData	Gtk object
GtkDialog	Create pop-up windows
GtkDrawingArea	Custom user interface elements
GtkEditable	Base class for text-editing widgets
GtkEntry	Single-line text entry field
GtkEventBox	Widget used to catch events for widgets that do not have their own window
GtkFileSelection	Prompt the user for a file or directory name
GtkFixed	Container that supports fixed sizes and positions of its children
GtkFontSelection	Widget for selecting fonts
GtkFontSelectionDialog	Dialog box for selecting fonts
GtkFrame	Bin with a decorative frame and optional label
GtkGammaCurve	Gamma curve
GtkHandleBox	Widget for detachable window portions
GtkHButtonBox	Container for arranging button horizontally
GtkHBox	Horizontal container box
GtkHPaned	Container with two panes arranged horizontally

Table 6-12. GTK+ Widgets and Objects *(continued)*

Widgets and Objects	Description
GtkHRuler	Horizontal ruler
GtkHScale	Horizontal slider widget for selecting a value from a range
GtkHScrollbar	Horizontal scroll bar
GtkHSeparator	Horizontal separator
GtkImage	Images
GtkInputDialog	Configure devices for the Xinput extension
GtkInvisible	Invisible feature
GtkItem	Select items
GtkItemFactory	Create and manage Gtk items
GtkLabel	Widget that displays a small to medium amount of text
GtkLayout	Layout widget
GtkList	List widget
GtkListItem	List item
GtkMenu	Drop-down menu widget
GtkMenuBar	Menu bar
GtkMenuItem	Menu item
GtkMenuShell	Base class for menu objects
GtkMisc	Base class for widgets with alignments and padding
GtkNotebook	Notebook widget
GtkObject	Create, manage, and delete Gtk objects
GtkOptionMenu	Widget used to choose from a list of valid choices
GtkPacker	Pack widgets
GtkPaned	Base class for widgets with two adjustable panes
GtkPixmap	Display a graphical image or icon
GtkPlug	Top level for embedding into other processes
GtkPreview	Display RGB or grayscale data
GtkProgress	Progress widget
GtkProgressBar	Progress bar
GtkRadioButton	Button radio widget
GtkRadioMenuItem	Menu radio item

6

Table 6-12. GTK+ Widgets and Objects *(continued)*

Widgets and Objects	Description
GtkRange	Range widget
GtkRuler	Draw ruler
GtkScale	Base class for GtkHScale and GtkVScale
GtkScrollbar	Scroll bar
GtkScrolledWindow	Scroll bars for its child widget
GtkSeparator	Base class for GtkHSeparator and GtkVseparator
GtkSocket	Container for widgets from other processes
GtkSpinButton	Retrieve an integer or floating-point number from the user
GtkStatusbar	Report messages of minor importance to the user
GtkTable	Pack widgets in regular patterns
GtkTearoffMenuItem	Menu item used to tear off and reattach its menu
GtkText	Text widget that can display and manipulate text
GtkTipsQuery	Query tips
GtkToggleButton	Toggle buttons
GtkToolbar	Button bars
GtkTooltips	Tips for widgets
GtkTree	Treelist widget
GtkTreeItem	Tree item
GtkVButtonBox	Button box
GtkVBox	Vertical container box
GtkViewport	Viewport
GtkVPaned	Container with two panes arranged vertically
GtkVRuler	Vertical ruler
GtkVScale	Vertical slider widget for selecting a value from a range
GtkVScrollbar	Vertical scroll bar
GtkVSeparator	Vertical separator
GtkWidget	Structure, macros, and functions to manage Gtk widgets
GtkWindow	Functions to create and manage windows

Table 6-12.   GTK+ Widgets and Objects *(continued)*

Type casting is used extensively throughout a GTK program to ensure that the object is passed to a function with its correct type. It also tests to see if the object can be correctly cast. Widgets are defined by using functions that dynamically allocate a widget structure for that widget and return a pointer. This pointer is usually defined as a pointer to the generic type GtkWidget. However, when you pass the widget to another function for processing, you have to cast this pointer to point to an object of the appropriate type. For example, in the Hello program, window is a pointer to a GtkWidget. After the gtk_window_new function returns a pointer to a widget structure for a window, the window pointer is then used in the gtk_signal_connect to pass the widget structure as one of type GtkObject, and then later to the gtk_container_set_border_with function as a structure of type GtkContainer. The casting macros GTK_OBJECT and GTK_CONTAINER are used to cast the widget to the appropriate type for that function argument. Several of the commonly used macros are listed in Table 6-13.

```
GtkWidget *button;
gtk_init(&argc, &argv);

window = gtk_window_new (GTK
                          _WINDOW_TOPLEVEL);

    gtk_signal_connect (GTK_OBJECT (window),
"delete_event", GTK_SIGNAL_FUNC (delete_event), NULL)

        gtk_container_set_border_width (GTK_CONTAINER
                                        (window), 10);
```

GTK_WIDGET(widget)
GTK_OBJECT(object)
GTK_SIGNAL_FUNC(function)
GTK_CONTAINER(container)
GTK_WINDOW(window)
GTK_BOX(box)

Table 6-13. Gtk Macros

Packing Widgets

When you place several widgets, like buttons and text boxes, inside an object, like a window or dialog, you will want to position them at specific places on the object. You do this with a method called "packing." You pack buttons into a window, placing them at certain locations on it. Packing makes use of unseen widgets called boxes. These operate like invisible frames within which you position objects. With horizontal boxes you can place widgets horizontally side by side, and with a vertical box you place widgets vertically. You can also place boxes next to each other or inside one another to construct complex formats.

You use the gtk_hbox_new command to create a horizontal box and the gtk_vbox_new to create a vertical box. The declaration for the gtk_hbox_new is shown here. The homogenous argument is used to specify if each object is to have the same size (height for vertical boxes and width for horizontal boxes). The spacing argument is the space you want between objects.

```
GtkWidget *gtk_hbox_new (gint homogeneous,
                         gint spacing);
```

You can pack widgets into a box from either end using the gtk_box_pack_start and gtk_box_pack_end command. Packing operations provide a great deal of flexibility, and there may be options for positioning widgets. The gtk_box_pack_start function has the following arguments: box is the box, child is the object you are packing into the box, expand is an option to expand the object to fill the box (TRUE or FALSE), fill allows extra space for the object, and padding provides spacing between the object and the box.

```
void gtk_box_pack_start( GtkBox    *box,
                         GtkWidget *child,
                         gint      expand,
                         gint      fill,
                         gint      padding );
```

The following code segment shows a very simple packing operation for two buttons. First, a horizontal box is created and its pointer is assigned to a box. The button1 button is created with ftk_button_new_with_label and given the label OK. This button is then packed to the box widget with gtk_box_pack_start. Gtk_widget_show will then designate button1 as ready to display. The same process is used to create and pack button2 to the box

widget. The mybox widget is then added to the window widget
with gtk_container_add.

```
GtkWidget *mybox;
GtkWidget *button1;
GtkWidget *button2;
GtkWidget *mywindow;


mybox = gtk_hbox_new (TRUE, 2);

button1 = gtk_button_new_with_label ("OK");
gtk_box_pack_start (GTK_BOX (mybox), button1,
                    TRUE, 0, 1);
gtk_widget_show (button1);

button2 = gtk_button_new_with_label ("Cancel");
gtk_box_pack_start (GTK_BOX (mybox), button2,
                    TRUE, 0, 1);
gtk_widget_show (button2);

gtk_container_add (GTK_CONTAINER (window), mybox);
```

Instead of using a single box container to pack objects, you can
use tables. These are grids with sections arranged in rows and
columns. You create a table with the gtk_table_new function. It
takes as its arguments the number of rows and columns. If the
homogeneous argument is TRUE, then the sections will all be the
same size as the largest one in the table; if FALSE, then each row
is adjusted to the widest in its row and the largest in its column.

```
GtkWidget *gtk_table_new( gint rows, gint columns,
                          gint homogeneous );
```

The numbering for the table begins with 0. Coordinates are
measured in terms of the edges of the section. You can think of
these as the lines making up the table. The coordinates indicate
the sections that the object will take up. Left and right
coordinates indicate the width in terms of sections and the top
and bottom coordinates indicate the height. For example, the
width of the first section is 0,1 and its height is also 0,1. For the
first section in the second row, the height would be 1,2. Use the
gtk_table_attach_defaults function to pack an object into the table
with defaults for padding and fill.

```
void gtk_table_attach_defaults( GtkTable   *table,
                                GtkWidget *child,
                                gint       left_attach,
                                gint       right_attach,
                                gint       top_attach,
                                gint       bottom_attach );
```

The following code creates a new table and packs a button to the upper-left section. In a 2 × 2 table, the width of the first section in the first row and column is 0,1 and the height is 0,1. For the second section in the first row the width would be 1,2 with a height of 0,1.

```
mytable = gtk_table_new (2, 2, TRUE);
gtk_table_attach_defaults (GTK_TABLE(mytable),
                           button1, 0, 1, 0, 1);
```

Drag and Drop

To receive data from a drop, you first determine the types of data you want to receive. These MIME types are specified in an array of GtkTargetEntry structures. Such a structure holds the MIME type, flag, and info field to identify the type numerically.

To set up a widget for dragging, you use the gtk_drag_dest_set function. You pass the widget along with the array of GtkTargetEntry structure and an argument indicating the type of action that is allowed. Such actions include GDK_ACTION_ DEFAULT, GDK_ACTION_COPY, GDK_ACTION_MOVE, GDK_ACTION_LINK, and GDK_ACTION_ASK. You then use a gtk_signal_connect function to bind the drag_data_received signal to the widget and a function you've written to handle the drag-and-drop operation (see the Gtk documentation for a more detailed analysis).

To send data with a drag operation, you also create a GtkTargetEntry array with MIME types and a mask for the start mouse button, GDK_BUTTON1_MASK I GDK_BUTTON3_MASK for the first mouse button. With the gtk_drag_source_set function, you set up the widget for dragging. Then, with the gtk_signal_ connect function, you need to bind the drag_data_get signal to the widget along with a drag handling function.

art_affine.h	Affine operations
art_alphagamma.h	Alphagamma tables
art_bpath.h	Bezier paths
art_filterlevel.h	"Filter levels" for image rendering
art_gray_svp.h	Rendering sorted vector paths to a grayscale buffer
art_misc.h	Miscellaneous libart declarations
art_pathcode.h	Path operators (moveto, lineto, etc.)
art_pixbuf.h	Pixel buffers
art_point.h	Point data types (i.e., X,Y coordinate pairs)
art_rect.h	Rectangle data types
art_rect_svp.h	Bounding box computation for sorted vector paths
art_rect_uta.h	Bounding rectangles from a microtile array
art_rgb.h	Basic RGB drawing primitives (run-filling)
art_rgb_affine.h	Affine transformation of RGB buffers
art_rgb_bitmap_affine.h	Affine transformation of bitmaps
art_rgb_pixbuf_affine.h	Affine transformation of generic pixel buffers
art_rgb_rgba_affine.h	Affine transformation of RGBA buffers
art_rgb_svp.h	Rendering sorted vector paths to RGB buffers
art_svp.h	Sorted vector path data type
art_svp_ops.h	Sorted vector path set operations (union, intersection, etc.)
art_svp_render_aa.h	Anti-aliased sorted vector path rendering
art_svp_vpath.h	Sorting an unsorted vector path
art_svp_vpath_stroke.h	"Strokes" a vector path yielding a sorted vector path
art_svp_wind.h	Winding rules for sorted vector paths
art_uta.h	Microtile array data type
art_uta_ops.h	Microtile array set operations (union, etc.)

Table 6-14. Gtk and Gnome Header Files

art_uta_rect.h	Conversion from a rectangle to a microtile array
art_uta_svp.h	Conversion from a sorted vector path to a microtile array
art_uta_vpath.h	Conversion from a vector path to a microtile array
art_vpath.h	Vector path data type
art_vpath_bpath.h	Bezier path to vector path conversion
art_vpath_svp.h	Sorted vector path to vector path conversion
gdk.h	Gdk function declarations
gdkcursors.h	Gdk built-in cursor IDs
gdki18n.h	Portability wrappers for iswalnum() and iswspace()
gdkkeysyms.h	Gdk keysym names (GDK_space, GDK_Up, etc.)
gdkprivate.h	Private Gdk types
gdkrgb.h	Gdk's GdkRGB module
gdktypes.h	Gdk type declarations
gdkx.h	Declarations for Gdk-to-X mapping
glib.h	glib header
gnome-about.h	GnomeAbout widget
gnome-animator.h	GnomeAnimator widget
gnome-app-helper.h	GnomeApp add-ons, including GnomeUIInfo menu/toolbar generation
gnome-app-util.h	User messages, via dialog or status bar
gnome-app.h	GnomeApp widget
gnome-appbar.h	GnomeAppBar widget
gnome-calculator.h	GnomeCalculator widget
gnome-canvas-image.h	GnomeCanvasImage canvas item
gnome-canvas-line.h	GnomeCanvasLine canvas item
gnome-canvas-load.h	Routine to load a PNG with alpha transparency
gnome-canvas-polygon.h	GnomeCanvasPolygon canvas item
gnome-canvas-rect-ellipse.h	GnomeCanvasRect and GnomeCanvasEllipse canvas items
gnome-canvas-text.h	GnomeCanvasText canvas item

Table 6-14.   Gtk and Gnome Header Files *(continued)*

gnome-canvas-util.h	Miscellaneous canvas-related routines
gnome-canvas-widget.h	GnomeCanvasWidget canvas item
gnome-canvas.h	GnomeCanvas widget, GnomeCanvasItem base class and GnomeCanvasGroup item
gnome-client.h	GnomeClient session management interface
gnome-color-picker.h	GnomeColorPicker widget
gnome-config.h	Configuration file API
gnome-dateedit.h	GnomeDateEdit widget
gnome-defs.h	Miscellaneous libgnome macros
gnome-dentry-edit.h	GnomeDEntryEdit object
gnome-dentry.h	**.desktop** file handling
gnome-dialog-util.h	Dialog convenience functions
gnome-dialog.h	GnomeDialog widget
gnome-dns.h	Asynchronous DNS lookups
gnome-dock-band.h	GnomeDockBand widget
gnome-dock-item.h	GnomeDockItem widget
gnome-dock-layout.h	GnomeDockLayout object
gnome-dock.h	GnomeDock widget
gnome-entry.h	GnomeEntry widget
gnome-exec.h	Convenience wrappers to exec child processes
gnome-file-entry.h	GnomeFileEntry widget
gnome-fileconvert.h	Routine that attempts to convert between MIME types
gnome-font-picker.h	GnomeFontPicker widget
gnome-font-selector.h	GnomeFontSelector widget
gnome-geometry.h	Convenience functions for geometry strings (e.g., 1000x1000+0+0)
gnome-guru.h	Obsolete "wizard" widget
gnome-help.h	gnome_help_goto() and friends
gnome-history.h	Recently used file history
gnome-href.h	GnomeHRef widget
gnome-i18n.h	Gnome internationalization macros
gnome-i18nP.h	Library-internal internationalization (private)

Table 6-14. Gtk and Gnome Header Files *(continued)*

gnome-ice.h	Code to handle an ICE connection
gnome-icon-entry.h	GnomeIconEntry widget
gnome-icon-item.h	GnomeIconTextItem canvas item (don't use; library-private)
gnome-icon-list.h	GnomeIconList widget
gnome-icon-sel.h	GnomeIconSelection widget
gnome-init.h	gnome_init() and variants
gnome-less.h	GnomeLess widget
gnome-mdi-child.h	GnomeMDIChild object
gnome-mdi-generic-child.h	GnomeMDIGenericChild object
gnome-mdi-session.h	Session management support for GnomeMDI
gnome-mdi.h	GnomeMDI object
gnome-messagebox.h	GnomeMessageBox widget
gnome-metadata.h	Facilities for associating data with files
gnome-mime-info.h	Get information about registered MIME types
gnome-mime.h	Determine MIME type of a file
gnome-number-entry.h	GnomeNumberEntry widget
gnome-paper-selector.h	GnomePaperSelector widget
gnome-paper.h	Deprecated interface for paper size configuration (use gnome-print instead)
gnome-pixmap-entry.h	GnomePixmapEntry widget
gnome-pixmap.h	GnomePixmap widget
gnome-popt.h	Argument-parsing-related declarations
gnome-popup-help.h	Routine to add pop-up help to a widget
gnome-popup-menu.h	Convenience routines to create right-click pop-up menus
gnome-preferences.h	Routines to load and save certain Gnome-wide preferences
gnome-procbar.h	GnomeProcBar widget
gnome-properties.h	Experimental interface for handling preferences
gnome-property-entries.h	Auxiliary routines for experimental gnome-properties.h interface
gnome-propertybox.h	GnomePropertyBox widget
gnome-regex.h	Wrapper for regcomp() that caches compiled regular expressions

Table 6-14. Gtk and Gnome Header Files *(continued)*

gnome-remote.h	Remote command execution (user configures the remote execution command on a per-host basis)
gnome-score.h	Routines to load and save high scores
gnome-scores.h	GnomeScores widget
gnome-sound.h	Routines to play sounds
gnome-spell.h	GnomeSpell widget
gnome-startup.h	Routines to allow "locking" during session startup
gnome-stock.h	Gnome stock pixmap widgets and declarations
gnome-triggers.h	Register events and actions to trigger when the events happen
gnome-types.h	Assorted type declarations
gnome-uidefs.h	Assorted macros
gnome-url.h	gnome_url_show() to display an URL using a user-configured method
gnome-util.h	Lots of useful utility functions
gnome-winhints.h	Gnome window manager hints
gnome.h	Includes all the public libgnome and libgnomeui headers
gnorba.h	libgnorba header file
gtk-clock.h	GtkClock widget
gtk-ted.h	GtkTed widget
gtk.h	Includes the public Gtk+ headers and gdk.h
gtkaccelgroup.h	Accelerator key support
gtkaccellabel.h	GtkAccelLabel widget
gtkadjustment.h	GtkAdjustment object
gtkalignment.h	GtkAlignment widget
gtkarg.h	GtkArg type
gtkarrow.h	GtkArrow widget
gtkaspectframe.h	GtkAspectFrame widget
gtkbbox.h	GtkButtonBox widget
gtkbin.h	GtkBin widget
gtkbindings.h	Keybinding support for GTK_RUN_ACTION signals

Table 6-14.   Gtk and Gnome Header Files *(continued)*

gtkbox.h	GtkBox widget
gtkbutton.h	GtkButton widget
gtkcalendar.h	GtkCalendar widget
gtkcauldron.h	Experimental dialog-creation routines
gtkcheckbutton.h	GtkCheckButton widget
gtkcheckmenuitem.h	GtkCheckMenuItem widget
gtkclist.h	GtkCList widget
gtkcolorsel.h	GtkColorSelection widget
gtkcombo.h	GtkCombo widget
gtkcompat.h	Compatibility macros for renamed or removed functions
gtkcontainer.h	GtkContainer widget
gtkctree.h	GtkCTree widget
gtkcurve.h	GtkCurve widget
gtkdata.h	GtkData object
gtkdial.h	GtkDial widget
gtkdialog.h	GtkDialog widget
gtkdnd.h	Gtk+ drag-and-drop interface
gtkdrawingarea.h	GtkDrawingArea widget
gtkeditable.h	GtkEditable widget
gtkentry.h	GtkEntry widget
gtkenums.h	Enumerations used in Gtk+
gtkeventbox.h	GtkEventBox widget
gtkfeatures.h	Macros to identify Gtk+ library version
gtkfilesel.h	GtkFileSelection widget
gtkfixed.h	GtkFixed widget
gtkfontsel.h	GtkFontSelection widget
gtkframe.h	GtkFrame widget
gtkgamma.h	GtkGammaCurve widget
gtkgc.h	Graphics context cache interface
gtkhandlebox.h	GtkHandleBox widget
gtkhbbox.h	GtkHButtonBox widget
gtkhbox.h	GtkHBox widget
gtkhpaned.h	GtkHPaned widget
gtkhruler.h	GtkHRuler widget
gtkhscale.h	GtkHScale widget

Table 6-14. Gtk and Gnome Header Files *(continued)*

gtkhscrollbar.h	GtkHScrollbar widget
gtkhseparator.h	GtkHSeparator widget
gtkimage.h	GtkImage widget
gtkinputdialog.h	GtkInputDialog widget
gtkintl.h	Gtk+ internationalization
gtkitem.h	GtkItem widget
gtkitemfactory.h	GtkItemFactory object
gtklabel.h	GtkLabel widget
gtklayout.h	GtkLayout widget
gtklist.h	GtkList widget
gtklistitem.h	GtkListItem widget
gtkmain.h	Gtk+ main loop
gtkmarshal.h	Gtk+ signal marshalers
gtkmenu.h	GtkMenu widget
gtkmenubar.h	GtkMenuBar widget
gtkmenufactory.h	GtkMenuFactory (use item factory instead)
gtkmenuitem.h	GtkMenuItem widget
gtkmenushell.h	GtkMenuShell widget
gtkmisc.h	GtkMisc widget
gtknotebook.h	GtkNotebook widget
gtkobject.h	GtkObject base class
gtkoptionmenu.h	GtkOptionMenu widget
gtkpacker.h	GtkPacker widget
gtkpaned.h	GtkPaned widget
gtkpixmap.h	GtkPixmap widget
gtkpixmapmenuitem.h	GtkPixmapMenuItem widget
gtkplug.h	GtkPlug widget
gtkpreview.h	GtkPreview widget
gtkprogress.h	GtkProgress widget
gtkprogressbar.h	GtkProgressBar widget
gtkradiobutton.h	GtkRadioButton widget
gtkradiomenuitem.h	GtkRadioMenuItem widget
gtkrange.h	GtkRange widget
gtkrc.h	Gtk+ rc file parsing
gtkruler.h	GtkRuler widget

Table 6-14. Gtk and Gnome Header Files *(continued)*

gtkscale.h	GtkScale widget
gtkscrollbar.h	GtkScrollbar widget
gtkscrolledwindow.h	GtkScrolledWindow widget
gtkselection.h	Selection-handling routines
gtkseparator.h	GtkSeparator widget
gtksignal.h	Signal-related declarations
gtksocket.h	GtkSocket widget
gtkspinbutton.h	GtkSpinButton widget
gtkstatusbar.h	GtkStatusbar widget
gtkstyle.h	GtkStyle type and themed drawing routines
gtktable.h	GtkTable widget
gtktearoffmenuitem.h	GtkTearoffMenuItem widget
gtktext.h	GtkText widget
gtkthemes.h	Theme engine data type
gtktipsquery.h	GtkTipsQuery widget
gtktogglebutton.h	GtkToggleButton widget
gtktoolbar.h	GtkToolbar widget
gtktooltips.h	GtkTooltips object
gtktree.h	GtkTree widget
gtktreeitem.h	GtkTreeItem widget
gtktypebuiltins.h	Gtk+ built-in type IDs
gtktypeutils.h	Gtk+ type system routines
gtkvbbox.h	GtkVButtonBox widget
gtkvbox.h	GtkVBox widget
gtkviewport.h	GtkViewport widget
gtkvpaned.h	GtkVPaned widget
gtkvruler.h	GtkVRuler widget
gtkvscale.h	GtkVScale widget
gtkvscrollbar.h	GtkVScrollbar widget
gtkvseparator.h	GtkVSeparator widget
gtkwidget.h	GtkWidget base class
gtkwindow.h	GtkWindow widget
libgnome.h	Includes all public libgnome headers
libgnomeui.h	Includes all public libgnomeui headers
zvtterm.h	ZvtTerm widget

Table 6-14. Gtk and Gnome Header Files *(continued)*

Glib

Both GDK and GTK make use of lower-level functions in the Glib library. Glib is the GNU library that is an enhanced version of the standard C libraries. Glib includes string functions, byte operations, memory allocation functions, and so on. It also includes predefined data structures such as linked lists, hash tables, variable size arrays, trees, keyed lists, and even relational database tables. For detailed documentation on Glib, check **www.gtk.org** or **developer.gnome.org**. Table 6-15 lists the kinds of functions that make up the Glib library.

Glib includes the type definitions used in Gnome applications. Here, you find the definitions for types like gint, gchar, and gboolean.

```
char          gchar;
short     gshort;
long      glong;
int       gint;
char      gboolean;
unsigned char     guchar;
unsigned short    gushort;
unsigned long     gulong;
unsigned int      guint;
float     gfloat;
double    gdouble;
long double gldouble;
void*  gpointer;
gint8
guint8
gint16
guint16
gint32
guint32
```

Strings are defined using the type GString. This operates like the C string, but can expand automatically in size. The idea is to prevent runtime errors that can result from large strings copied into smaller ones. The smaller string will automatically expand to the size of the larger string. Like C, strings are still NULL terminated, '\0'.

6

```
struct GString
{
  gchar *str; /* Points to the string's current
\0-terminated value. */
  gint len; /* Current length */
};
```

To create a GString you use the g_string function. This takes as its argument the address of a string (ghar*) and returns a pointer to a GString. For an empty string, use NULL.

```
GString *g_string_new( gchar *init );
```

There are corresponding string manipulation functions such as g_string_assign to copy a string, g_string_free to erase a string, and g_string_append to append one string to another. There are also g_string_sprintf and g_string_sprintfa for use with formatted strings.

For input and output operations, you can use g_print to print a string.

To print standard error messages, you can use g_strerror instead or perror. To directly print an error message and exit the program, you can use g_error. To just display an error message, you can use g_warning. For simple messages, you can use g_message.

Data structures like doubly linked lists can be managed using Glib functions. To create a linked list, you define a variable of type GList* and use g_list_append to add elements, g_list_instert to insert, and g_list_remove to delete an element on doubly linked lists. For singly linked lists, you use g_slist_append, g_slist_insert, and g_slist_remove. To manage memory, you use g_malloc and g_free.

GDK

The Gimp Drawing Toolkit (GDK) is an implementation of the lower-level X Window System libraries. It operates as an interface between Gtk and the X Window System. Instead of calling X Window System functions directly, Gtk makes calls to GDK functions, which in turn call the appropriate X Window System functions. Such a design also provides portability for Gtk. Versions

GLib Fundamentals	Description
Basic types	Standard GLib types, defined for ease of use and portability
Limits of basic types	Portable method of determining the limits of the standard types
Standard macros	Commonly used macros
Type conversion macros	Portable method for storing gint & guint values in gpointer variables
Byte order macros	Portable way to convert between different byte orders
Miscellaneous macros	Specialized macros

GLib Core Application Support	
The main event loop	Manages all available sources of events
Threads	Thread abstraction; including mutexes, conditions and thread private data
Dynamic loading of modules	Portable method for dynamically loading 'plug-ins'
Memory Allocation	General memory-handling
IO Channels	Portable support for using files, pipes, and sockets
Message output and debugging functions	Functions to output messages and help debug applications
Message logging	Support for logging messages

GLib Utilities	
String utility functions	String functions
Date and time functions	Calendrical calculations and miscellaneous time stuff
Hook functions	Support for manipulating lists of hook functions
Miscellaneous utility functions	Selection of portable utility functions
Lexical scanner	General-purpose lexical scanner
Automatic string completion	Support for automatic completion using a group of target strings

6

Table 6-15. GLIB

GLib Fundamentals	Description
Timers	Functions to time operations
Windows compatibility functions	Functions to support portability to the Windows environment

GLib Data Types

Memory chunks	Efficient way to allocate groups of equal-sized chunks of memory
Doubly linked lists	Linked lists containing integer values or pointers to data, with the ability to iterate over the list in both directions
Singly linked lists	Linked lists containing integer values or pointers to data, limited to iterating over the list in one direction
Hash tables	Associations between keys and values so that given a key the value can be found quickly
Strings	Text buffers that grow automatically as text is added
String chunks	Efficient storage of groups of strings
Arrays	Arrays of arbitrary elements that grow automatically as elements are added
Pointer arrays	Arrays of pointers to any type of data, which grow automatically as new elements are added
Byte arrays	Arrays of bytes, which grow automatically as elements are added
Balanced binary trees	Sorted collection of key/value pairs optimized for searching and traversing in order
N-ary trees	Trees of data with any number of branches
Quarks	Two-way association between a string and a unique integer identifier
Keyed data lists	Lists of data elements that are accessible by a string or GQuark identifier
Datasets	Associate groups of data elements with particular memory locations

Table 6-15.   GLIB *(continued)*

GLib Fundamentals	Description
Relations and tuples	Tables of data that can be indexed on any number of fields
Caches	Allows sharing of complex data structures to save resources
Memory allocators	Allocates chunks of memory for GList, GSList, and GNode

Table 6-15. GLIB *(continued)*

of Gdk have been written for other window systems, such as Windows. Table 6-16 lists the kinds of functions making up the GDK.

The X Window System structures its interface around the concept of an X Window. This concept literally denotes the shapes and segments you see on the screen. The main X Window is the root window, which is the entire background screen. All windows are logically placed in a hierarchical tree where the root window is the root of this tree and all other windows are arranged below it. Application windows that show on the screen are children of the parent root window. Components of a particular window like the title bar are in turn children of the window they belong to. The X server performs actual actions on the windows such as resizing them, moving them, or capturing events like mouse clicks and menu selections. Gtk uses Gdk to access the X Window System. Gdk contains a simple X Window wrapper, called GdkWindow, through which X Windows are accessed. Gtk+ widgets usually have a corresponding GdkWindow. Actions on a widget are translated through Gdk and its corresponding GdkWindow into X Window operations.

The low-level functions used by the X Window System are containers in a library called Xlib. The Gdk library, in turn, contains functions that are simple wrappers for corresponding Xlib functions. The aim is to hide the lower-level complex tasks actually performed by the X Window System from the Gtk functions. This in effect enables Gtk+ to be transportable. Instead of Xlib, Gdk can be rewritten for other window libraries such as Windows or the Mac, requiring little or no change to Gtk.

It is important to keep in mind the difference between a GtkWindow and a GdkWindow. GtkWindow is a Gtk widget used for application top-level windows. A GdkWindow, on the other hand, is just a simple wrapper for an X Window. An X Window is an object managed by the X server that already knows how to handle windows. GdkWindow merely contains the ID for the window being managed by the X server along with some local information like the size. It functions as a handle for referencing a server-managed object.

Table 6-16 breaks down the Gdk functions by category, giving you some idea of the tasks they perform. In most cases, you will never have to directly invoke a Gdk function. These are automatically invoked by Gtk+ functions as needed.

Component	Description
General	Initialization, display, keyboard, and event functions
Bitmaps and pixmaps	Offscreen drawables
Images	Image structure and functions
GdkRGB	RGB image functions
Colormaps and colors	Manipulation of colors and color maps
Fonts	Loading and manipulating fonts
Drawing primitives	Functions to draw primitive figures such as lines and rectangles
Graphics contexts	Functions to set graphic features
Visuals	Manipulation of visuals
Windows	Functions to control windows
Selections	Functions to control selections
Properties and atoms	Functions to manage properties and atoms
Input methods	Functions for managing input methods
Input contexts	Input context structures and functions
Color contexts	Color context structures and functions
Points, rectangles, and regions	Functions to manage points, rectangles, and regions
Threads	Thread functions

Table 6-16. GDK Components

Component	Description
Key values	Functions for manipulating keyboard codes
Input devices	Functions for handling input devices
Events	Functions, types, and masks for GDK events
Event structures	GDK event structures
Cursors	Define cursors
Input	Callbacks on file descriptors
Drag and drop	Functions to control drag-and-drop operations

Table 6-16.   GDK Components *(continued)*

6

Chapter 7
KDE Programming

KDE is organized on a C++ object model with C++ objects
containing functions with which you can modify the object. Many
of the functions are inherited, and others are defined for a
particular type of object. In a KDE program, you define an object
and then use its public and private functions to modify it. For
example, you can create a menu object and then use the menu
object's functions to add new menu items to it. As a C++
object-oriented program, KDE applications use a set of
hierarchical object classes contained in the KDE and QT libraries.
Classes lower in the hierarchy will inherit members from those
they are connected to higher in the hierarchy. You can create your
own classes and have them inherit members (functions) from
these predefined KDE classes. KDE uses the QT Toolkit and
currently relies on it directly. Unlike Gnome, which can have its
lower-level functions managed by any toolkit, KDE relies solely
on the QT Toolkit. Currently, KDE programming is essentially
QT programming.

KDE and QT programming relies on an extensive set of classes,
each of which usually has a significant number of member
functions that manage objects of that class. There are far more
than can be listed within the size limitations of this book. Table
7-5 lists all the KDE user interface classes, but these in turn have
an extensive number of member functions. For a complete listing,
it is strongly advised that you use the documentation profiled on
the KDE developer's site, **developer.kde.org**. This site includes
detailed tutorial, complete reference materials for the KDE API as
well as KOM (KDE Object Manager) documentation and QT
reference material. Each class is described in detail along with the
class type declaration including their member function
declarations and definitions. In addition, consult the KDE and QT
header files. The **.h** files contain a complete listing of the KDE and
QT classes along with detailed comments describing their
member functions.

A widget like a window or a button is just an object. You can
define a window object using a KDE or QT window class or a
button using a KDE or QT button class. There are several kinds of
classes depending on the type of window or button you want. To
create a complex widget like a window that contains other

315

widgets like toolbars and menus, you define the sub-widgets as children of the main widget. When you define a toolbar you specify a particular window object as its parent. A sub-widget can in turn have its own sub-widgets, its own children. A menubar can have a window as its parent and individual menus as its children.

When you declare a C++ object you usually include arguments, in addition to the class and object name. These arguments are passed to a special function called a constructor that is executed when the object is defined. It performs any needed setup or initialization operation object. For widgets one of these arguments is usually the address of its parent widget. A toolbar will be defined with one of its argument's being the address of a window object that is its parent. If the widget is a top level one with no parent, the argument is NULL. With a series of simple object definitions you can easily create a complex widget.

KDE Libraries

A KDE program is simply a C++ program compiled with KDE and QT libraries. You use the g++ compiler on your source coder files as you would any other C++ program. There are several KDE libraries, each with an extensive set of classes. Currently, there are two versions of these libraries, those for KDE release 1.1 and those for the more recent KDE 2.0. Table 7-2 lists the KDE 1.1 libraries and Table 7-1 lists the KDE 2.0 libraries. In addition, Table 7-3 lists the classes for the KDE 2.0 kdecore library. Most programs will need at least the kdecore and kdeui libraries. Kdeui holds the KDE user interface classes for KDE widgets (see Table 7-5). The 2.0 release of KDE also includes the KOffice suite. To compile programs that take advantage of KOffice components, you use the KDE Object Manager (KOM) libraries (see Table 7-4).

KDE Applications and Widgets

To create a KDE application, you simply create an object of type Kapplication in your program. It must be defined before you define any other KDE objects. The class declaration for Kapplication is contained in the **kapp.h** file. The definition of a Kapplication object takes as its arguments argc and argv. These operate as they do in

Components	Description
kdecore	Core KDE classes that are not related to the user interface
kdeui	KDE user interface classes such as widgets
kded	The KDE daemon; provides centralized access to various standard KDE services
khtml	The KDE HTML component
jscript	JavaScript support
kfile	High-level access to the KDE network-aware file abstraction
kimgio	Support for various bitmap image formats
kom	The KDE Object Model
kparts	Support for reusable, embeddable, extendable applications
kpartsui	User interface classes for KParts
kspell	Easy access to the spell checker
kformula	The Equation Editor

Table 7-1.　KDE 2.0

7

Components	Description
kdecore	Core KDE classes that are not related to the user interface
kdeui	KDE user interface classes such as widgets
khtmlw	The KDE HTML component; note the HTML component in KDE 2.0 is different
kfile	High-level access to the KDE network-aware file abstraction
kimgio	Support for various bitmap image formats
kspell	Easy access to the spell checker
kab	Access to the KDE address book

Table 7-2.　KDE 1.1

KAccel	Configurable key binding support.
KApplication	Controls and provides information to all KDE applications.
KCharsets	KCharsets is a small class to help you solve some charset related problems.
KColorGroup	A KColorGroup provides seven colors for widgets: foreground, background, light, mid, dark, text, and base.
KConfig	KDE Configuration Management class.
KConfigBackEnd	KDE Configuration file loading/saving abstract base class.
KConfigBase	KDE Configuration Management abstract base class.
KConfigGroupSaver	Helper class for easier use of KConfig/KSimpleConfig groups.
KConfigINIBackEnd	Class for KDE INI-style configuration file loading/saving.
KDebugDialog	Control debug output at runtime.
KDesktopFile	KDE Desktop File Management class.
KEntry	map/dict/list node entry.
KEntryKey	Key structure holding both the actual key and the group to which it belongs.
KfontStruct	KDE font structure
KfontStructList	Font list class
KGlobal	Accessors to KDE global objects.
KGlobalAccel	The KGlobalAccel class handles global keyboard accelerators.
KIconLoader	Icon loader with caching.
KkeyEntry	Key code members
Klocale	Class for supporting locale settings and national language.
KPixmap	Offscreen paint device with extended features.
KProcess	Child process invocation, monitoring, and control.
KProcessController	A class for internal use by KProcess only.
KprotocolManager	Protocols supported by KDE

Table 7-3. KDE Core 2.0

KRegExp	Regular expression matching with back references.
KRegExpPrivate	Used internally by KRegExp.
KRootProp	Access to KDE desktop resources stored on the root window.
KServerSocket	Monitor a port for incoming TCP/IP connections.
KShared	Share methods
KSharedPtr	Can be used to control the lifetime of an object that has derived KShared.
KShellProcess	A class derived from KProcess to start child processes through a shell.
KSimpleConfig	KDE Configuration Management class with deletion ability.
KSocket	A TCP/IP client socket.
KStandardDirs	Site-independent access to standard KDE directories.
KStartParams	A class for simple command-line argument access.
KStdAccel	Convenient methods for access to the common accelerator keys in the key configuration.
KStyle	Extends the QStyle class with virtual methods to draw KDE widgets
KURL	Mention that KURL has some restrictions regarding the path encoding.
KWM	Class for interaction with the window and session manager.
KWinModule	Base class for KDE window manager modules.
KZoneAllocator	Zone allocation
QSharedPtr	Can be used to control the lifetime of an object that has derived QShared.
Q_EXPORT	This class acts like a union.
kFSDither	Floyd-Steinberg dithering.
kauto_array	Automatic array

Table 7-3.   KDE Core 2.0 *(continued)*

KFileNotifier	Notifier for a file event.
KOMAggregate	Provides additional interfaces for a component.
KOMAggregateFactory	Class KOMAggregateFactory.
KOMApplication	Base class for all applications in KOM.
KOMApplicationIf	KOMApplicationIf class
KOMAutoLoader	The KOMAutoLoader class.
KOMBase	The base class of KOM.
KOMBoot	Template class KOMBoot.
KOMBuiltinAggregate	KOMMBuiltinAggregate struct.
KOMBuiltinPlugin	KOMBuiltinPlugin struct.
KOMComponent	A component with the possibility for dynamic extensions.
KOMComponentFactory	The KOMComponentFactory class.
KOMContainer	A KOMContainer acts as repository for KOM::Base types.
KOMDerivedInterface	KOMDerivedInterface struct.
KOMDynamicAggregate	KOMDynamicAggregate struct.
KOMDynamicPlugin	KOMDynamicPlugin struct
KOMPlugin	Changes the implementation of the functionality of a component.
KOMPluginFactory	Class KOMPluginFactory.
KOMShutdownManager	This class will launch a (q)timer after all watched KOMBase (or derived) objects have been destroyed.
KOMVar	KOM Var methods
KTimerNotifier	Notifier for a timer event.

Table 7-4. KOM

C programs, referencing any command line arguments the user enters. The following example defines an application object called myapp:

```
KApplication myapp( argc, argv );
```

Declarations for different kinds of KDE and QT objects are located in separate header files. Whenever you define an object of a particular type, be sure to include the header file that has its class declaration. Table 7-6 lists the different KDE header files, and Table 7-10 lists the QT header files. For example, to create a main application window, you use KTMainWindow class and you need to include the **ktmainwindow.h** header file.

```
#include <ktmainwindow.h>
```

The header files are also extremely helpful as a reference source. They list all the member functions for a particular class and include detailed comments describing each function and its use. The header files will be located in the KDE include directory. Currently for Red Hat, this is the standard include directory, **/usr/include**. On OpenLinux and other distributions, it may be the special KDE directory such as **/opt/kde/include**.

To define a main window for your application, you use the KTMainWindow class. The following example creates a main window object called mywin:

```
KTMainWindow mywin = KTMainWindow();
```

If you create an application where the main window is the primary interface and you want the application to close when that window closes, you have to make it the main widget for the application. For this, you use the application object's setMainWidget function. The main widget could be any widget you want. The following example sets the main widgets to the mywin window.

```
myapp.setMainWidget(mywin);
```

When you define a widget, you will also be defining any of its member functions contained in its class declaration. See the **developer.kde.org** documentation for a complete description of all KDE class declarations, including their member functions. Many of these member functions are designed to let you change the display features of a widget, such as its color or initial size. For example, to control the display size of the KTMainWindow widget, you use its setGeometry function as shown here:

```
mywin.setGeometry(100,100,200,100);
```

Any widget that you want displayed, you have to explicitly instruct KDE to show it. For this, you use your widget's show member function. For example, to have the mywin window display, you execute its show function as shown here:

7

```
mywin.show();
return myapp.exec();
```

Once you have defined all your widgets and made any modifications, you can then run the application. You do this with the Kapplication object's exec member function. When the user closes the application, control returns to the main function, which can then terminate the program.

```
myapp.exec();
```

The following program creates a simple KDE application that displays a window:

```
#include <kapp.h>
#include <ktmainwindow.h>

int main( int argc, char **argv )
{
  KApplication myapp( argc, argv );
  KTMainWindow mywin = KTMainWindow();
  mywin.setGeometry(100,100,200,100);

  myapp.setMainWidget(mywin);
  mywin.show();
  return myapp.exec();
}
```

Widgets	Description
DialogBase	This base class provides basic functionality needed by nearly all dialogs.
KAboutContributor	Every person displayed is stored in a KAboutContributor object.
KAboutDialog	KAboutDialog is a DialogBase with predefined main widget.
KAboutWidget	KAboutWidget is the main widget for KAboutDialog.
KAccelMenu	This class simplifies the use of KAccel and KKeyDialog with menus.

Table 7-5.   KDE 2.0 kdeui (User Interface)

Widgets	Description
KActCfgListItem	An item in the action configuration widget.
KActItemCfg	Action configuration widget
KAction	A named user action.
KActionConfigWidget	Widget for user to configure actions.
KActionMenuBuilder	Easy building of pop-up menu items using KUIActions.
KApplet	KDE Panel Applet class.
KAuthIcon	This is the base class from which different authorization icon widgets that actually do something should be derived.
KButton	Provides active raise/lower buttons.
KButtonBox	Container widget for buttons.
KColorButton	A pushbutton to display or allow user selection of a color.
KColorCells	A table of editable color cells.
KColorCombo	Combobox for colors.
KColorDialog	KDE Color Selection dialog.
KColorDrag	KColorDrag for XDnd'ing objects of type application/x-color.
KcolorPatch	
KConfigWidget	The base widget for a setup dialog box.
KContainerLayout	Alternative layout manager widget.
KControlApplication	Common base for setup applications.
KControlDialog	KControlDialog is a QTabDialog that is internally used by Kcontrol applications.
KCursor	A QCursor wrapper allowing "themed" cursors.
KDatePicker	A widget for selecting dates.
KDateTable	Draws a calendar table.
KDialog	Dialog box with extended modeless support.
KDirectionButton	KDirectionButton.
KDualColorButton	A widget for selecting two related colors.
KEdGotoLine	Edit goto line class
KEdReplace	Edit replace class

Table 7-5.   KDE 2.0 kdeui (User Interface) *(continued)*

7

Widgets	Description
KEdSrch	Edit search class
KEdit	Edit class
KFloatValidator	KFloatValidator—see QValidator for more details.
KFontChooser	Widget for interactive font selection.
KFontDialog	Dialog for interactive font selection.
KGradientSelector	Gradient selector widget
KHSSelector	Widget for hue/saturation selection.
KIconLoaderButton	This is a button that uses KIconLoaderDialog.
KIconLoaderCanvas	Internal display class for KIconLoaderDialog.
KIconLoaderDialog	Dialog box for interactive selection of icons.
KIntNumInput	KIntNumInput combines a QSpinbox and optionally a QSlider with a label to make an easy-to-use control for setting some integer parameter.
KIntSpinBox	Integer spin box class
KIntValidator	Integer validation class (see Qvalidator)--.
KKeyButton	A pushbutton that looks like a keyboard key.
KKeyChooser	The KKeyChooser widget is used for configuring dictionaries of key/action associations for KAccel and KGlobalAccel.
KKeyDialog	The KKeyDialog class is used for configuring dictionaries of key/action associations for KAccel and KGlobalAccel.
KLed	A round led widget.
KLedLamp	A CDE-style LED lamp widget.
KLineEdit	KDE line input widget.
KLineEditDlg	Dialog for user to enter a single line of text.
KMenuBar	Floatable menu bar.
KMessageBox	Easy MessageBox dialog box.
KNumCheckButton	Provides a different type of Check button.
KPalette	Pallete class
KPixmapEffect	This class includes various pixmap-based graphical effects.

Table 7-5. KDE 2.0 kdeui (User Interface) *(continued)*

Widgets	Description
KPopupMenu	Pop-up menu with title.
KProgress	A progress indicator widget.
KRadioGroup	Class for group of radio buttons in toolbar.
KRestrictedLine	Restricted editline: Only selected characters are valid input.
KrootPermsIcon	Root permission icon
KRuler	A ruler widget.
KSelector	1D value selector with contents drawn by derived class.
KSeparator	Standard horizontal or vertical separator.
KSplitList	A list box capable of multicolumns.
KSplitListItem	A list box item for KSplitList.
KStatusBar	KDE statusbar widget.
KStatusBarItem	Internal class for use in KStatusBar.
KStatusBarLabel	Internal class for use in KStatusBar.
KStyleMenuBarInternal	Menu bar style
KTMLayout	Special layout manager for KTMainWindow.
KTMLayoutIterator	Auxiliary class for KTMLayout.
KTMainWindow	KDE top-level main window.
KTabBar	KTabBar.
KTabButton	KTabButton.
KTabCtl	Tabbed dialog box with extended features.
KTabListBox	A multicolumn listbox feature: user-resizable columns.
KTabListBoxColumn	List box widget column
KTabListBoxItem	List box widget item
KTabListBoxTable	List box widget table
KThemeBase	This is a base class for KDE themed styles.
KThemeCache	A very simple pixmap cache for theme plug-ins.
KThemePixmap	This class adds simple time management to KPixmap for use in flushing KThemeCache.
KThemeStyle	This is a class for KDE themed styles.
KToolBar	Floatable toolbar with autoresize.
KToolBarButton	A toolbar button.
KToolBarItem	A toolbar item.

7

Table 7-5.   KDE 2.0 kdeui (User Interface) *(continued)*

Widgets	Description
KToolBoxManager	Class for own window management.
KTopLevelWidget	Old KDE top-level window.
KUIActions	Unified UI action manager.
KURLCompletion	URL completion helper.
KURLLabel	A drop-in replacement for QLabel that displays hyperlinks.
KValueSelector	Dialog for color value selection.
KWMModuleApplication	Base class for KDE window manager modules.
KWizard	General-purpose multipage dialog box.
KWritePermsIcon	Write permission icon
KXYSelector	2D value selector.
QXEmbed	Embeded QT

Table 7-5. KDE 2.0 kdeui (User Interface) *(continued)*

Compiling

To compile a source code file, you may need to specify the KDE and QT include directories. If not already defined, you can configure your system to assign to the KDEDIR and QTDIR shell variables the Kde and QT directory paths.

```
g++ -c -I$KDEDIR/include -I$QTDIR myapp.cpp
```

To create an application with the linker, you need to specify the KDE library's directory and the specific KDE libraries you want to use along with the QT library. In this example, the kdecore and kdeui libraries are used. These are the KDE core library and the KDE user interface library. qt is the QT library.

```
g++ -L$KDEDIR/lib -lkdecore -lkdeui -lqt -o myapp
myapp.o
```

On Red Hat Linux, the QT libraries for 6.0 are placed in the **/usr/lib/qt** directory. KDE libraries are mixed with other libraries

kab.h
kabapi.h
kaccel.h
kapp.h
kaudio.h
kbutton.h
kbuttonbox.h
kcharsets.h
kckey.h
kclipboard.h
kcolorbtn.h
kcolordlg.h
kcolorgroup.h
kcombiview.h
kcombo.h
kconfig.h
kconfigbase.h
kconfigdata.h
kcontainer.h
kcontrol.h
kcursor.h
kdatepik.h
kdatetbl.h
kdbtn.h
kde.pot
kdebug.h
kdir.h
kdirlistbox.h
keditcl.h
keyvaluemap.h
kfilebookmark.h
kfiledetaillist.h
kfiledialog.h
kfilefilter.h
kfileinfo.h

7

Table 7-6.   KDE Header Files

kfileinfocontents.h
kfilepreview.h
kfilesimpleview.h
kfm.h
kfmclient_ipc.h
kfmipc.h
kfontdialog.h
kglobalaccel.h
kiconloader.h
kiconloaderdialog.h
kimgio.h
kintegerline.h
kkeydialog.h
kled.h
kledlamp.h
klined.h
klocale.h
kmenubar.h
kmisc.h
kmsgbox.h
knewpanner.h
knotebook.h
kpanner.h
kpixmap.h
kpoint.h
kpopmenu.h
kpreview.h
kprocctrl.h
kprocess.h
kprocio.h
kprogress.h
kquickhelp.h
krect.h
kremotefile.h
krestrictedline.h

Table 7-6.   KDE Header Files *(continued)*

krootprop.h
kruler.h
ksconfig.h
kselect.h
kseparator.h
ksimpleconfig.h
ksize.h
kslider.h
ksock.h
kspell.h
kspelldlg.h
kspinbox.h
kstatusbar.h
kstdaccel.h
kstring.h
ktabbar.h
ktabctl.h
ktablistbox.h
ktmainwindow.h
ktoolbar.h
ktoolboxmgr.h
ktopwidget.h
ktreelist.h
kurl.h
kurllabel.h
kwizard.h
kwm.h
kwmmapp.h
kaffe:
Arrays.h
java_lang_Object.h
java_lang_String.h
java_lang_Thread.h
java_lang_ThreadGroup.h
java_lang_Throwable.h

Table 7-6.   KDE Header Files *(continued)*

jmalloc.h
jni.h
jni_cpp.h
jsyscall.h
jtypes.h
native.h

Table 7-6.   KDE Header Files *(continued)*

in the **/usr/lib** directory. You will not have to specify a KDE
library, and for QT, you specify the **/usr/lib/qt** directory.

```
g++ -L/usr/lib/qt -lkdecore -lkdeui -lqt -o myapp
myapp.o
```

Caldera OpenLinux, along with other distributions, currently
defines the KDE libraries to be in the **/opt/kde** directory.

Signals and Slots

KDE and QT use signals and slots to allow one widget to
communicate with another. Signals and slots are member functions
defined in a class that have special capabilities. Signals are emitted
by an object when it is activated by some event occurring on it. For
example, when a user clicks on a button object, the button will
emit a clicked signal. This signal can then be picked up by any
other object set up to receive it. Such an object will have slots that
are designated to receive the signal. A slot is just a member
function that executes when the object receives a certain signal.

In effect, slots operate like event handlers and signals can be
thought of as events. In fact, KDE and QT do not operate like
standard event-driven GUIs. Instead, the process of event
handling is implemented as messages sent and received by
objects. Instead of focusing on the processing of an event when it
occurs, objects manage their own event tasks as they occur,
whether that is receiving or sending signals. A KDE widget emits
a signal when an event occurs on it or it changes state for some
reason. There are several possible signals, among the more
common of which are the activated and clicked signals. So, when

an activated signal occurs on a menu item widget, the processing function will execute the corresponding function for that item. For example, given a window with a menu that has an Exit item, when a user clicks on an Exit item in the File menu a function to exit the program should be executed. The Exit item emits a signal that is then received by the main window object, which then executes the slot function associated with the Exit item.

The connection between the signal from an emitting object to a slot function in a receiving object is created with the object's connect function. The connect function sets up a connection between a certain signal in a given object with a specific slot function in another object. Its first argument is the object, the second is the signal, and the last is the callback function. To specify the signal, you use the SIGNAL macro on the signal name with its parameters. For the callback command function, you use the SLOT macro. Using connect operations, you can also connect a signal to several slots and connect several signals to just one slot. In the following example, the clicked signal on the buttonhi object is connected to the myhello slot function in the mywin object:

```
connect(buttonhi, SIGNAL(clicked()), mywin,
SLOT(myhello()));
```

Classes composed of several widgets like an application window will often have connections from signals from the different widgets to the main widget. Connect operations are usually placed with the class declaration of the main widget for connecting signals from its subwidgets to itself. In this case, the main widget (object) can then be referenced with the C++ **this** pointer reference, which always references the class being declared.

```
connect(buttonhi, SIGNAL(clicked()), this,
SLOT(myhello()));
```

Furthermore, any class that includes slots or signals must also include a special reference named Q_OBJECT. This enables the Meta Object Compiler preprocessor to set up any signals and slots declared in the class.

Meta Object Compiler: MOC

Though the code for entering signal and slot functions, as well as their connection, may appear straightforward to the programmer, it actually requires much more complex C++ coding. Signal and slot functions need to be preprocessed by the Meta Object Compiler (MOC) to generate the C++ code that can implement the signal and slot message connection process. You then include the output of MOC in your source code file for compiling. This means that you should place the class declarations for any classes that have signals and slots in separate header files. You can then preprocess these header files and include the output in the source code. You cannot combine the member function definitions with the class declaration. To compile, the class declaration has to first be preprocessed by MOC before it can be combined correctly with the member function definitions. This necessitates placing the class declaration in a separate file from the member functions so that the class declaration can be separately preprocessed by MOC. Table 7-7 lists the different MOC options.

To declare a class that contains either signals or slots, you would first declare the class in a header file like **myobj.h**. You do not place the definitions of any of the member functions in the header file, only the class declaration. Note that the class declaration will include declarations of the member functions, structures, and

Option	Description
-o *file*	Write output to file rather than to stdout.
-f	Force the generation of an #include statement in the output. This option is only useful if you have header files that do not follow the standard naming conventions.
-i	Do not generate an #include statement in the output. You should then #include the meta object code in the **.cpp** file.
-nw	Do not generate any warnings.
-ldbg	Write lex debug information on stdout.
-dbg	Treat all nonsignal members as slots, for internal debugging purposes.
-p path	Makes the MOC prepend path/ to the file name in the generated #include statement.
-q path	Makes the MOC prepend path/ to the file name of qt #include files in the generated code.

Table 7-7. MOC Options

variables. In a separate source code file you would place the definition of member functions, like **myobj.cpp**. A member function definition is the actual code for the function. For these definitions to be correctly compiled, you have to include the MOC preprocessed version of its object declaration, not the actual declaration itself. To generate the preprocessed MOC versions, you use the class declaration header file and the MOC command, such as

```
moc myobj.h -o myobj.moc
```

In the particular source code files where you are defining member functions for this object, you would include the MOC version of the header file that contains the object declaration, not the header file itself. So you would include **myobj.moc** in the **myobj.cpp** source code file, not **myobj.h**. For any other source code files where you are generating an object of that class, say with a **new** operation, you just include the header file, not the MOC file. So, for any source code file where you only need the class declaration, you include the header file, such as **myobj.h**. But for any source code where you are defining members that are part of that object, you include the MOC file, such as **myobj.moc**. For example, suppose in the **main.cpp** file a myobj object is generated as a variable, whereas in a **myobj.cpp** file there are function definitions for member functions for the myobj class. Furthermore, the class definition for myobj is in the **myobj.h** header file and the MOC version of **myobj.h** is in the **myobj.moc** file. In the **main.cpp** file, you would include the **myobj.h** file (not **myobj.moc**), and in the **myobj.cpp** file you would include the **myobj.moc** file (not **myobj.h**).

The following example is a simple hello world program that displays a button in the main window and then will display a message box with Hello World when clicked. Notice that the Hellowin class has two slots declared: myhello and myexit. The declaration also includes Q_OBJECT. The declaration for Hellowin is placed in the **hellowin.h** header file. All the member function definitions are placed in the **hellowin.cpp** file. To compile this program, you first preprocess the **hellowin.h** header file with MOC. Then, you can compile the **hellowin.cpp** file. Notice that this file includes the **hellowin.moc** file, not the **hellowin.h** file. The compile operations are shown here:

```
Moc -o hellowin.moc  hellowin.h
g++ -L/usr/lib/qt -lkdecore -lkdeui -lqt -o hellowin
                hellowin.cpp
```

A better organization would place the member function definitions in a separate source code file of their own, leaving the main function in its own source code file. In this case, you would include **hellowin.h** with the main function and **hellowin.moc** with the member function definitions.

Display of the Hello World message is handled by a KMsgBox object. This class implements a simple dialog box with messages and several buttons, if you want them. In addition to a simple message dialog box, KMsgBox also supports dialogs with Yes/No buttons and Yes/No/Cancel buttons. Be sure to include **kmsgbox.h**. For About dialogs you can use KAboutDialog.

hellowin.h

```
#include <kapp.h>
#include <ktmainwindow.h>
#include <qpushbutton.h>
#include <kmsgbox.h>

class Hellowin : public KTMainWindow
{
  Q_OBJECT
public:
  Hellowin ();
  void closeEvent(QCloseEvent *);
public slots:
  void myhello();
  void myexit();
private:
  QPushButton *buttonhi;
  QPushButton *buttonExit;
};
```

myhello.cpp

```
#include <kapp.h>
#include <ktmainwindow.h>
#include <qpushbutton.h>
#include "hellowin.moc"
#include <kmsgbox.h>

Hellowin::Hellowin () : KTMainWindow()
{
  buttonhi = new QPushButton("Hello", this);
  buttonhi->setGeometry(45,30,50,25);
```

```
  buttonhi->show();
  connect(buttonhi, SIGNAL(clicked()), this,
SLOT(myhello()));

  buttonExit = new QPushButton("Exit", this);
  buttonExit->setGeometry(105,30,50,25);
  buttonExit->show();
  connect(buttonExit, SIGNAL(clicked()), this,
SLOT(myexit()));
}

void Hellowin::closeEvent(QCloseEvent *)
{
  kapp->quit();
}

void Hellowin::myhello()
{
  KMsgBox::message(0,"Important","Hello World!");
}

void Hellowin::myexit()
{
  close();
}

int main( int argc, char **argv )
{
  KApplication myapp ( argc, argv, "Hello World!" );
  Khello mywin;
  Mywin.setGeometry(100,100,200,100);

  myapp.setMainWidget( w );
  mywin.show();
  return myapp.exec();
}
```

Menus

For menus, you create a KDE menu bar and then add QT menus
with their menu items to it. You will need to include the
qpopupmenu.h header file for the menus and the **kmenubar.h**
header file for the menu bar.

```
#include <qpopupmenu.h>
#include <kmenubar.h>
```

You then define a menu bar object or a pointer to one, and do the same for your menus. The class for a menubar is KmenuBar and the class for a menu is QpopupMenu. The following example defines pointers to a menu bar and a menu:

```
KMenuBar *mymenubar;
QPopupMenu *myfilemenu;
```

If you defined pointers, you can create the menu and menubar objects with the new operation as shown here. KmenuBar takes as its argument its parent. When defined in a class like a window where you want the class itself to be the parent, you use the **this** pointer.

```
mymenubar = new KMenuBar(this);
myfilemenu = new QPopupMenu;
```

You can then add the menu to the menu bar with the menubar's insertItem member function. The first argument is the label you want displayed on the menu bar for the menu and the second argument is the address of the menu object. The following example adds myfilemenu to the mymenubar:

```
mymenubar->insertItem("File", myfilemenu);
```

Then, to add items to a particular menu, you use the menu object's insertItem member function. Its first argument is the label you want displayed for the item; then, the next two arguments are references to a slot function to be executed when the item emits a signal. This is the same as the slot arguments in the connect function. The insertItem's second argument is the address of the object that holds the slot function, and the third argument is the slot function in that object to be executed. The following example creates an Exit item in the myfilemenu menu and connects it to the myexit slot function in the current object (denoted by the **this** pointer):

```
myfilemenu->insertItem("Exit", this, SLOT(myexit()));
```

Status and Toolbars

The KDE status bar widget is KStatusBar. To create a status bar, you create a KstatusBar object and assign its address to a pointer you want to use to reference the object. KstatusBar takes as its argument the address of its parent. In the following example, the parent is the class it is being defined in, which is referenced with the special **this** pointer (commonly used for subwidgets):

```
statusbar= new KStatusBar(this);
```

To set the text you want initially displayed on the status bar, you use the KstatusBar class's insertItem method. This takes as its first argument the text you want displayed and as a second argument an identifier. To change the status bar message, you use the changeItem function.

```
statusbar->insertItem("My hello program", 0);
statusbar->changeItem("My New Hello Program", 0);
```

To attach the status bar to the window object you use the KTMainWindow class's setStatusBar function. This takes the address of the statusbar object and an identifier as its arguments.

```
setStatusBar(statusbar, 0);
```

Then, to have the status bar displayed, you use the show function.

```
statusbar->show();
```

To create a toolbar, you define a KToolBar object, assigning its address to a pointer you want to use to reference the object. In this example, the user creates a toolbar object and assigns its address to mytoolbar:

```
mytoolbar = new KToolBar(this);
```

For a toolbar, you also need to manage the icons you want to use in it. To load icons, you use a KIconLoader object that you create with a getIconLoader method, as shown here. The KIconLoader object will load and cache the toolbar icons, searching for them in specified KDE icon directories. Be sure to include the **kiconloader.h** header file.

```
KIconLoader *myloader = myapp->getIconLoader();
```

To add a button to the toolbar, you use the insertButton method. This takes as its first argument the icon you want to use for the button. For this argument, you have to first load the icon using the KIconLoader object's loadIcon method. This method takes as its argument the file name of the icon. The following example loads the file for the Exit icon:

```
loader->loadIcon("filenew.xpm")
```

The second argument is the command identifier, the third is a flag to indicate whether the button is enabled, and the last is the tooltip text. The following example adds an Exit button to a toolbar with the hint "Exit program":

```
mytoolbar->insertButton(loader->loadIcon("exit.xpm"),
0, TRUE,"Exit Program");
```

It is helpful to allow for international support by wrapping the tooltip text in the klocale->translate function.

```
klocale->translate("Exit Program")
```

To connect an icon in the toolbar with an object's slot function, you use the toolbar object's addConnection function. This takes as its first argument the identifier of the icon in the toolbar. The identifier is the number you used as the second argument with the interButton function when you added the icon to the toolbar. The remaining arguments are similar to the connect function, the signal, the object holding the slot function, and the slot function.

```
mytoolbar->addConnection(0, SIGNAL(clicked()),this,
SLOT(myexit()));
```

Use an insertButton operation for each button you want to add. Once you have added your button, use the KTMainWindow's addToolBar function to add the toolbar to the window. Then use the toolbar object's setBarPos to position it and the show method to display it.

```
addToolBar(toolbar);
toolbar->setBarPos(KToolBar::Top);
toolbar->show();
```

The following program illustrates the use of complex widgets. The hellowin program creates a window with a toolbar, menus, and a status bar. The toolbar has two icons, one for exiting the program and one for displaying the "Hello World" message. The status bar displays a program description. The menu bar has a File menu with entries for displaying a "Hello World" dialog box and also for exiting the program.

hellowin.h

```
/************* hellowin.h ******************/
#include <kapp.h>
```

```
#include <ktmainwindow.h>
#include <qpushbutton.h>
#include <kmenubar.h>
#include <ktoolbar.h>
#include <kstatusbar.h>
#include <qpopupmenu.h>

class Hellowin : public KTMainWindow
{
  Q_OBJECT
public:
  Hellowin();
  void closeEvent(QCloseEvent *);
public slots:
  void myhello();
  void myexit();
private:
  QPushButton *hellobutton;
  QPushButton *exitbutton;
  KMenuBar *mymenubar;
  QPopupMenu *filemenu;
  KToolBar *mytoolbar;
  KStatusBar *mystatusbar;
};
```

hellowin.cpp

```
/************ Hellowin.cpp ****************/
#include "hellowin.moc"
#include <kmsgbox.h>
#include <kpixmap.h>
#include <kiconloader.h>


Hellowin::Hellowin() : KTMainWindow()
{

mytoolbar = new KToolBar(this);
KIconLoader *myloader = kapp->getIconLoader();

QPixmap hellopic =
myloader->loadIcon("/usr/share/toolbar/stamp.xpm", 0,
0);
mytoolbar->insertButton(hellopic,1, TRUE,"Hello
                    window", 0);
mytoolbar->addConnection(1, SIGNAL(clicked()),this,
```

7

```
                                   SLOT(myhello()));

QPixmap exitpic = myloader->loadIcon("exit.xpm",
                                 0, 0);
mytoolbar->insertButton(exitpic,0, TRUE,"Exit
                       Program", 0);
mytoolbar->addConnection(0, SIGNAL(clicked()),
                       this, SLOT(myexit()));

mytoolbar->setBarPos(KToolBar::Floating);
addToolBar(mytoolbar, 0);
mytoolbar->show();

mystatusbar = new KStatusBar(this);
mystatusbar->insertItem("My hello program", 0);
setStatusBar (mystatusbar);
mystatusbar->show();

filemenu = new QPopupMenu();
filemenu->insertItem("&Hello", this,
                             SLOT(myhello()));
filemenu->insertItem("E&xit", this, SLOT(myexit()));

mymenubar = new KMenuBar(this);
mymenubar->insertItem("&FILE", filemenu);
}

void Hellowin::closeEvent(QCloseEvent *)
{
  kapp->quit();
}

void Hellowin::myhello()
{
  KMsgBox::message(0,"World Message","Hello World!");
}

void Hellowin::myexit()
{
  close();
}
```

```
main.c
#include <kapp.h>
#include <ktmainwindow.h>
#include "hellowin.h"

int main( int argc, char **argv )
{
    KApplication myapp( argc, argv, "Hello World!" );
    Hellowin *mywin = new Hellowin();
    mywin->setGeometry(100,100,200,100);
    myapp.setMainWidget( mywin );
    mywin->show();
    myapp.exec();
    return 0;
}
```

To compile the program, it is best to use a Makefile as shown here. Notice how the MOC file is created.

```
hellowin: main.o hellowin.o hellowin.moc
    g++ -lkdecore -lkdeui -lqt -o hellowin main.o
hellowin.o

hellowin.o: hellowin.cpp
    g++ -c -I/usr/include -I/usr/include/qt
hellowin.cpp

main.o: main.cpp
    g++ -c -I/usr/include -I/usr/include/qt
main.cpp

hellowin.moc: hellowin.h
    moc hellowin.h -o hellowin.moc
```

7

QT Programming

KDE currently relies directly on the QT Toolkit. Using just QT objects, you can create an interface with a similar look and feel as KDE. You can create a QT application using just QT objects and the QT libraries. This section provides a basic introduction to QT programming. Both the KDE development site at **developer.kde.org** and the QT Web site at **www.trol.com** provide very detailed documentation and tutorials on QT programming. It is strongly recommended that you consult these resources for a detailed presentation of QT programming and API references.

QT Application

A QT program is a C++ program. The QT libraries provide extensive definitions of QT classes with which you can define QT objects in your program. You can also use these classes to create your own, inheriting their predefined capabilities. Table 7-8 lists the QT classes and Table 7-9 lists the commonly used QT widgets. To create a QT application, you have to define a Qapplication object. Each application has to have at least one Qapplication object. This Qapplication object is used to manage application features like the font and cursor. To include the Qapplication class declaration in your program, you just have to include the **qapplication.h** file. Specific QT classes and groups of classes are defined in various QT header files. Table 7-10 lists these header files. The name of the header file indicates the kind of class defined in it.

```
#include <qapplication.h>
```

You can then choose from various objects to include in your application, such as windows, buttons, and menus. To define a particular object, you first declare its class and then, as you would traditionally declare a variable, you define an object of that class. In non-C++ terms, you can think of the class as the type and an object as a variable of that type. QT provides numerous class declarations, each placed in its own header file. To declare a class, you just have to include its header file. For example, to declare the QpushButton (a button), you include the **qpushbutton.h** file.

```
#include <qpushbutton.h>
```

Widgets like buttons will automatically implement default features with which they can maintain their own look and feel. You can modify these features, changing the aspects like the color or the text displayed. When you define a widget object like a button, you also have to provide as arguments the name you want to give to the object and the widget's parent. If it is not part of another widget, then you can use NULL, 0, to indicate that it has no parent. The arguments are passed to a constructor function that will be executed to perform certain initialization operations on the widget. For example, the following definition of the mybutton button widget will display "Click Me" and indicate that it has no parent:

```
QPushButton mybutton( "Click Me", 0 );
```

A QT program is essentially a C++ program. You define your classes and any member functions, and then define the main function where the program starts. Here, you place the definition for your Qapplication object. This definition has to occur before any other QT widget (object) definitions. For the Qapplication widget definition, you include the (argv, argc) arguments. These have the same functionality as in other C++ programs. Other widgets will take different sets of arguments. The following example defines the Qapplication widget called myapp and a button widget called mybutton.

```
QApplication myapp( argc, argv );
QPushButton mybutton( "Click Me", 0 );
```

To make a widget into the application's main widget, you use the Qtapplication's setMainWidget member function. The main widget is the one that you want to use to control closing the application. When you close the main widget, you close the application also. The main widget is usually the application's main window. Closing that window will close the application. The argument for this function is the address of the widget, which you can obtain with the **&** operator.

```
myapp.setMainWidget( &mybutton );
```

Once you have defined your widgets and changed any features, you then need to specify that the widget is to be displayed. You use this with the widget's show member function. The following example will indicate that the mybutton button is to be displayed:

```
mybutton.show();
```

When you have finished constructing your application and specifying the widgets to be displayed, you can then turn control over to QT to manage the execution of the application with the Qapplication widget's exec member function. At this point, the application is run and all the widgets displayed. QT will manage events, invoking the appropriate widget connected to them. When the user closes the application's main widget, control returns to the program. You can then end the program with a final return statement in the main function.

```
myapp.exec();
return 0;
```

The following program illustrates the basic structure of a QT program:

```
#include <qapplication.h>
#include <qpushbutton.h>

int main( int argc, char **argv )
{
    QApplication myapp( argc, argv );
    QPushButton mybutton( "Click Me", 0 );
    mybutton.resize( 100, 30 );

    myapp.setMainWidget( &hello );
    mybutton.show();
    return myapp.exec();
}
```

QT Signals and Slots

Traditionally, GUI toolkits use a method of events that activate callback functions. When an event occurs, its associated callback function is executed. QT replaces this approach with a system of signals and slots. The event activation process is reformulated as a message communication process between two objects. Since they are merely communicating messages, signals and slots can be made very robust. They can take a varying number of arguments of different types, and you can connect any number of signals to the same slot as well as slots to signals. Signals and slots can be used in any classes that inherit from the QObject class, such as QWidget. Any object can contain both signals to send messages and slots to receive messages.

When an event occurs on a widget, it will emit a signal. That is all it does. It does not set up a connection to another object. To be able to receive a message from a signal, an object sets up a slot. A slot is just a member function that is executed when the object receives a signal. Conceptually, it is used to obtain information about a change in the other objects.

A slot does not know if there are actually any signals connected to it, and a signal does not know if there are any slots to receive it. You use the connect function to set up a connection between a signal in one object and a slot in another. You can connect as many signals as you want to a single slot, and a signal can be connected to any number of slots. Each QT object can have signals to send messages and slots to receive messages. The connect functions will set up a connection between two objects, connecting a signal from one to a slot in another. In the following example, the clicked signal for the mybutton object is connected to the quit slot of the myapp object:

```
QObject::connect( &mybutton, SIGNAL(clicked()),
&myapp, SLOT(quit()) );
```

When an event occurs on an object, the emit operation uses the signal function to send out a message. When a signal is emitted by an object, any slots connected to it are immediately executed. Slots are simply member functions in a class. They differ only in that they can be connected to a signal. They can be also called as regular functions. You make slots protected, private, or public and thereby control what objects can have their signals connect to them.

```
private signals:
    void mysignal();
private slots:
    void myslot1();
    void myslot2();
```

The signal and slot terms in a class definition will be replaced with code acceptable to the C++ compiler by the MOC preprocessor. Any source code files that contain classes with signal and slot definitions have to be preprocessed by the MOC. In addition, any class with slots and signals has to include the term Q_OBJECT in their class declaration. This is used by MOC. The Meta Object Compiler (MOC) also generates code that initializes the meta object. The meta object contains names of all signal and slot members along with pointers to these functions.

Windows

To create an application window, you use the QmainWindow class. The following example creates a new application window and assigns its address to the mw pointer:

```
QMainWindow * mywin = new QmainWindow;
```

A QMainWindow widget includes several member functions for setting different features. With the setCaption member, you can set the window title.

```
 mywin->setCaption( "My Document" );
```

To have your application close automatically when you close your last open window, you can connect the application widget's lastWindowClosed signal to its quit slot, as shown here. Signals and slots are discussed in the next section.

```
myapp.connect( &myapp, SIGNAL(lastWindowClosed()),
&myapp, SLOT(quit()) );
```

The following program shows the implementation of a QT window:

```
#include <qapplication.h>
#include <qmainwindow.h>

int main( int argc, char **argv )
{
    QApplication myapp( argc, argv );
    QMainWindow mywin;
    mywin.setCaption( "Document 1" );
    myapp.connect( &myapp,
                SIGNAL(lastWindowClosed()),
                &myapp, SLOT(quit()) );
    myapp.setMainWidget( &mywin );
    mywin.show();
    return myapp.exec();
}
```

Parent-Child Objects

You construct a QT interface using objects that you place in hierarchical structures, with lesser objects designated as dependent on a major object. For example, a window would be a major object that in turn would have lesser objects like menus, toolbars, and slider bars dependent on it. The major object is the parent and the lesser objects are its children. When you create a major widget like a window, you can also create lesser widgets like toolbars that you can then attach to the window. You do this by making the lesser widget, such as the toolbar, a child of the major widget (like the window). A child widget can in turn be a parent to its own child widgets. In constructing a QT interface you place widgets in a hierarchical structure of parent widgets and their children. The hierarchical structure for the QT classes is shown at the end of this chapter.

To create a complex widget like a window with its dependent children, you first define the parent widget. Then, when you define a widget that you want to be a child of that parent, you place the address of the parent widget as an argument in the widget's definition. The following example defines a button widget named quit and makes it a child of the box widget. The box widget now includes the button widget. Notice that the **&** operator is used to obtain the address of the parent widget.

```
QPushButton mybutton( "Quit", &mywin );
```

When you display the parent widget, all its child widgets are automatically displayed. In the following example, the show member function for the box widget will also "show" the mybutton button:

```
myapp.setMainWidget( &mywin );
mywin.show();
```

The following program shows a button as a child of a window:

```
#include <qapplication.h>
#include <qmainwindow.h>
#include <qpushbutton.h>
#include <qfont.h>

int main( int argc, char **argv )
{
    QApplication myapp( argc, argv );
    QMainWindow *mywin = new QMainWindow;
    QPushButton mybutton( "Click Me", mywin );

    mywin->setCaption( "My Document" );
    myapp.connect( &myapp,
                SIGNAL(lastWindowClosed()),
                &myapp, SLOT(quit()) );
    myapp.setMainWidget(mywin);
    mybutton.setFont( QFont( "Times", 14, QFont::Bold
) );

    mywin->show();
    return myapp.exec();
}
```

7

Layout Widgets

With layout widgets, you can easily position the child widgets (such as buttons or text) on a parent widget (such as a window). In addition to positioning, they provide default sizes, resizing, and updating the widgets' display. There are several easy-to-use widgets available. QHBox positions widgets in a horizontal row, QVBox positions them vertically in a column, and QGrid positions them in a table. For more detailed control, you can use QgridLayout, QHBoxLayout, and QVBoxLayout.

Creating Your Own Widgets

Creating your own widgets is a simple matter of defining a QT-compliant class and then creating an object of the class. Such a class has to be derived from a QT base class such as Qwidget. You specify such a derivation by making the QT base class for your new class. In the following example, the user creates a mywidget class, deriving it from the QWidget class. Mywidget will inherit member functions and variables from the QWidget class.

```
class MyWidget : public QWidget
{
};
```

You can declare whatever public and private members, including functions and variables, you may want for your class. The definitions of member functions are usually placed after the class definition. A common member function found in most classes is the constructor. This function bears the same name as the class and is automatically invoked whenever an object of that class is defined. You can think of a constructor as a kind of initialization function that takes care of any initial setup tasks you want performed on a new object of this class. In the following example, a constructor function is declared in the mywidget class.

```
class MyWidget : public QWidget
{
public:
    MyWidget( QWidget *parent=0, const char *name=0 );
};
```

In the constructor functions for your own QT widgets, you need
to include an argument for the address of the widget you
want to be the parent. The default is NULL, 0. If the parent is
NULL, it automatically becomes a top-level widget, rather than
a child of another. The second argument is the name to be given
to the particular widget being created of this class. Instead of
writing the code to handle these, you can just pass them on to
the QWidget constructor that is inherited by your class. To
do this, you place the QWidget constructor with its arguments
in your class' constructor function, attaching after the
function arguments.

```
MyWidget::MyWidget( QWidget *parent, const char *name )
        : QWidget( parent, name )
```

In the constructor function, you would place the definitions for
any child objects that you want to make up your widget. For
example, if you are creating a window widget, you would write a
construction function for it in which you would define components
like a menu, toolbars, or a status bar. You can set features for
these widgets such as size and color, and also set up any
signal/slot connections for them as needed. The following
example is a constructor function definition for mywidget:

```
MyWidget::MyWidget( QWidget *parent, const char *name )
        : QWidget( parent, name )
{
    QPushButton *quit = new QPushButton( "Quit",
                                this, "quit" );
    quit->setFont( QFont( "Times", 18, QFont::Bold )
);
    connect( quit, SIGNAL(clicked()), qApp,
                        SLOT(quit()) );
}
```

Suppose you want to construct your own application window with
menus and toolbars that you design. QmainWindow only provides
a bare window. To create an application window with your own
menus, toolbars, and other widgets, you define a new window
class of your own and have it inherit the QmainWindow class.
Your new window class will include the QmainWindow members
as well as any new ones you define in it. The following example

creates a new window class called MyAppWindow that is based on the QmainWindow class:

```
#include <qmainwindow.h>

class QToolBar;
class QPopupMenu;

class MyAppWindow: public QMainWindow
{
    Q_OBJECT
public:
    MyAppWindow ();
    ~ MyAppWindow ();
protected:
    void closeEvent ( QCloseEvent* );
private slots:
    void newfile();
    void openfile();
private:
    QToolBar *mytoolbar;
    QMenuBar *mymenubar;
};
```

The MyAppWindow class is based on the QmainWindow and will inherit its public members. The class includes a constructor and a destructor for setting up the window and shutting it down. It also has a toolbar and menu bar, declared as private members. This class definition includes slots. These are functions that will be executed when a certain object emits a signal. For example, when a user selects a New item on a menu or clicks on a New button on the toolbar, the newfile function (slot) is executed. The "private slots:" label is not a C++ term. It needs to be preprocessed by the Meta Object Compiler (MOC) to generate readable C++ code. To indicate that this class has MOC terms in it, you place the Q_OBJECT term in the class definition.

```
#include <qapplication.h>
#include <qmainwindow.h>
#include <qpushbutton.h>

class QToolBar;
class QPopupMenu;

class MyAppWindow: public QMainWindow
```

```
{
    Q_OBJECT
public:
    MyAppWindow ();
    ~ MyAppWindow ();
protected:
    void closeEvent ( QCloseEvent* );
private slots:
    void newfile();
    void openfile();
private:
    QToolBar *mytoolbar;
    QToolBar *mymenubar;
};
```

For the widget that you make your main widget, you may need to reference actions on your application widget. For example, if you make a window the main widget for your application, you may want to be able to close the application by just clicking on a Quit button on the window's toolbar. To do this, you have to connect the toolbar's Quit button to the application's quit function. This involves creating a clicked signal connection from the button to the application's quit slot. However, the window widget will not know that name of the application widget. To handle this problem, QT creates a special pointer called qApp that will reference a program's application widget. The window widget will use qApp to reference the application widget and its quit function. In the following example, the connect function connects a clicked signal on a window toolbar's Quit button with the application's quit function (slot). When the user clicks on the Quit button on the window's toolbar, the entire application will close.

```
connect(quit, SIGNAL(clicked()), qApp, SLOT(quit())
);
```

Toolbars

To create a toolbar, you use the QtoolBar widget. It takes as its arguments the parent and the name of the toolbar. The following example defines a toolbar and assigns its address to the mytoolbar pointer:

```
QToolBar mytoolbar;
mytoolbar = new QToolBar( this, "file operations" );
```

Once you have created the toolbar, you can then define the images you want to use for its buttons. For this, you use the QPixmap object. This function takes as its argument the name of the image file. The following example defines a file open image:

```
Qpixmap openfile("openfile.xpm");
```

For a toolbar button, you use the QtoolButton widget. This widget takes several arguments: the image, the name you want displayed on the button, the text displayed for the button, the object holding its connected slot function, the slot function in that object that you want executed when the button is activated, the toolbar, and the help tip string). The following example creates a new toolbar button called fileOpen. It uses the openIcon image and will display the text "Open File." The button is placed in the mytools toolbar and will execute the load function when activated. The **this** argument is a special pointer to the class that the current function call is part of. The function (slot) you want executed when this button is activated is defined within the same object as your button definition, you can use the **this** pointer to specify the slot function's object.

```
QToolButton * fileOpen = new QToolButton( openicon,
"Open File",
              0, this, SLOT(myload()), mytoolbar,
"open file" );
```

Menus

To create a menu bar, you use the QMenuBar class. This takes as its arguments the address of the parent widget and the name of the menu bar.

```
mymenubar = new QMenuBar( this, "file operations" );
```

To create a menu, you use the QPopupMenu widget. You can then use the menubar's insertItem function to add the menu to it. insertItem takes as its arguments the label for the menu and the menu. The following example creates a File menu and adds it to the menu bar:

```
QPopupMenu * myfile = new QPopupMenu(mymenubar);
mymenubar->insertItem( "&File", myfile );
```

To add an entry to a particular menu, you use the menu's own insertItem member function. The menu insertItem function takes as its first argument the label for the item. The following two arguments reference the object and slot functions that the menu item will signal when activated. These operate much like the last two arguments in a connect function. The object is the object to be signaled and the function is the function in that object to be executed (slot). The last argument is a keyboard alternate. The following example adds New and Open entries to the myfile menu. The New item will have the label "New" with the N underlined; when activated, it will execute the mynewdoc function, and its keyboard alternate is a CTRL-N. Be sure to include the **qkeycode.h** file.

```
myfile->insertItem( "&New", this, SLOT(mynewdoc()),
                        CTRL+Key_N );
openid = myfile->insertItem( openIcon, "&Open", this,
            SLOT(myload()), CTRL+Key_O );
```

The insertItem function will return an identifier for that menu item. You can use it to enable such features as What's This help, as shown here:

```
myfile->setWhatsThis( openid, "Opening a file" );
```

To insert a line between items, you use the menu's insertSeparator function.

```
myfile->insertSeparator();
```

To create a Quit entry that will close the application, you use qApp to reference the application widget. Then, use closeAllWindows to close the application.

```
myfile->insertItem( "&Quit", qApp, SLOT(
closeAllWindows() ), CTRL+Key_Q );
```

Dialog Boxes

To create a simple dialog box, you can use the Qmessagebox widget. You can then generate dialog boxes with different features using the Qmessagebox member functions (methods). For example, if you just want to display a message, receiving no information back from the user, then you can use the QmessageBox widget's about function. It simply takes the parent object, the message title, and the message as its arguments. You can use escape sequences for newlines and tabs, \n and \t.

```
QMessageBox::about( this, "Qt Message box example",
"This example demonstrates simple use of ""The
message box.");
```

For dialogs where you want the user to select one of several buttons you use the QmessageBox 's information function. This takes several arguments: its parent object, its title, the message text, and the buttons you want displayed. For separate lines on the message, place each line in its own string. The following example creates a simple message box with two lines of text and three buttons: OK, Cancel, Apply:

```
QMessageBox::information( this, "Save notice","The
        document has been changed since " "the last
save.", "OK", "Cancel", "Apply",0, 1 )
```

The message box will return the number of the button selected. You can then use this result to select the action you want to take.

```
res = QMessageBox::information( this, "Save
notice","The document has been changed since " "the
last save.", "OK", "Cancel","Apply",0, 1 )
        switch( res) {
        case 0:
            myok();
            break;
        case 1:
        default:
            break;
        case 2:
            myapply();
            break;
        }
```

Click and Drag

To initiate a drag operation, you first have to define an object of the QdragObject subclass. There are different types of objects for various types of media. For example, you use the QtextDrag object for text and QimageDrag for images. You then use the drag member function to drag the object.

```
void MyWidget::startDragging()
{
    QDragObject *mydrag = new QTextDrag(
```

```
myHighlightedText(), this );
    mydrag ->dragCopy();
  }
```

To enable a widget to receive a dragged object, you execute the setAcceptDrops(TRUE) operation for the widget. This is usually executed in the object's constructor. You can also override the event-handler functions dragEnterEvent(), dragMoveEvent(), dragLeaveEvent(), and dropEvent(). With QdragObject, you also have access to the Clipboard accessed through the Qclipboard object. This object has two functions, setData and data. With setData you can place text in the Clipboard, and with the data function you can copy text from it.

Classes	Description
QAccel	Handles keyboard accelerator and shortcut keys
QApplication	Manages the GUI application's control flow and main settings
QArray	Template class that provides arrays of simple types
QAsciiCache	Template class that provides a cache based on char* keys
QAsciiCacheIterator	Iterator for QAsciiCache collections
QAsciiDict	Template class that provides a dictionary based on char* keys
QAsciiDictIterator	Iterator for QAsciiDict collections
QAsyncIO	Encapsulates I/O asynchronicity
QBitArray	Array of bits
QBitmap	Monochrome (1-bit depth) pixmaps
QBitVal	Internal class, used with QBitArray
QBoxLayout	Lines up child widgets horizontally or vertically
QBrush	Defines the fill pattern of shapes drawn by a QPainter
QBuffer	I/O device that operates on a QByteArray
QButton	The abstract base class of button widgets, providing functionality common to buttons

Table 7-8.   QT API Classes

Classes	Description
QButtonGroup	Organizes QButton widgets in a group
QCache	Template class that provides a cache based on QString keys
QCacheIterator	Iterator for QCache collections
QCDEStyle	CDE Look and Feel
QChar	A Unicode character
QCheckBox	Checkbox with a text label
QCheckListItem	Implements checkable list view items
QChildEvent	Event parameters for child object events
QClipboard	Access to the window system Clipboard
QCloseEvent	Parameters that describe a close event
QCollection	The base class of all Qt collections
QColor	Colors based on RGB
QColorDialog	The QColorDialog provides a dialog widget for specifying colors
QColorGroup	Group of widget colors
QComboBox	Combined button and pop-up list
QCommonStyle	Encapsulates common Look and Feel of a GUI
QConnection	Internal class, used in the signal/slot mechanism
QConstString	A QString that uses constant Unicode data
QCString	Abstraction of the classic C zero-terminated char array (char*)
QCursor	Mouse cursor with an arbitrary shape
QCustomEvent	Support for custom events
QDataPump	Moves data from a QDataSource to a QDataSink during event processing
QDataSink	A QDataSink is an asynchronous consumer of data
QDataSource	A QDataSource is an asynchronous producer of data
QDataStream	Basic functions for serialization of binary data to a QIODevice
QDate	Date functions

Table 7-8. QT API Classes *(continued)*

Classes	Description
QDateTime	Combines QDate and QTime into a single class
QDialog	The base class of dialog windows
QDict	Template class that provides a dictionary based on QString keys
QDictIterator	Iterator for QDict collections
QDir	Traverses directory structures and contents in a platform-independent way
QDoubleValidator	Range checking of floating-point numbers
QDragEnterEvent	The event sent to widgets when a drag-and-drop first drags onto it
QDragLeaveEvent	The event sent to widgets when a drag-and-drop leaves it
QDragMoveEvent	Event sent as a drag-and-drop is in progress
QDragObject	The QDragObject encapsulates MIME-based information transfer
QDropEvent	Event sent when a drag-and-drop is completed
QDropSite	Provides nothing and does nothing
QEvent	Base class of all event classes; event objects contain event parameters
QFile	I/O device that operates on files
QFileDialog	The QFileDialog provides a dialog widget for inputting file names
QFileIconProvider	Icons for QFileDialog to use
QFileInfo	System-independent file information
QFocusData	Maintains the list of widgets that can take focus
QFocusEvent	Event parameters for widget focus events
QFont	Font used for drawing text
QFontDialog	The QFontDialog provides a dialog widget for selecting a text font
QFontInfo	General information about fonts
QFontMetrics	Font metrics information about fonts

7

Table 7-8. QT API Classes *(continued)*

Classes	Description
QFrame	The base class of widgets that can have a frame
QGArray	Internal class for implementing the QArray class
QGCache	Internal class for implementing QCache template classes
QGCacheIterator	An internal class for implementing QCacheIterator and QIntCacheIterator
QGDict	Internal class for implementing QDict template classes
QGDictIterator	An internal class for implementing QDictIterator and QIntDictIterator
QGL	Namespace for miscellaneous identifiers in the Qt OpenGL Extension
QGLayoutIterator	The abstract base class of internal layout iterators
QGLContext	Encapsulates an OpenGL rendering context
QGLFormat	The display format of an OpenGL rendering context
QGList	Internal class for implementing Qt collection classes
QGListIterator	The QGListIterator is an internal class for implementing QListIterator
QGLWidget	Widget for rendering OpenGL graphics
QGrid	Performs geometry management on its children
QGridLayout	Lays out widgets in a grid
QGroupBox	Group box frame with a title
QHBox	Performs geometry management on its children
QHBoxLayout	Lines up widgets horizontally
QHButtonGroup	Organizes QButton widgets in a group with one horizontal row
QHeader	Table header
QHGroupBox	Organizes QButton widgets in a group with one horizontal row
QHideEvent	The event sent after a widget is hidden

Table 7-8. QT API Classes *(continued)*

Classes	Description
QIconSet	Set of icons (normal, disabled, various sizes), for example for buttons
QImage	Hardware-independent pixmap representation with direct access to the pixel data
QImageConsumer	An abstraction used by QImageDecoder
QImageDecoder	Incremental image decoder for all supported image formats
QImageDrag	The QImageDrag provides a drag-and-drop object for transferring images
QImageFormat	Incremental image decoder for a specific image format
QImageFormatType	Factory that makes QImageFormat objects
QImageIO	Parameters for loading and saving images
QIntCache	Template class that provides a cache based on long keys
QIntCacheIterator	Iterator for QIntCache collections
QIntDict	Template class that provides a dictionary based on long keys
QIntDictIterator	Iterator for QIntDict collections
QIntValidator	Range checking of integers
QIODevice	The base class of I/O devices
QIODeviceSource	A QIODeviceSource is a QDataSource that draws data from a QIODevice
QKeyEvent	Parameters that describe a key event
QLabel	Displays a static text or pixmap
QLayout	The base class of geometry specifiers
QLayoutItem	The abstract items that a QLayout manipulates
QLayoutIterator	Iterators over QLayoutItem
QLCDNumber	Displays a number with LCD-like digits
QLineEdit	Simple line editor for inputting text
QList	Template class that provides doubly linked lists
QListBox	List of selectable, read-only items

7

Table 7-8.   QT API Classes *(continued)*

Classes	Description
QListBoxItem	This is the base class of all list box items
QListBoxPixmap	List box items with a pixmap
QListBoxText	List box items with text
QListIterator	Iterator for QList collections
QListView	Implements a list/tree view
QListViewItem	Implements a list view item
QListViewItemIterator	Iterator for collections of QListViewItems
QLNode	Internal class for the QList template collection
QMainWindow	Typical application window, with a menu bar, some tool bars, and a status bar
QMap	Value-based template class that provides a dictionary
QMapConstIterator	Iterator for QMap
QMapIterator	Iterator for QMap
QMenuBar	Horizontal menu bar
QMenuData	Base class for QMenuBar and QPopupMenu
QMessageBox	Displays a brief message, an icon, and some buttons
QMimeSource	An abstract piece of formatted data
QMimeSourceFactory	An extensible supply of MIME-typed data
QMotifStyle	Motif Look and Feel
QMouseEvent	Parameters that describe a mouse event
QMoveEvent	Event parameters for move events
QMovie	Incrementally loads an animation or image, signaling as it progresses
QMultiLineEdit	Simple editor for inputting text
QNPInstance	A QObject that is a Web browser plug-in [Qt NSPlugin Extension]
QNPlugin	The plug-in central factory [Qt NSPlugin Extension]
QNPStream	A stream of data provided to a QNPInstance by the browser [Qt NSPlugin Extension]
QNPWidget	A QWidget that is a Web browser plug-in window [Qt NSPlugin Extension]

Table 7-8. QT API Classes *(continued)*

Classes	Description
QObject	The base class of all Qt objects that can deal with signals, slots, and events
QPaintDevice	Of objects that can be painted
QPaintDeviceMetrics	Information about a paint device
QPainter	Paints on paint devices
QPaintEvent	Event parameters for paint events
QPalette	Color groups for each widget state
QPen	Defines how a QPainter should draw lines and outlines of shapes
QPicture	Paint device that records and replays QPainter commands
QPixmap	Off-screen pixel-based paint device
QPixmapCache	Application-global cache for pixmaps
QPlatinumStyle	Platinum Look and Feel
QPNGImagePacker	Creates well-compressed PNG animations
QPoint	Defines a point in the plane
QPointArray	Array of points
QPopupMenu	Pop-up menu widget
QPrinter	Paint device that paints on a printer
QProgressBar	Horizontal progress bar
QProgressDialog	Provides feedback on the progress of a slow operation
QPtrDict	Template class that provides a dictionary based on void* keys
QPtrDictIterator	Iterator for QPtrDict collections
QPushButton	Pushbutton with a text or pixmap label
QQueue	Template class that provides a queue
QRadioButton	Radio button with a text label
QRangeControl	Integer value within a range
QRect	Defines a rectangle in the plane
QRegExp	Pattern matching using regular expressions or wildcards
QRegion	Clip region for a painter
QResizeEvent	Event parameters for resize events

Table 7-8. QT API Classes *(continued)*

7

Classes	Description
QScrollBar	Vertical or horizontal scroll bar
QScrollView	Scrolling area with on-demand scroll bars
QSemiModal	The base class of semimodal dialog windows
QSessionManager	Access to the session manager
QShared	The QShared struct is internally used for implementing shared classes
QShowEvent	The event sent when a widget is shown
QSignal	Can be used to send signals without parameters
QSignalMapper	A QSignalMapper object bundles signals from identifiable senders
QSimpleRichText	A small displayable piece of rich text
QSize	Defines the size of a two-dimensional object
QSizeGrip	Corner grip for resizing a top-level window
QSizePolicy	A layout attribute describing horizontal and vertical resizing
QSlider	Vertical or horizontal slider
QSocketNotifier	Support for socket callbacks
QSortedList	Allows sorting of elements that implement operator
QSpacerItem	A QLayoutItem that represents blank space
QSpinBox	Spin box widget, sometimes called up-down widget, little arrows widget, or spin button
QSplitter	QSplitter implements a splitter widget
QStack	Template class that provides a stack
QStatusBar	Horizontal bar suitable for presenting status messages
QStoredDrag	Simple stored-value drag object for arbitrary MIME data
QStrIList	Doubly linked list of char* with case-insensitive compare
QString	Abstraction of Unicode text and the classic C zero-terminated char array(char*)
QStringList	A list of strings

Table 7-8. QT API Classes *(continued)*

Classes	Description
QStrList	Doubly linked list of char*
QStyle	Encapsulates common Look and Feel of a GUI
QStyleSheet	A collection of styles for rich text rendering and a generator of tags
QStyleSheetItem	Encapsulates a text format
Qt	Namespace for miscellaneous identifiers that need to be global-like
QTab	The structures in a QTabBar
QTabBar	Tab bar, for use in tabbed dialogs, for example
QTabDialog	Stack of tabbed widgets
QTableView	This is an abstract base class for implementing tables
QTabWidget	Stack of tabbed widgets
QTextBrowser	A rich text browser with simple navigation
QTextCodec	Provides conversion between text encodings
QTextDecoder	State-based decoder
QTextDrag	The QTextDrag provides a drag-and-drop object for transferring plain and Unicode text
QTextEncoder	State-based encoder
QTextIStream	A convenience class for input streams
QTextOStream	A convenience class for output streams
QTextStream	Basic functions for reading and writing text using a QIODevice
QTextView	A sophisticated single-page rich text viewer
QTime	Time functions
QTimer	Timer signals and single-shot timers
QTimerEvent	Parameters that describe a timer event
QToolBar	Simple toolbar
QToolButton	Pushbutton whose appearance has been tailored for use in a QToolBar
QToolTip	Tooltips (sometimes called balloon help) for any widget or rectangular part of a widget

7

Table 7-8. QT API Classes *(continued)*

Classes	Description
QToolTipGroup	Collects tooltips into natural groups
QTranslator	Internationalization support for text output
QUriDrag	Provides for drag-and-drop of a list of URI references
QValidator	Validation of input text
QValueList	Value-based template class that provides doubly linked lists
QValueListConstIterator	Iterator for QValueList
QValueListIterator	Iterator for QValueList
QVBox	Performs geometry management on its children
QVBoxLayout	Lines up widgets vertically
QVButtonGroup	Organizes QButton widgets in a group with one vertical column
QVGroupBox	Organizes QButton widgets in a group with one vertical column
QWhatsThis	Simple description of any widget, for example, answering the question "what's this?"
QWheelEvent	Parameters that describe a wheel event
QWidget	The base class of all user interface objects
QWidgetItem	A QLayoutItem that represents widget
QWidgetStack	Stack of widgets, where the user can see only the top widget
QWindowsStyle	Windows Look and Feel
QWizard	Framework for easily writing wizards
QWMatrix	Two-dimensional transformations of a coordinate system
QXtApplication	Allows mixing of Xt/Motif and Qt widgets [Qt Xt/Motif Extension]
QXtWidget	Allows mixing of Xt/Motif and Qt widgets [Qt Xt/Motif Extension]

Table 7-8. QT API Classes *(continued)*

Widgets	Description
QButtonGroup	Organizes QButton widgets in a group
QCheckBox	Checkbox with a text label
QComboBox	Combined button and pop-up list
QFrame	The base class of widgets that can have a frame
QGroupBox	Group box frame with a title
QHButtonGroup	Organizes QButton widgets in a group with one horizontal row
QHGroupBox	Organizes QButton widgets in a group with one horizontal row
QHeader	Table header
QLCDNumber	Displays a number with LCD-like digits
QLabel	Displays a static text or pixmap
QLineEdit	Simple line editor for inputting text
QListBox	List of selectable, read-only items
QListView	Implements a list/tree view
QMainWindow	Typical application window, with a menu bar, some toolbars, and a status bar
QMenuBar	Horizontal menu bar
QMultiLineEdit	Simple editor for inputting text
QPopupMenu	Pop-up menu widget
QProgressBar	Horizontal progress bar
QProgressDialog	Provides feedback on the progress of a slow operation
QPushButton	Pushbutton with a text or pixmap label
QRadioButton	Radio button with a text label
QScrollBar	Vertical or horizontal scroll bar
QSizeGrip	Corner-grip for resizing a top-level window
QSlider	Vertical or horizontal slider
QSpinBox	Spin box widget, sometimes called up-down widget, little arrows widget, or spin button
QSplitter	QSplitter implements a splitter widget
QStatusBar	Horizontal bar suitable for presenting status messages
QTabBar	Tab bar, for use in tabbed dialogs, for example

Table 7-9. QT Widgets

Widgets	Description
QTabWidget	Stack of tabbed widgets
QTextBrowser	A rich text browser with simple navigation
QTextView	A sophisticated single-page rich text viewer
QToolBar	Simple toolbar
QToolButton	Pushbutton whose appearance has been tailored for use in a QToolBar
QVButtonGroup	Organizes QButton widgets in a group with one vertical column
QVGroupBox	Organizes QButton widgets in a group with one vertical column

Table 7-9. QT Widgets *(continued)*

qabstractlayout.h
qaccel.h
qapplication.h
qarray.h
qasciicache.h
qasciidict.h
qasyncimageio.h
qasyncio.h
qbitarray.h
qbitmap.h
qbrush.h
qbuffer.h
qbutton.h
qbuttongroup.h
qcache.h
qcdestyle.h
qcheckbox.h
qclipboard.h

Table 7-10. QT Headers

qcollection.h
qcolor.h
qcolordialog.h
qcombobox.h
qcommonstyle.h
qconnection.h
qcstring.h
qcursor.h
qdatastream.h
qdatetime.h
qdialog.h
qdict.h
qdir.h
qdragobject.h
qdrawutil.h
qdropsite.h
qevent.h
qfile.h
qfiledialog.h
qfileinfo.h
qfocusdata.h
qfont.h
qfontdialog.h
qfontinfo.h
qfontmetrics.h
qframe.h
qgarray.h
qgcache.h
qgdict.h
qgl.h
qglist.h
qglobal.h
qgrid.h
qgroupbox.h
qhbox.h
qhbuttongroup.h

7

Table 7-10. QT Headers *(continued)*

qheader.h
qhgroupbox.h
qiconset.h
qimage.h
qintcache.h
qintdict.h
qiodevice.h
qlabel.h
qlayout.h
qlcdnumber.h
qlineedit.h
qlist.h
qlistbox.h
qlistview.h
qmainwindow.h
qmap.h
qmenubar.h
qmenudata.h
qmessagebox.h
qmime.h
qmotifstyle.h
qmovie.h
qmultilineedit.h
qnamespace.h
qnp.h
qobject.h
qpaintdevice.h
qpaintdevicemetrics.h
qpainter.h
qpalette.h
qpen.h
qpicture.h
qpixmap.h

Table 7-10. QT Headers *(continued)*

qpixmapcache.h
qplatinumstyle.h
qpngio.h
qpoint.h
qpointarray.h
qpopupmenu.h
qprinter.h
qprogressbar.h
qprogressdialog.h
qptrdict.h
qpushbutton.h
qqueue.h
qradiobutton.h
qrangecontrol.h
qrect.h
qregexp.h
qregion.h
qscrollbar.h
qscrollview.h
qsemimodal.h
qsessionmanager.h
qshared.h
qsignal.h
qsignalmapper.h
qsimplerichtext.h
qsize.h
qsizegrip.h
qsizepolicy.h
qslider.h
qsocketnotifier.h
qsortedlist.h
qspinbox.h

7

Table 7-10.   QT Headers *(continued)*

qsplitter.h
qstack.h
qstatusbar.h
qstring.h
qstringlist.h
qstrlist.h
qstyle.h
qstylesheet.h
qtabbar.h
qtabdialog.h
qtableview.h
qtabwidget.h
qtextbrowser.h
qtextcodec.h
qtextstream.h
qtextview.h
qtimer.h
qtoolbar.h
qtoolbutton.h
qtooltip.h
qtranslator.h
qvalidator.h
qvaluelist.h
qvbox.h
qvbuttongroup.h
qvgroupbox.h
qwhatsthis.h
qwidget.h
qwidgetstack.h
qwindowdefs.h
qwindowsstyle.h
qwizard.h
qwmatrix.h
qxt.h

Table 7-10. QT Headers *(continued)*

The following shows the QT Class inheritance hierarchy.

```
QAsyncIO
        QDataSink
        QDataSource
                QIODeviceSource
    QBitVal
    QChar
    QCollection
        QGCache
                QAsciiCache
                QCache
                QIntCache
        QGDict
                QAsciiDict
                QDict
                QIntDict
                QPtrDict
        QGList
                QList
                        QStrList
                                QStrIList
                QQueue
                QStack
    QColor
    QColorGroup
    QConnection
    QCursor
    QDataStream
    QDate
    QDateTime
    QDir
    QDropSite
    QFileInfo
    QFocusData
    QFont
    QFontInfo
    QFontMetrics
    QGArray
        QArray
                QPointArray
    QGCacheIterator
        QAsciiCacheIterator
        QCacheIterator
        QIntCacheIterator
```

7

```
QGDictIterator
     QAsciiDictIterator
     QDictIterator
     QIntDictIterator
     QPtrDictIterator
QGL
     QGLContext
     QGLFormat
     QGLWidget
QGListIterator
     QListIterator
QIconSet
QImage
QImageConsumer
QImageDecoder
QImageFormat
QImageFormatType
QImageIO
QIODevice
     QBuffer
     QFile
QLayoutItem
     QLayout
     QSpacerItem
     QWidgetItem
QLayoutIterator
QListBoxItem
     QListBoxPixmap
     QListBoxText
QListViewItemIterator
QLNode
QMap
QMapConstIterator
QMapIterator
QMenuData
     QMenuBar
     QPopupMenu
QMimeSource
     QDragObject
     QDropEvent
QMimeSourceFactory
QMovie
QNPlugin
QNPStream
QPaintDevice
```

```
        QPicture
        QPixmap
            QBitmap
        QPrinter
        QWidget
QPaintDeviceMetrics
QPalette
QPixmapCache
QPoint
QRangeControl
        QScrollBar
        QSlider
        QSpinBox
QRect
QRegExp
QRegion
QShared
        QGLayoutIterator
QSimpleRichText
QSize
QSizePolicy
QString
        QConstString
Qt
        QBrush
        QEvent
            QChildEvent
            QCloseEvent
            QCustomEvent
            QDragLeaveEvent
            QDropEvent
                QDragMoveEvent
                        QDragEnterEvent
            QFocusEvent
            QHideEvent
            QKeyEvent
            QMouseEvent
            QMoveEvent
            QPaintEvent
            QResizeEvent
            QShowEvent
            QTimerEvent
            QWheelEvent
        QListViewItem
            QCheckListItem
```

7

```
QObject
      QAccel
      QApplication
            QXtApplication
      QClipboard
      QDataPump
      QDragObject
            QImageDrag
            QStoredDrag
                  QUriDrag
            QTextDrag
      QFileIconProvider
      QLayout
            QBoxLayout
                  QHBoxLayout
                  QVBoxLayout
            QGridLayout
      QNPInstance
      QSessionManager
      QSignal
      QSignalMapper
      QSocketNotifier
      QStyle
            QCommonStyle
                  QMotifStyle
                        QCDEStyle
                  QWindowsStyle
                        QPlatinumStyle
      QStyleSheet
      QTimer
      QToolTipGroup
      QTranslator
      QValidator
            QDoubleValidator
            QIntValidator
      QWidget
            QButton
                  QCheckBox
                  QPushButton
                  QRadioButton
                  QToolButton
            QComboBox
            QDialog
                  QColorDialog
                  QFileDialog
```

```
            QFontDialog
            QMessageBox
            QTabDialog
            QWizard
        QFrame
            QGrid
            QGroupBox
                QButtonGroup
                        QHButtonGroup
                        QVButtonGroup
                    QHGroupBox
                    QVGroupBox
                QHBox
                    QVBox
                QLCDNumber
                QLabel
                QMenuBar
                QPopupMenu
                QProgressBar
                QScrollView
                    QListBox
                    QListView
                    QTextView
                        QTextBrowser
                QSpinBox
                QSplitter
                QTableView
                    QMultiLineEdit
                QWidgetStack
        QGLWidget
        QHeader
        QLineEdit
        QMainWindow
        QNPWidget
        QScrollBar
        QSemiModal
            QProgressDialog
        QSizeGrip
        QSlider
        QStatusBar
        QTabBar
        QTabWidget
        QToolBar
        QXtWidget
```

7

```
        QPainter
        QPen
        QPixmap
        QStyleSheetItem
        QToolTip
        QWhatsThis
QTab
QTextCodec
QTextDecoder
QTextEncoder
QTextStream
        QTextIStream
        QTextOStream
QTime
QValueList
QValueListConstIterator
QValueListIterator
QWMatrix
```

Appendix A
Perl: Quick Reference

The Practical Extraction and Report Language (Perl) is a scripting language originally designed to generate reports on very large files. Perl was designed as a core program to which features could be easily added. Over the years, Perl's capabilities have been greatly enhanced. It can now control network connections, process interactions, and even support a variety of database management files.

Perl has a comprehensive set of file-handling commands. It supports scalar and associative arrays with a complete set of commands for manipulating both kinds of arrays. Perl includes the standard set of arithmetic, relational, and assignment operators, as well as a complete set of control structures for conditions and loops. Perl supports complex pattern matching using special characters and string-manipulation functions.

Web Sites

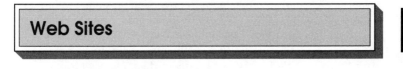

A

www.perl.com
language.perl.com
reference.perl.com
conference.perl.com
republic.perl.com
www.perl.com/CPAN/CPAN.html
www.cis.ufl.edu/Perl

Newsgroups

comp.lang.perl.announce
comp.lang.perl.misc
comp.lang.perl.modules
comp.lang.perl.tk
comp.infosystems.www.authoring.cgi

File Commands

Command	Function
open(*file-handle, permission-with-filename***)**	Open a file.
close(*file-handle***)**	Close a file.
<*filename***>**	Read from a file.
<STDIN>	Read from the standard input.
<>	Read from files whose filenames were provided in the argument list when the program was invoked.
print <*file-handle*> *text* ;	Write to a file. (If *file-handle* is not specified, write to standard output. If no *text* is specified, write contents of **$_**.)
printf <*file-handle*> " *format-str* ", *values* ;	Write formatted string (*format-str*) to a file. Use conversion specifiers to format *values*. (If *file-handle* is not specified, write to standard output. If no *values* are specified, use contents of **$_**.)
sprintf *str-variable* " *format-str* ", *values* ;	Write formatted *values* to a string (*str-variable*). Use conversion specifiers to format *values*. (If no *values* are specified, use contents of **$_**.)

Permissions

Permission	Function
< *filename*	Set read permission.
> *filename*	Set write permission.
+> *filename*	Set read and write permissions.
>> *filename*	Append. (Add written data to the end of the file.)
command		Read data from an input pipe.
	command	Send data out through an output pipe.

Command-Line Options

Option	Function
-e	Enter one line of a Perl program.
-n	Read from files listed on the command line.
-p	Output to standard output any data read.

Array Operations (@*array*)

Scalar Arrays

Operation	Function
push(*array, value-list*)	Add elements to the end of an *array*.
pop(*array*)	Remove the last element from the end of an *array*.
shift(*array, value-list*)	Add an element to the beginning of an *array*.
unshift(*array*)	Remove an element from the beginning of an *array*.
sort(*array*)	Sort an *array* alphabetically in ascending order.
reverse(*array*)	Sort an *array* alphabetically in descending order.
split(*delim, str*)	Split a string (*str*) into an array of elements. (*delim* can be either a pattern or a string. It is used as the delimiter to separate the string (*str*) into element values.)
join(*delim, array*)	Combine *array* elements into one string.
grep(*array, pattern*)	Search the elements in an *array* for the *pattern*.
splice(*array, index*)	Use **splice** to delete an element from an *array*. Number *index* from 0.
splice(*array, index, num*)	Use **splice** to delete a consecutive number (*num*) of elements from an *array*.

A

Operation	Function
splice(*array*, *num*,0, *str*)	Use **splice** to insert an element into an *array* with the value of *str*.
splice(*array*,**$#argv**,0, *str*)	Use **splice** to add a new element to the end of an *array*.

Associative Arrays

Operation	Function
keys(%*assoc-array*)	Generate a list of all the index strings in an associative array (*assoc-array*).
values(%*assoc-array*)	Generate a list of all the values of the elements in an associative array (*assoc-array*).
each(%*assoc-array*)	Return both the value of the next element in an associative array (*assoc-array*) and the element's index string.
delete(%*assoc-array*, *index-string*)	Delete an element with the specified index from an associative array (*assoc-array*).

General Array

Operation	Function
undef(*array*)	Delete an *entire* array (scalar or associative).

Operators

Arithmetic Operators

Operator	Description
*	Multiplication
/	Division

Operator	Description
+	Addition
-	Subtraction
%	Modulo; results in the remainder of a division
**	Power

Relational Operators

Operator	Description
>	Greater than
<	Less than
>=	Greater than or equal to
<=	Less than or equal to
==	Equal in **let**
!=	Not equal

Increment Operators

Operator	Function
++	Increment variable by one.
--	Decrement variable by one.

Arithmetic Assignment Operators

Operator	Function
+=	Increment by specified value.
-=	Decrement by specified value.
/=	Make variable equal to itself divided by specified value.
*=	Make variable equal to itself multiplied by specified value.
%=	Make variable equal to itself remaindered by specified value.

String Comparison Operators

Operator	Description
gt	Greater than
lt	Less than
ge	Greater than or equal to
le	Less than or equal to
eq	Equal
ne	Not equal

Logical Operators

Operator	Function
expression **&&** *expression* *expression* **and** *expression*	The logical AND condition returns a true 0 value if both *expressions* return a true 0 value; if one returns a nonzero value, then the AND condition is false and also returns a nonzero value. Execution stops at the first false expression. The **and** operation is the same as **&&** but has a lower precedence.
expression | | *expression* *expression* **or** *expression*	The logical OR condition returns a true 0 value if one or the other *expression* returns a true 0 value; if both *expressions* return a nonzero value, then the OR condition is false and also returns a nonzero value. Evaluation stops at the first true expression. The **or** operation is the same as | | but has a lower precedence.
! *command* **not** *command*	The logical NOT condition inverts the true or false value of the expression. The **not** operation is the same as **!** but has a lower precedence.

File Test Operators

Operator	Returns
-e	True if file exists.
-f	True if file exists and is a regular file.
-s	True if file is not empty.
-z	True if file is empty (zero in size).
-r	True if file is readable.
-w	True if file can be written to (modified).
-x	True if file is executable.
-d	True if filename is a directory name.
-B	True if file is a binary file.
-T	True if file is a text file.

Assignment Operator

Operator	Function
=	Assign a value to a variable.

Control Structures

A

Condition Control Structures: if, else, elsif, case

Structure	Function

LABEL:{
    statements;
}
	A block is a collection of *statements* that can be labeled (*LABEL*) and that are enclosed within opening and closing braces. The statements are executed sequentially.

if(*expression*) {
    statements;
}
	if executes statements if its test *expression* is true. *Statements* must be included within a block.

Structure	Function

if(*expression*) {
    statements;
}
else(*expression*) {
    statements;
}
	if-else executes *statements* if the test *expression* is true; if false, then the **else** *statements* are executed.

if(*expression*) {
    statements;
}
elsif(*expression*) {
    statements;
}
else(*expression*) {
    statements;
}
	elsif allows you to nest **if** structures, enabling selection among several alternatives; at the first true **if** *expression*, its *statements* are executed and control leaves the entire **elsif** structure.

unless(*expression*) {
    statements;
}
	unless executes *statements* if its test *expression* is false.

test **?** *stat1* : *stat2*	Conditional expression, which, if true, executes *stat1*, **else** *stat2*.

LABEL:{
if(*expr*){
    statements;
    last *LABEL*};
        }
	Simulate a **switch** structure by using listed **if** *statements* within a block with the **last** statement referencing a *LABEL* for the block.

Loop Control Structures: while, until, for, foreach

Structure	Function

LABEL:**while**(*expression*) {
    statements;
}
	while executes *statements* as long as its test *expression* is true. *LABEL* is optional.

do{ *statements*; } **until**(*expression*)	**until** executes *statements* as long as its test *expression* is false.

Structure	Function

foreach *variable* (*list-values*)
{
   statements;
}
	foreach is designed for use with lists of values (*list-values*) such as those generated by an array; the *variable* operand is consecutively assigned the values in the list.

for(*init-expr; test-expr; incr-expr*)
{
   statements;
}
	The **for** control structure executes *statements* as long as the test expression (*test-expr*) is true. The first expression, *init-expr,* is executed before the loop begins. The third expression, *incr-expr*, is executed within the loop after the *statements*.

LABEL: *block-or-loop*	Label a *block* or *loop*. Used with the **next**, **last**, and **redo** commands.
next	Skip remainder of loop and start next iteration. Will execute any **continue** block. (Like the C **continue** command.)
continue {*statements*;}	Execute **continue** block as last *statements* in a loop. Executed even if a **next** statement starts next iteration.
redo *LABEL*	Reexecute loop even if test fails. Skips **continue** block.
last *LABEL*	Exit block or loop. Skips **continue** block, if any. (Like the C **break** statement.)

A

Functions

Function Name/Syntax	Function
sub *function-name*;	Declare a function (*function-name*).

sub *function-name* {
   statements;
}
	Define a function with the name *function-name*.

Function Name/Syntax	Function
& *function-name*(*arg-list*)	Call a function (*function-name*) with arguments specified in the argument list (*arg-list*).
@_	Hold the values of arguments passed to the current function. **$_** and **index** reference an argument. **$_[0]** is the first argument.
$#_	Number of arguments passed to the current function

String Operations

Operation	Function
string . *string*	Concatenate *string*s.
string **x** *num*	Repeat a *string* a number (*num*) of times.

String Functions

Function Name/Syntax	Function
chomp(*string*)	Remove trailing newline.
substr(*string*, *start-pos*, *length*)	Return a substring of the specified *string*, beginning at the start position (*start-pos*) for the *length* specified.
substr(*string*, *start-pos*, *length*) = *string*	Replace the specified *string*, beginning at the start position (*start-pos*), with the assigned *string*.
length(*string*)	Find the length of a *string*.
index(*string*, *pattern*)	Find the position of a *pattern* in a *string*.
rindex(*string*, *pattern*)	Find the last position of a *pattern* in a *string*.

Pattern-Matching Operations

Operators

Operation	Function
variable =~ /*reg-expr*/	Find the occurrence of the regular expression (*reg-expr*) in the string *variable*.
variable !~ /*reg-expr*/	Check to see if the regular expression (*reg-expr*) does not occur in string *variable*.
/*reg-express*/	Match a pattern using a regular expression (*reg-express*).

Options

Option	Function
i	Perform case-insensitive pattern matching.
m	Treat string as multiple lines.
s	Treat string as single line.
x	Extend a pattern's legibility with white space and comments.

Regular Expressions

Special Characters

Character	Function
^	Match the beginning of a line.
$	Match the end of a line.
*c**	Match on zero or more sequential instances of the preceding character (*c*).

Character	Function
.	Match on any single character.
c+	Match on at least one or more sequential instances of the preceding character (*c*).
c?	Match on zero or just one instance of the preceding character (*c*).
c{*num*}	Specify the number (*num*) of repeated sequential instances of the preceding character (*c*) to match on.
c{*min*,*max*}	Specify a minimum (*min*) and maximum (*max*) number of repeated sequential instances of the preceding character (*c*) to match on.
[*character-list*]	Match classes of *characters*.
[*character-character*]	Match ranges of *characters*.
[^*char-list*] [^*char-char*]	Match any characters not in the character list (*char-list*) or the range (*char-char*) specified.
reg-exp | *reg-exp*	Match on any of the specified regular expressions (*reg-exp*). (Functions as a logical OR operation.)
(*pattern-segment*) *n*	Specify a segment of a pattern (*pattern-segment*) that can then be referenced with the *n* code. (**1** references the first segment, **2** the second, and so on. Used with **s**/// substitution.)

Escape Characters

Character	Description
w	Any alphanumeric character: [a-bA-B0-9]+
d	Any digit: [0-9]+
s	White spaces (spaces, tabs, newlines, and form feeds: [\n\t\r\f]+)
b*word*	Words
W	Characters that are not alphanumeric: [^a-bA-B0-9]+

Character	Description
\D	Characters other than digits: [^0-9]+
\S	Characters other than white spaces: [^\n\t\r\f]+
\Bpattern	Any pattern that is not a word

Subroutine Components

Component	Description
@_	An array to hold a list of arguments. (Arrays are combined into single elements of this array.)
sub name {statements;}	A subroutine definition.
sub name;	A subroutine declaration.
sub name (type-list);	A prototype declaration.
function-name;	A function call.
function-name(arguments);	A function call.
&function-name arguments;	A function call.
my(object-list)	A local variable restricted to a subroutine or block.
local(object-list)	A local version of a global object, known to the current subroutine and block, as well as other subroutines called.
\@array-name	An array reference (used in an argument list to maintain the integrity of an array).

A

Appendix B
Tcl and Tk

Tcl is a general-purpose command language developed by John Ousterhout in 1987 at the University of California, Berkeley. Originally designed to customize applications, it has become a fully functional language in its own right. As with Perl, you can write Tcl scripts, developing your own Tcl programs. Tcl is often used in conjunction with Tk to create graphical applications. Tk is used to create the graphical elements such as windows, and Tcl performs the programming actions such as managing user input. Like Java, Tcl and Tk are cross-platform applications.

Tcl is an interpreted language that, like Perl, operates within its own shell. **tclsh** is the command for invoking the Tcl shell. Within this shell, you can execute Tcl commands. You can also create files within which you can invoke the Tcl shell and list Tcl commands, effectively creating a Tcl program. A significant advantage to the Tcl language and its applications is the fact that it is fully compatible with the C programming language. Tcl libraries can be incorporated directly into C programs.

The Tk applicaton extends Tcl with commands for creating and managing graphic objects such as windows, icons, buttons, and text fields. Tk commands create graphic objects using the X-Window system. It is an easier way to program X-Window objects than using the X11 toolkit directly. With Tk, you can easily create sophisticated window-based user interfaces for your programs.

B

The Tk language is organized according to different types of graphic objects such as windows, buttons, menus, and scroll bars. Such objects are referred to as *widgets.* Each type of widget has its own command with which you can create a widget. For example, you can create a button with the **button** command or a window with the **window** command. A type of widget is considered a *class,* and the command to create such a widget is called a *class command.* The command will create a particular instance of that class, a particular widget of that type.

Tk operates under the X-Window system, within which it uses its own shell—the **wish** shell—to execute Tk commands. To run Tk programs, you first start up your X-Window system and then start

up the wish shell with the **wish** command. This will open a
window in which you can run Tk commands.

Tcl and Tk Software Products

Current versions of Tcl and Tk, as well as the other products listed
here, are available free of charge from the Tcl/Tk Web site, at
http://sunscript.sun.com:

Product	Description
Tcl	The Tcl programming language and interpreter (current version 8.0): tcl8.0.tar.gz
Tk	The Tk programming language (current version 8.0): tk8.0.tar.gz
SpecTcl	Tcl/Tk GUI builder; creates GUI user interfaces: SpecTcl1.1.tar.gz
Tcl Plugin	The Tcl/Tk Web page plugin (current version 2.0); viewer for Tcl/Tk applications (Tclets): tclplugin1.1.386.rpm
TclHttpd	Tcl/Tk Web server: tclhttpd.tar.Z

Tcl List Operations

Command	Function
set *list values*	Create a *list* and assign *values* to it.
lsearch(*list, pattern*)	Search for a *pattern* in elements of a *list*.
lindex(*list, index*)	Return the value of the *index*ed element in a *list*.
llength(*list*)	Return the number of elements in a *list*.
linsert(*list, index, value-list*)	Insert a new element into a *list* after the *index*.

Command	Function
lreplace(*list, index, value-list*)	Replace element *index*ed with a new value.
lappend(*list, value-list*)	Append new values to the end of the *list*.
concat(*lists*)	Combine elements of several *lists* into one list.
list(*lists*)	Combine *lists* into a larger list whose elements are the respective lists.
split(*str, delim*)	Split a string (*str*) into a list, using delimiter (*delim*) to separate values.
join(*list*)	Join elements of a *list* into a string.
lsort(*list*)	Sort the *list* alphabetically or numerically.

Common Tcl Commands

Assignments and Variables

Command	Function
set	Assign a value to a variable.
global	Declare global variables.
incr	Increment a variable by an integer value.
unset	Delete variables.
upvar	Reference a variable in a different scope.
variable	Declare namespace variables.
array	Perform array access operations like searches.
expr	Define math expressions.

B

Control Structures and Procedures

Structure/Procedure	Function/Description
if	Conditional command, extend with **else** and **elseif** blocks
switch	Switch selection structure.
while	The **while** loop.
for	The **for** Loop, like the C **for** loop.

Structure/Procedure	Function/Description
foreach	Loop through a list, or lists, of values.
break	Force a loop exit.
continue	Skip remainder of block and continue with next loop iteration.
proc	Define a Tcl procedure.
return	Return a value from a procedure.
source	Read and execute Tcl commands in another file.
uplevel	Execute a command in a different scope.

File Commands

Command	Function
file	Obtain file information.
open	Open a file.
close	Close a file.
eof	Check for end of file.
fcopy	Copy from one file to another.
flush	Flush output from a file's internal buffers.
glob	Match filenames using **glob** pattern characters.
read	Read blocks of characters from a file.
seek	Set the seek offset of a file.
tell	Return the current offset of a file.
socket	Open a TCP/IP network connection.

Input/Output Commands

Command	Function
format	Format a string with conversion specifiers (like **sprintf** in C).
scan	Read and convert elements in a string using conversion specifiers (like **scanf** in C).
gets	Read a line of input.
puts	Write a string to output.

String Commands

Command	Function
binary	Convert between strings and binary data.
regexp	Match on string using regular expressions.
regsub	Perform substitutions using patterns with regular expressions.
split	Split a string up into list elements.
string	Operate on strings.
subst	Perform substitutions on a string.

System Commands

Command	Function
catch	Trap errors.
cd	Change the working directory.
clock	Return the time and format date strings.
error	Raise an error.
eval	Evaluate a list of arguments as a command.
exec	Execute a Unix command.
exit	End the program and exit.
pwd	Return the current working directory.
info	Query the state of the Tcl interpreter.
trace	Check values of variables.

B

Tk Commands

Event Operations

Command	Function
bind	Associate Tcl scripts with X events.
bindtags	Bind commands to tags.
selection	Select a widget or text with a mouse.

Geometry Managers

Command	Function
pack	Pack widgets next to each other.
grid	Pack widgets in a grid of rows and columns.
place	Place widgets in positions in a frame.

Window Operations

Command	Function
destroy	Close a Tk window.
toplevel	Select a top-level window.
wm	Set window features.
uplevel	Move up to a previous window level.

Standard Tk Widgets

Widget	Description
button	A button
canvas	A canvas window
checkbutton	A check button
entry	An input box
frame	A simple widget whose primary purpose is to act as a spacer or container for complex window layouts
image	An image widget for displaying pictures
label	A label
listbox	A list box with selectable lists of items
menu	A menu
menubutton	A menu button to access the menu
message	A message
radiobutton	A radio button
scrollbar	A scroll bar
text	An editable text box
scale	A scale

Standard Tk Options

Option	Function
-anchor	Specify how information is displayed in the widget. (Must be one of the following values: n, ne, e, se, s, sw, w, nw, or center.)
-background	Specify the normal background color to use when displaying the widget.
-bitmap	Specify a bitmap to display in the widget.
-borderwidth	Specify the width of the 3-D border to draw around the outside of the widget.
-cursor	Specify a mouse cursor to use for the widget.
-font	Specify the font to use when drawing text inside the widget.
-foreground	Specify the normal foreground color to use when displaying the widget.
-geometry	Specify the desired geometry for the widget's window.
-highlightbackground	Specify a color to display in the traversal highlight region when the widget does not have the input focus.
-highlightcolor	Specify a color to use for the traversal highlight rectangle that is drawn around the widget when it has the input focus.
-image	Specify an image to display in the widget.
-insertbackground	Specify a color to use as background in the area covered by the insertion cursor.
-justify	Justify multiple lines of text displayed in a widget.
-orient	Specify the orientation for widgets that can position themselves, such as scroll bars.
-padx	Specify how much extra space to request for the widget in the X-direction.

B

Option	Function
-pady	Specify how much extra space to request for the widget in the Y-direction.
-relief	Specify the 3-D effect desired for the widget.
-selectbackground	Specify the background color to use when displaying selected items.
-text	Specify a string to be displayed inside the widget.
-textvariable	Specify the name of a variable.
-troughcolor	Specify a color to use for the rectangular trough areas in widgets, such as scroll bars and scales.
-underline	Specify an integer index of a character to underline in the widget.
-xscrollcommand	Specify a command used to communicate with horizontal scroll bars.
-yscrollcommand	Specify a command used to communicate with vertical scroll bars.

Button Options

Option	Function
-command	Specify a Tcl command to associate with the button.
-selectimage	Specify an image to display when a check button is selected.
-height	Specify the height for a button.
-selectcolor	Specify the background color to use when a button is selected.
-state	Specify one of three states for a radio button: normal, active, or disabled.
-variable	Specify a global variable to set to indicate whether or not a button is selected.
-width	Specify the width for the button.

Appendix C
TeX and LaTeX

TeX is a professional-level typesetting application for formatting text. It reads a standard character file containing text with tags that instruct TeX how to format that text. TeX generates a device-independent (dvi) file that can then be converted to various forms of output such as a PostScript file or an X-Window display. There are basic lower-level TeX commands that can be combined by macros to perform more complex tasks such as formatting headings and paragraph. You can design your own TeX macros for any given document. TeX has been popularly used to typeset technical documents that have complex mathematical formulas. It is also portable across any Unix or Linux system.

LaTeX is a set of TeX macros that provides easy-to-use formatting capabilities. Instead of detailing a complex set of TeX commands, you can use a corresponding LaTeX macro. LaTeX macros allow you to focus on formatting the general layout of the text.

TeX and LaTeX Mathematical Symbols

Command	Symbol	Description
^{expr}	x^j	Superscript
\alpha	α	Alpha
\delta	δ	Delta
\beta	β	Beta
\epsilon	ϵ	Epsilon
\sigma	σ	Sigma
\mu	μ	Mu
\theta	θ	Theta
\prod	Π	Product
\pi	π	Pi
\sum	Σ	Summation
\int	$\int$	Integral
\subset	$\subset$	Subset

Command	Symbol	Description
\supset	⊃	Superset
\Delta	Δ	Delta
\equiv	≡	Equivalent
\neq	≠	Not equal
\leq	≤	Less than or equal
\geq	≥	Greater than or equal
\div	÷	Division
\bullet	•	Bullet
\times	×	Times
\ast	*	Asterisk
\ldots	...	Horizontal ellipsis

TeX

Commands

Documents

Command	Function
\bye	End a TeX document.

Paragraphs

Command	Function
\par or *empty-line*	Start a new paragraph with the first line indented.
\noindent	Start a new paragraph with no first-line indent.

Predefined Fonts

Command	Function
\rm	Set in Roman.
\tt	Set in typewriter font.
\bf	Set in boldface.
\it	Set in italics.
\sl	Set in slanted font.

Defining a Font

Command	Function
\font *fontname*=*font*	Define a font. (*fontname* is the TeX name you give to the font. *font* is the font's actual name.)

Spacing

Command	Function
\hskip *num-measure*	Insert a space of the specified size into a line.
\vskip *num-measure*	Insert a line of the specified size between lines.
\smallskip	Insert a small empty line between lines.
\medskip	Insert a medium empty line between lines.
\bigskip	Insert a large empty line between lines.
\hfill	Fill empty space on a line. (Used to flush text left or right on a line.) \hfill *text*　　　　Flush right *text* \hfill　　　　Flush left \hfill *text* \hfill　　Center
\vfill	Fill empty space between lines.

Spacing Measures

Measure	Description
em	Width of a character, font-dependent
in	Inches
pt	Points
mm	Millimeters

Page Layout

Command	Function
\headline={*text*}	Set *text* as a header.
\footline={*text*}	Set *text* as a footer.
\hsize=*num-measure*	Set paragraph text box size.

Command	Function
\baselineskip= *num-measure*	Set regular spacing between lines.
\parskip= *num-measure*	Set regular spacing between paragraphs.

Groups

Command	Function
\begingroup	Begin a grouping.
\endgroup	End a grouping.
{*text*} {*command* *text*}	Create a grouping (Has the same effect as using **\begingroup** and **\endgroup**. *Command*s in the group apply only to *text* in the group.)

Positioning Objects

Command	Function
\topinsert *object* **\endinsert**	Position an *object* such as a figure at the top of the page.
\pageinsert *object* **\endinsert**	Position an *object* on a page of its own.

Macros

Command	Function
\def*macro-name*{*text*}	Define a new macro.
\def*macro-name* *parameter-list*{*text*}	Define a new macro with parameters.
#*num**	Define a parameter for a macro. Used in *parameter-list*. **\def\myn#1#2{My name is #1 #2}**

Special Characters

Command	Function
c	Quote a single character (*c*).
tex-command	Execute a TeX command.
%*tex-comment*	Add a comment.

Command	Function
{*text*}	Group *text*.
#*num*	Define a parameter.
$*formula*$	Embed a mathematical *formula* within text.
$$*formula*$$	Display a mathematical *formula* on its own line.
text^{*suptext*}	Make *suptext* a superscript of *text*.
*text*_{*subtext*}	Make *subtext* a subscript of *text*.
&	Specify a formate file.
\\	Insert a newline, or line break.
space	Separate a word.
empty-line	Separate a paragraph.

LaTeX

Document Classes

Class	Description
article	Short documents such as journal articles
book	Book-length documents with chapters
letter	Personal or business letters
report	Long reports with several chapters
slides	Slides

Document Class Macros

Command	Function
\documentclass{*classname*}	Define the document class for this file.
\begin{*document*}	Begin the body of a document.
\end{*document*}	End the body of a document.

Options

Option	Function
11pt	Print in 11 point.
12pt	Print in 12 point.
oneside	Print on one side of the page (not for the **letter** class).
twoside	Print on two sides of the page (not for the **letter** class).
openright	Start chapters on odd pages.
openany	Start chapters on either odd or even pages.
leqno	Number formulas on the left side.
draft	Output in draft mode.
fleqn	Flush an equation to the left.
leqno	Place the equation number to the bottom left.
letterpaper, a4, paper	Specify paper sizes.

Environments

Tables and Graphics

Environment	Function
figure	Number and position a figure or picture. (Use **caption** to label.)
table	Number and position a table. (Use **caption** to label.)
tabular	Create a table.
picture	Create a drawing.

Line Formats

Environment	Function
center	Center lines.
flushleft	Left-align lines.
flushright	Right-align lines.
tabbing	Reset tabs.

Environment	Function
minipage	Set up a mini-page.
titlepage	Set up a special title page.

Lists

Environment	Function
enumerate	Create a numbered list. (Use \item for entries.)
itemize	Create a bulleted list. (Use \item for entries.)
description	Create a labeled list. (Use \item for entries.)
list{*label*}{*spacing*}	Create a list with a specified *label* (can be a LaTeX command) and specified *spacing*. (Use \item for entries.)

Math

Environment/ Environment Symbol	Function
equation	Number and position an equation.
math or $	Embed a math formula within text.
displaymath or $$	Display a math formula on its own line.
array	Arrange math formulas in rows and columns.
eqnarray	Arrange math formulas in rows and columns, and label each row with an equation number.
theorems	Label and number a theorem.

C

Specialized Environments

Environment	Function
letter	Create a letter. (This environment is used within the **letter** document class.)
quote	Quote a paragraph.
quotation	Quote several paragraphs.
verbatim	Display text exactly as entered.
verse	Display text as verse.
theBibliograph	Create a bibliography.

Commands

Counters

Command	Function
\addtocounter{*counter*}{*value*}	Add a *value* to a *counter*.
\alph{*counter*}	Print the value of a *counter* using alphabetic characters.
\arabic{*counter*}	Print the value of a *counter* using numbers.
\roman{*counter*}	Print the value of a *counter* using Roman numerals.
\newcounter{*name*}	Define a new *counter*.
\setcounter{*counter*}{*value*}	Assign new *value* to a *counter*.
\stepcounter{*counter*}	Increment a *counter*.
\usecounter{*counter*}	Use a *counter* in a **list** environment.
\value{*counter*}	Use the value of a *counter* in an expression.

Page Style and Headers

Command	Function		
\pagestyle{*style*}	Define the placement of headers and footers for the entire document. *style* can be any of the following:		
	empty	No header or footer.	
	plain	Print only page number in footer.	
	headings	Print even and odd headers.	
	myheadings	Define your own headers.	
\thispagestyle{*style*}	Define the placement of headers and footers for this page only.		
\markboth{*even-header*}{*odd-header*}	Set your own even and odd headers.		

Command	Function
\markright{*single-header*}	Set your own header.
\twocolumn	Start a new page with two columns.
\onecolumn	Start a new page with one column.
\item [*label*]	Define a list item within a **list** environment such as **enumerate**, **itemize**, or **description**.

Paragraphs and Lines

Command	Function
empty-line, \par	Start and indent a new paragraph.
\indent	Indent a paragraph.
\noindent	Do not indent a paragraph.
\centering	Center a paragraph.
\raggedright	Left-justify a paragraph.
\raggedleft	Right-justify a paragraph.
\linebreak	Break a line.
\newline	Break a line prematurely.
\nolinebreak	Do not break a line.
\newpage	Start a new page.
\nopagebreak	Do not make a page break here.
\pagebreak	Make a page break here.
\verb	Print text exactly as typed (verbatim).

C

Font Styles

Command	Function
\rm	Set in Roman.
\it	Set in italic.
\em	Emphasize text (toggles between \it and \rm).
\bf	Set in boldface.
\sl	Set in slanted font.
\sf	Set in sans serif font.
\sc	Set in small caps.
\tt	Set in typewriter font.

Font Sizes

Command	Function
\tiny	Set in very small font size.
\scriptsize	Set in script font size.
\footnotesize	Set in footnote size.
\small	Set in small font size.
\normalsize	Set in default font size.
\large	Set in large font size.
\Large	Set in initial caps.
\LARGE	Set in all caps.
\huge	Set in huge font size.
\Huge	Set in initial caps.

Character Operations

Command	Function
_{text}	Display text in subscript. (Use math mode for expressions.)
^{text}	Display text in superscript. (Use math mode for expressions.)
\symbol{number}	Display the symbol for a number in the character set.
\underline{text}	Underline text.
\ldots	Display an ellipsis (works in all modes).

Section Headings

Command	Function
\section{heading-text}	Add a section heading.
\subsection{heading-text}	Add a subsection heading.
\subsubsection{heading-text}	Add a sub-subsection heading.
\paragraph{heading-text}	Add a paragraph heading.
\subparagraph{heading-text}	Add a subparagraph heading.
\appendix	Add an appendix.
\part{part-title}	Add a part heading.
\chapter{chapter-title}	Add a chapter title.
\tableofcontents	Use headings to create a table of contents.

Titles

Command	Function
\maketitle	Make a title for the document.
\title{*title-text*}	Define the title.
\author{*author-name*}	Define the author.
\date	Generate the date.

Footnotes

Command	Function
\footnote[*number*] {*footnote-text*}	Create a footnote. (As an option, you can specify your own *number* for the footnote.)
\footnotemark	Place a footnote reference within a paragraph (uses **footnotetext**).
\footnotetext{*text*}	Place a footnote mark within a paragraph.
\label{*label-name*}	Mark text for a cross-reference using *label-name*.
\ref{*label-name*}	Create a cross-reference specifying a section.
\pageref{*label-name*}	Create a cross-reference specifying a page.

Math

Command	Function
\;	Insert a thick space.
\:	Insert a medium space.
\,	Insert a thin space.
\!	Insert a negative thin space.
\cdots	Place a horizontal ellipsis at the center of a line.
\ddots	Display a diagonal ellipsis.
\vdots	Display a vertical ellipsis.
\ldots	Display an ellipsis (works in all modes).
\frac{*num*}{*den*}	Generate a fraction with *num* divided by *den*.

Command	Function
\overbrace{*text*}	Generate. a brace over *text*.
\underbrace{*text*}	Generate *text* with a brace underneath.
\overline{*text*}	Overline *text*.
\underline{*text*}	Underline *text* (works in all modes).
\sqrt[*root*]{*arg*}	Generate the square root of the *root*'s argument (arg).

Environments

Command	Function
\caption{*text*}	Insert a caption. (Use with **figure** and **table** environments.)
\begin{*environment-name*}	Begin an environment and label it *environment-name*. Apply the environment's formatting to the following text.
\end{*environment-name*}	Close an environment.

tabular Environment (Tables)

Command	Function
\cline{*coli-colj*}	Draw a horizontal line spanning columns indicated by range starting from *coli* to *colj*.
\hline	Draw a horizontal line spanning all columns.
\multicolumn{*cols*}{*align*}{*text*}	Create an entry that spans the specified number of columns or create a customized entry. *align* is the alignment (l, r, or c).
\vline	Draw a vertical line.

picture Environment (Pictures)

Command	Function
\put(*x coord*,*y coord*){*objects*}	Perform the actual drawing of *objects*, placing the objects at the given coordinates.

Command	Function
\circle[*]{diameter}	Create a circle of size *diameter*.
\oval(*width,height*)[*position*]	Create an oval of size *width* and *height*, and place any text within it. (Text can be positioned at different quadrants using combinations of **t**, **b**, **l**, and **r** for *position* option.)
\line(*x slope,y slope*){*length*}	Draw a line of specified *length* and *slope*.
\vector(*x slope,y slope*) {*length*}	Draw a line with an arrow at the end of the specified *length* and *slope*.
\makebox(*width,height*) [*position*]{*text*}	Create a box of size *width* and *height* and place any *text* within it. (Text can be positioned at different quadrants using combinations of **t**, **b**, **l**, and **r** for *position* option.)
\framebox(*width,height*) [*position*]{*objects*}	Create a box of size *width* and *height* and place it around specified *objects*. Text can be positioned at different quadrants using combinations of **t**, **b**, **l**, and **r** for *position* option.
\dashbox{*dash-length*} (*width,height*){*text*}	Create a dashed box of size *width* and *height* and place any *text* within it. Length of dashes (*dash-length*) can be specified.
\frame{...}	Place a frame directly around an object with no space in between.
\multiput(*x coord,y coord*) (*delta x,delta y*){*number of copies*}{*object*}	Draw multiple copies of an object.

letter Environment (Letters)

Command	Function
\begin{letter} {*name* \\ *address* \\ *city, state zip*}	Begin a **letter** environment, starting a new letter. (Separate address components with a \\.)
\address{*return-address*}	Add your return address.

Command	Function
\cc{*name* \\ *name* \\ *etc.*}	Create a cc list. Separate entries with a \\.
\closing{*text*}	End letter *text* and specify farewell text such as "Sincerely."
\encl{*enclosure-list*}	Add a list of enclosed material. Separate entries with a \\.
\location{*address*}	Add the organization's *address*. (Appears only if the **firstpage** page style is used.)
\makelabels{*number*}	Make address labels. (Labels are entered in the preamble.)
\name{*name*}	Add a *name* to be included in the return address.
\opening{*text*}	Start the letter *text* and specify an opening salutation such as "Dear Sir."
\ps	Add a postscript.
\signature{*name*}	Add a printed *name* for a signature.
\startbreaks	Allow page breaks.
\stopbreaks	Disallow page breaks.
\telephone{*number*}	Add a telephone *number*. (Appears only if the **firstpage** page style is used.)

theBibliograph Environment (Bibliographies)

Command	Function
\bibitem[*label*]{*cite_key*}	Create a bibliographic entry using *label*. If the label is missing, use enumerated labels. (Use *cite_key* to create a list of citations.)
\cite[*text*]{*key_list*}	Refer to a bibliography item. (The *key_list* is a list of citation keys.)
\nocite{*key_list*}	Add *key_list*.

Defining New Commands, Environments, and Fonts

Command	Function
\newcommand{cmd}[args] [default]{definition}	Define a new command.
\renewcommand{cmd}[args] [default]{definition}	Change the definition of an existing command.
\newenvironment{env_name} [args][default]{begdef}{enddef}	Define a new environment.
\renewenvironment{env_name} [args]{begdef}{enddef}	Change the definition of an existing environment.
\newtheorem{env_name} [numbered_like]{caption}	Define a new environment that handles theorems.
\newfont{cmd}{font_name}	Create a new command to reference a font.

Using Packages and Including Files

Command	Function
\usepackage{package}	Load in a LaTeX package.
\include{file}	Conditionally include a file.
\includeonly{file-list}	Determine which files are included.
\input{file}	Unconditionally include a file.

C

INDEX